D1190282

How to LIVE LIFE *Laughing!*

HANK RUSSELL

maranatha publications

Over 30 Years of Publishing

FIRST EDITION

Cover Design by John D. Weiner

To Order Online Visit Our Website:
https://www.weinermedia.com

To Order by Phone Please Contact :
Maranatha Publications 352-375-6000

Or Write to:
Maranatha Publications
PO Box 1799
Gainesville, Florida, 32602

Library of Congress Cataloging in Publication Data has been applied for.

ISBN   978-0-93-855802-6

MARANATHA PUBLICATIONS
GAINESVILLE, FLORIDA

Dedication

I dedicate this book to my wonderful wife Grace Jarrell Williams Russell, who is an artist, writer, musician, and public speaker. She has drawn many architectural plans for houses that we have lived in and for many churches where we have served. She is a member of PAPA (Paducah Area Painters Alliance). Besides all of this, she the mother of our five children, whose talents and success reflect her personality and dynamic faith in God. She is rightly called "Amazing Grace."

Table of Contents

Forward

How to Live Life Laughing might sound like a foolish subject for a minister to be writing about, but living life joyfully is one of the great themes of the Bible. Everyone is familiar with the assurance that "laughter is the best medicine," yet how many people realize that this is a passage right out of the Bible. Having lived with Hank all these years, I have come to appreciate the value of a good sense of humor in helping cope with the difficulties of life.

For years friends and family have begged Hank to write some of his stories down. Finally, a couple of years or so ago, one of our children gave him some journals and said, "Take one of these with you and keep it handy so when a story comes to your mind you can write it down." He took the advice, and to please everyone, he wrote these stories down.

I have heard some of these stories many times, and I still get a lift from them. I know that God has filled Hank's heart with joy that enables him to approach life with a sense of humor. Not only has his sense of humor helped him cope with his own physical problems, it has helped him carry the burden of the problems of his congregations down through the years as well. Laughter helps. I highly recommend it to you.

It is great to live with and love a guy who manages to laugh even when it appears that there is nothing to laugh about. Although Hank has suffered many health problems over the years, including a life-threatening ear infection that lasted sixty-five years and three cancer operations, with the power of prayer and the help of medicine, the Lord has healed them all. Hank has found that in all life's challenges, faith and laughter are the greatest medicine. At the moment, we have been married 65 years and still we find something to laugh about every day.

Grace Russell

Introduction

Have you had a life changing experience with Jesus Christ? When happiness happens, life is enjoyed with better health. Hope by itself can be nothing more than delayed disappointment. Hope centered in Jesus Christ through his Holy Spirit can bring new life and joy.

When my boys started to drive the family car, I said, "I don't care how far you drive the car without gasoline, but I don't want you to drive it two feet without oil." Forgiveness is the oil in the crankcase of life. Don't go anywhere without it.

Advice to my children - learn from other peoples' mistakes. You will never live long enough to make them all yourself.

These narratives are really stories with double punch lines. One to make you laugh and another to make you think. You need both of these experiences in equal proportions. I warned you. Read them at your own risk.

This is not a perfect book. You, the reader, could have done a much better job than I have done. When you find a mistake or something I have left out, you have my permission to use the things below:

. Period	: Colon
"" Quotation marks	' Apostrophe
? Question mark	! Exclamation point
; Semicolon	- Dash

A Thought to Remember

Some of these stories are very old and were told to me long ago. A few of them are true, and some of them are fiction. Some of these stories are from my own personal experiences, and others I have repeated as they were told to me. As a reader, it's your job to figure out the difference. All of them are taken from my memory bank. These stories have been in the public domain for so long that no one is old enough to claim ownership of them.

If you have heard some of these stories before, you will know when to laugh, and hearing them again will make you feel well-read and educated in the field of humor. God bless you, and may "the joy of the Lord be your strength." ~ Nehemiah 8:10

"Sour godliness is the Devil's religion." ~ John Wesley

"Marriage is made in heaven, but so is thunder and lightening."

~ Anonymous

Dr. Henry E. Russell
622 Woodland Drive
Paducah, Kentucky, 42001
270-442-6671
270-217-2666

1

Laughter is Good Medicine

Many years ago, Norman Cousins was editor of the *Saturday Review of Literature*. He went to the doctor who gave him a gloomy report on his physical condition. Ready to die and in bad health, he rented a hotel room and checked out old films from the library - comedies such as Laurel and Hardy, slap stick, and so on. He forced himself to laugh, and finally, laughed himself back to health.

A woman anxious about her health checked in with the Lord. The Lord assured her that she had 40 years of good health left. She said that He also told her to relax, and He would watch out for her. So with the promise of years of long living, she decided to make some personal improvements. She lost 45 pounds, got a tummy tuck, got a face-lift, and a nose job. Last, she dyed her hair and started out on a new life. She was abruptly struck by a car and ended up in heaven where she sought out the Lord and asked, "I thought you were watching out for me, but you let me get hit by a car."

"Sorry," said the Lord, "but I didn't recognize you."

Don't loose your identity. Remember who you are! Learn to laugh even when there is nothing to laugh about. Someone reported that children laugh about 400 times a day, and adults laugh around 12 times a day. Have you ever counted the times you laugh each day? Aging can diminish laughter. The presence of pain can keep our nerves on edge. Medicine can help block pain, but laughter helps us when all else fails. Nehemiah records this thought for us to ponder, "Today is Holy to our Lord, so don't be sad. The joy that the Lord gives you will make you strong" (Neh. 8:10).

Can you believe that Nehemiah said this many, many years ago? Think about Nehemiah's life-style then. List all the things that he did not have – indoor plumbing, electricity, heat/air conditioning, automobiles, airplanes, good roads, and on and on the list goes. Many people who have all these things are still depressed. Worry and stress are making life miserable for a great number of people.

Look at the discovery the author of Proverbs made: "A happy heart makes the face cheerful" (15:13). The heart here means the center of our being. A healthy attitude makes a good disposition, and a good disposition makes for a joyful life. Again Proverbs declares, "A cheerful heart is good medicine" (17:22).

During WWII, the aircraft carrier was a great ship loaded with many airplanes going and coming. The noise on the carrier was deafening, blotting out voices and your ability to think. The engineers designed a soundproof cabin for those who were in command. They could go there to think and strategize and make decisions.

We all need a sound proof center in our lives. We can go there and shut out the noise and TV commercials. Here we can listen to the Voice of God, pray, and follow God's guidance for our lives. Here we can praise God and give thanks to Him.

Hear these words of Jesus: "These things I have spoken unto you, that in Me you might have peace. In the world you shall have tribulation; but be of good cheer; I have overcome the world" (John 16:3).

Scripture:

"I am not alone, because the Father is with me." ~ John 16:32b
These words gave me comfort when I was operated on for cancer of the liver at Vanderbilt Hospital in Nashville, Tennessee. They still help me celebrate God's Presence in my life.

Prayer:

O, Lord, thank You for Your love. It blesses my heart to know that Your love has the last word. Amen.

May God now bless you and give you assurance through the Presence of His Holy Spirit.

2

Determination

Years ago, *Collier's Magazine* was famous for its cartoons. Real cartoonists who are not politically biased can be the philosophers of our day. One of the cartoons of my childhood was unforgettable. The spring rains had come in earnest, and a flood had caused the family to take to the roof of their home. They were looking at a man's derby hat that kept bobbing back and forth in the water in front of their house.

One of the family members on the roof pointed to the moving hat and asked, "What is that?"

"Oh, that's grand-paw," another responded. "He said this morning, 'Come hell, or high-water, I'm going to mow the lawn today!' "

People who are able to make up their minds and remain focused on their desires can accomplish a lot. This focus always helps direct our activity and tells us when to continue with the plans we have and when to make new plans. The circumstances of life often send us in a new direction. Being able to change our minds without destroying our commitment to action is important and can produce new and enjoyable results.

Let us learn to live with disappointment. God can help us turn our disappointment into His appointment. Life will not always lead us where we want to go. Circumstances can change and alter our plans. But living in the center of God's will and walking with the company of the committed can produce joy and abundant life in us today.

Many times the simple can be profound. Living the simple life can free us from stress. The Bible is filled both with good advice and good news.

Jesus said, "Simply, let your *yes* be *yes* and your *no* be *no*"(Matt. 5:37). Such a statement requires a lot of thought on our part before we utter it. In fact, thinking before speaking can save us from a lot of unhappy experiences. Defining words to serve our purpose can be dangerous to their true meaning, and also to us, therefore we must remain honest.

The computer is a marvelous invention, but when it is used to replace our thinking, we can destroy our ability to think. We must not loose our ability to think. Using our mind to think is great mental exercise. Such behavior keeps us mentally healthy. We are never to old to learn and think.

Scripture:

"Apply your heart to instruction and you ears to the words of knowledge. Buy the truth, and sell it not." ~ Proverbs 23:12, 23

Prayer:

Lord, You are at the heart and center of my being; help me learn from You. Amen.

3

A Personal Appeal to God

One of my favorite stories concerns a church in Florida. The worship was in full swing when a deacon noticed a waterspout forming across the bay. On second glance, it looked like a pretty strong storm was brewing. A third look revealed to the deacon that the waterspout was headed for the little church. If you are familiar with a waterspout, you know that it can come up suddenly and descend upon a place and level a building. Since the deacon had knowledge that the Pastor and congregation were not aware of, he went to the pulpit and informed the minister of the possibility of an impending storm.

The wise pastor turned the worship service into a prayer meeting, and he eloquently prayed, "O Lord, we are facing a possible storm. Please send us the courage of the children of Abraham. O Lord, send us the strength of the children of Moses. O Lord, send us the wisdom of children of Solomon."

While the pastor and the people were praying, the deacon was watching the approaching storm. It looked deadly and fearful to him. He ran to the pulpit, took the mike away from the Pastor, and said, "O Lord, don't send nobody, You come Yourself - this ain't no job for children."

Facing the storms of life is not a job for the immature. As the Lord's people, we need to grow up. Disaster calls for people with unshakeable faith. Spiritual preparation produces moral and spiritual maturity. Faith teaches that the best of all is that God is with us. We can snatch victory from defeat by using our faith.

Jesus calmed the wind and the waves. Many times we see nature get out of control. Human nature also gets out of control. We will never learn to control nature until we are able to control human nature. Can you imagine what it would be like if a nation learned how to control the weather? The way we fight over the resources of the world is an indication of how we would behave if one of us learned how to control the weather. Let us surrender to the Holy Spirit and let God help us control our human nature. There's a great formula for our behavior. It is spelled "JOY!"

J esus First
O thers Second
Y ourself Last

Scripture:

"One day Jesus said to his disciples, 'Let's cross to the other side of the lake.' So they got into a boat and started out. As they sailed across, Jesus settled down for a nap. But soon a fierce storm came down on the lake. The boat was filling with water, and they were in real danger.

"The disciples went and woke him up, shouting, 'Master, Master, we're going to drown!' When Jesus woke up, He rebuked the wind and the raging waves. Suddenly the storm stopped and all was calm. Then He asked them, 'Where is your faith?' The disciples were terrified and amazed. 'Who is this man?' they asked each other. 'When he gives a command, even the wind and waves obey Him!' " ~ Luke 8:22-25

Prayer:

Lord, I surrender to Your Holy Spirit. As a wire surrenders to a dynamo so the electrical power can flow though it, so I surrender to you. May your message flow through me so You can bless others. Amen.

4

The Road to College and Beyond

In a certain town, a college student needed a job to help with his expenses. Since the college was located in this city, a part-time job was hard to come by. To his surprise one of the first ads he saw in the paper was a mysterious ad that described the job as part-time work at the city zoo. He answered the ad and gave himself a pep talk convincing himself that whatever the job was, even if it included cleaning the cages of animals, he would take it even if it was offensive to him.

When he was interviewed for the position, they measured him, checked his weight and decided that he was right for the job. "Our gorilla died and we cannot afford to buy another one. He was the most popular animal in the zoo. The kids loved him, so we ordered a gorilla suit, and we want to dress you up as a gorilla. We have some movies of him. You can study his behavior and imitate him. We will pay you well and you only have to appear a few afternoons a week for an hour or so. In fact, the pay is so good you can work your way through college."

The young man agreed. He put on the gorilla suit and entered the enclosed area marked "Fierce Gorilla." The young college boy did a great performance. In fact, he was the most popular animal at the zoo.

One day he attracted a large crowd of elementary students. He was performing for them when he accidentally fell into the lion's den next to his outdoor cage.

Desperately he began to yell, "Save me! Help me!"

The lion came roaring up to him and said, "Shut up! Be quiet! You aren't the only one working his way through college."

I worked my way through college disguised as a janitor, a yardman, a dishwasher, and an errand boy. Who we are is defined not by what we do but by the kind of character we have and the goals we hold. Money has its place, but it's a poor substitute for honesty, or a thoughtful personality where others are concerned. People spend millions of dollars defining their image, changing their names, and promoting themselves as something they are not.

The question is, do you like me, or do you like my image? Some people hide who they are from others, and especially from God. Then in one of life's great defining moments, they surrender to God. They confess everything to God, only to hear God say, "I knew all that stuff about you!" They respond, "Lord you mean you knew all about me and loved me anyway?"

I am not putting words in God's mouth when I tell you that He says, "Yes." When we turn to God in love, we discover that He first loved us. We just lacked the ability to recognize God's love for us!

Scripture:

"Therefore, since we have been justified through faith, we have peace with God through our Lord Jesus Christ, through whom we have gained access by faith into this grace in which we now stand. And we rejoice in the hope of the glory of God. Not only so, but we also rejoice in our sufferings, because we know that suffering produces perseverance, perseverance, character, and character, hope.

"And hope does not disappoint us, because God has poured out His love into our hearts by the Holy Spirit, whom He has given us. You see at just the right time, when we were still powerless, Christ died for the ungodly. Very rarely will anyone die for a righteous man, though for a good man someone might possibly dare to die. But God demonstrates His own love for us in this: while we were still sinners, Christ died for us." ~ Romans 5:1-8 (NIV)

Hope by itself, when deferred, can bring disappointment. But hope in Christ can be a rewarding experience.

Prayer:

Lord, You are my hope, my joy, and my peace. Amen!

5

Belief versus Fiction

In 1964, I met a certain elderly woman who lived in rural West Tennessee, who told me a story about what things were like when her grandmother was a little girl. Her folks lived in the country. In those days, there were no rural hotels. Some of the people who traveled were ministers. They would come to a rural community and stay in the home of church members while they preached at the local church. This woman's grandmother said her people always kept the traveling elders and preachers.

Those were the days of coal oil lamps. The light provided was a glass lamp filled with oil. A cloth wick was dropped in the kerosene. A burner was screwed on the glass base of the lamp. A small wheel enabled you to turn the wick up to a certain height. You then lit the cloth wick and placed a glass chimney over the flame. When you retired for the night, you would turn the flame down and blow out the lamp. To light the lamp, you had to find a match, strike it, turn up the wick, light it, and put on the glass chimney. It was an ordeal.

One of the ministers had physical problems. Whenever he had panic attacks, his traveling companion would get him fresh air. This always brought quick results. After retiring in a strange farmhouse in the darkness, the minister had a violent attack. He called for fresh air. His friend felt around for a window to open. "I've found a window," he told the minister, but I can't open it. The thing seems to be stuck."

"Well, if you can't open it," the minister stressed, "break out a pane!"

"OK. Here it goes." Crack! Crash! The glass fell. It was worth it! The fresh air calmed the minister, and he quickly fell asleep. The next morning when daylight came, they looked at the broken window that brought such relief and wonderful fresh air! To their dismay they found that in the darkness they had broken a glass door to the bookcase!

A hypochondriac always insisted that he was sick, even when the doctors assured him he was in good health. To make his point and have the last word, he had these words inscribed on his tombstone:

"SEE, I TOLD YOU I WAS SICK."

Thoughts affect our body, our mind, and the future of our life. Our mind can control our bodies. Our thoughts can guide our behavior. "As a man thinks in his heart, so is he" (Proverbs 23:7). Healing begins and continues at the center of our lives. Positive thoughts can produce good healthy results. Think like Jesus. Forgive. Love others, and be thankful for God's greatest gift - Life!

Scripture:

"Let this mind be in you that was also in Christ Jesus."~ Phil. 2:5

Prayer:

O Lord, please direct my thinking so I can live a healthy life.

6

Understanding

A certain man had a beautiful grandfather clock that he prized very much. It had been in his family for a long time, but one day it stopped working. He finally located a man who said he could repair it. The owner of the clock tried to remove the works from the cabinet but did not have the proper tools and was afraid that he would damage the clock beyond repair.

The repair shop agreed to repair the clock if it were brought to him in the cabinet, but the owner of the big grandfather clock had for his only transportation a Volkswagen. With difficulty and hard work, he managed to put the big clock in the tiny VW. He drove up in front of the clock repair shop, opened the door to the little car, and began to carry the big clock across the sidewalk and into the repair shop.

About that time a drunk came weaving down the sidewalk and accidentally, by perfect coordination, staggered into the owner carrying his clock. The big clock hit the pavement and broke into several pieces. The man carrying the clock also fell to the sidewalk. The drunk never fell, but looked over at the man on the sidewalk and all the pieces and declared, "Hey mister, why don't you wear a wrist watch like everybody else?"

Understanding is a frustrating word that can lead us off in all directions at the same time. An honest glance at ourselves, and considering our ability to walk in someone else's shoes, can soften the blows of life for all of us. Life can cause us to collide with other people in our day of activities. It is always healthy for us to look beyond ourselves and appreciate the role of other people in our journey.

While I was in Lambuth College, in Jackson, Tennessee, I served churches in Calvert City, Kentucky, and also Palma and Oakland. After the service at the Palma Church, I stood at the front door to greet the people. Many people came by to encourage me by complimenting the sermon. I knew they were being polite. The sermon lacked many things, among them being depth of understanding both of the scripture and human behavior. A dear lady stood beside me at the front door. After everybody left she said to me, "Compliments are like perfume. They are to be smelled and not swallowed."

Her observation has stayed with me for over 66 years. I've never forgotten it, and I still remember her warm and friendly love that accompanied this quote. I found them most helpful all my life. It is good to please people as much as you can, especially if you can make them happy, but pleasing everybody can be disastrous.

A man was building a boat beside the lake. People passed by and offered advice. The man took all the suggestions and incorporated them into the boat. He finally finished the boat and put it in the water. It promptly sank. He pulled the boat on the shore and started to build a new boat.

"What are you doing?" asked a passerby.

"I am building a boat."

The visitor began to offer a suggestion, but the builder said, "If you have any suggestions, please make them about that boat over there. That's everybody's boat. The thing sank."

"This is my boat, and I'm building it according to the best plan I know."

Time and understanding can come together and produce amazing results. Any clock or calendar should remind us to act toward God and understand that He has a plan for our life. Hosea's very old message is put in agricultural terms, but it can be applied to our personal life.

Scripture:

"Break up your fallow ground for it is time to seek the Lord." ~ Hosea 10:12

Prayer:

Lord, help me to spend more time with You. Amen.

7

Using God or Letting God Use You

A certain little boy began the habit of stretching the truth. Telling wild tales got him a lot of attention, but his mother was fearful that such behavior would lead to outright lying. One day he entered the house violently screaming,

"There is a big black bear in the back yard!"

His mother checked it out and saw only a big black dog. She said to her son, "Go upstairs to your room and get on your knees and pray to God. Ask Him to forgive you for saying that big, black dog was a bear."

The boy was gone for a short time and came back down stairs. His mother questioned him, "Did you ask God to forgive you for calling that big black dog a big black bear?"

"Yes," replied the boy, "and God said that the first time He saw that dog He thought it was a bear too!"

There is real danger in putting words into God's mouth. Perhaps a better method would be to ask God for guidance not approval of what we have already done. God can lead us in a new direction and help us to find new ways for the living of an abundant life. If we can conquer the "now" of our life, we can be certain that tomorrow will be fruitful. Now is the time to develop good healthy habits of living. Reading habits that include highlights of the Bible can assure us of good mental health.

As leaders, we need to provide better outlets for those around us. Too much TV that is laced with violence is not food for people of any age. One person defined adults as obsolete children. This may be true. Breaking out of thought patterns is a job for self-discipline. Others can help, but the best effort is what we do for ourselves.

Scripture:

Hosea describes those who try to con God: "They will be like the morning mist like the early dew that disappears, like chaff swirling from a threshing floor, like smoke rising out of a chimney." ~ Hosea 13:3

Hosea quotes God as saying: "O Israel, you have destroyed yourself, but in Me there is help for you." ~ Hosea 13:9

Prayer:

Dear Lord, forgive me for shooting myself in the foot. Help me to be kind to myself. Amen.

8

The Light is Attractive

Newfoundland, also called Cracker Neck, is a great northern country. The people there like to tell stories on themselves. Here is one of them:

There was a certain man and his wife who had many children. Much to the husband's frustration, he found that there was another child on the way. He loved and cared for all his children, but there comes a time when one more can be too much. As his wife's pregnancy grew to a close, the doctor was summoned. During the delivery, the husband became upset and frustrated. To keep him occupied the doctor gave him the job of holding the lantern.

"Hold the lantern over here," the doctor commanded. "There, you have a bouncing baby boy!" Startled the doctor hastily shouted, "Quick, bring the lantern over here. You have another one!"

Frustrated the father replied, "Quick, Doc, blow out the lantern. I think it's the light that's attracting them!"

The expectant father was right. It is the light that attracts all of us. Darkness is not attractive. It is the light that gets our attention. It is light that produces color. It is the light that makes all things bright and beautiful. It is the light that makes plants and animals grow. Jesus is the Light of the World. Our light is His reflected light. It is His light in us that makes us the light of the world. "If the light that is in us is darkness, then how great is that darkness?"

We are all more transparent than we think. Others can see through us. Therefore light a candle on the altar of your spirit, so God can shine through you. You can become a person of warmth and beauty. A positive and cheerful spirit is like a lighted candle within you.

Scripture:

Jesus said, "You are the light of the world. Let your light so shine before men, that they may see your good works and glorify your Father in heaven." ~ Matt. 5:14-16

Prayer:

Lord, help me take care of the light that is in me. Amen

9

What is a Vacation?

In a certain village at the foot of the mountain, a mother came in from the country every year, ready to give birth to a new child. It was always at the close of the harvest season, and her annual appearance at the village hospital was cause for concern. Finally, her doctor said to her, "Mrs. Brown, you have been coming here every year checking in the hospital, staying two weeks, and giving birth to a child. I think you have enough children. You need to stop doing this!"

"Oh, no, Doctor," Mrs. Brown replied. "Then I would miss the only rest I get all year!"

We all need a vacation from our job; it will help us get a new perspective on things. Getting a vacation from being retired is a little more difficult and calls for imagination and discipline. A vacation is a change that breaks the routine of your life. Not all changes are restful and refreshing. Routines of life are necessary, but they can become very dull. A vacation can change the way we see our job and ourselves.

In a southern town, a rural man was brought into court as a witness about an automobile accident. He was put on the stand and told this story.

"I was standing in the cotton fields learning on my hoe. These two cars were flying down the road, one of them ran slap dab into the other."

The witness was cross-examined and the lawyer questioned, "You said the cars were flying. Airplanes fly, cars do not! You didn't see two cars flying!"

"No sir, they weren't flying."

"You were wrong about the cars flying. I don't believe you can see very well. I don't believe you can see the length of this courtroom. How far can you see?"

"Well, sir, I can see the moon, how far away is that?"

St. Paul spelled out the human dilemma; "I do not understand my own actions, for I do not do what I want, but I do the very things I hate" (Rom.7:15). What is my mission in life? Do I understand it? Do I need to reevaluate it?

How seriously am I committed to my mission? Is my church the best place to express my commitment to Christ? Do my activities reflect the focus of my life's mission? Do I act on what I know? Acquiring knowledge is a good thing, but I need to put into practice what I already know! What kind of results do I want from my spiritual life?

Scripture:

"God's plan is to make known His secret to His people, this rich and glorious secret which He has for all peoples. And the secret is that Christ is in you, which means that you will share in the glory of God."~ Cols. 1:27

Prayer:

O Lord, since Christ is in me, may I not keep Him all bottled up, but help me let Christ out of my life so others can see Him and be blessed. Amen.

10

Seeing Through Someone Else's Eyes

A certain farmer grew weary of his farm and listed it in the paper for sale. The advertising department described the farm, its location, size, and natural beauty in glowing terms. When the farmer read the ad, he called his real estate agent and canceled the contract. The broker asked, "Why?" The farmer replied, "After you described my farm, I liked it so much I decided to keep it."

It has been my privilege to listen to a lot of people who have told me their problems. Some years ago, I started making a practice of listening to all their problems and then summarizing all they told me, asking them if I heard them correctly. Each one agreed that what I told them was exactly what they had told me. Immediately after I started to implement the summarization process in my counseling, I began to notice a change of attitude in all the people I listened to.

At the end of my summary, each person declared that he or she had been helped. I asked one person who thanked me for helping him, just how I had helped. He said, "Well, when I told you all the things that angered me and made me come unglued, it really distressed me. But, when you told them all back to me, the problem didn't seem that distressing. When I told you all this, these events were a major problem, but when you summarized my problems and said them back to me, they did not seem that important."

In the year 2000, the doctor told me I had bladder cancer and also told me to come back the next day for surgery. He said, "You have bladder cancer, but I'm not worried about it." On the way home to our condo in Panama City Beach, Florida, I told Grace,

"If he had cancer of the bladder, I wouldn't be worried about it either!"

The truth is that I would be concerned about anybody I knew who had cancer of the bladder. I thank God for a competent doctor and the prayer of thousands of people whose faithful prayers aided God in my healing process. Problems are always bigger to the one who is suffering from them than they seem to everyone else. Sometimes our problems are genuinely overwhelming, but sometimes, when we hear them spoken back to us from others, we can see that we have blown them out of proportion and have let them dominate us.

Scripture:

"Finally, brethren, whatever things are true, whatever things are noble, whatever things are just, whatever things are pure, whatever things are lovely, whatever things are of good report, if there is any virtue and if there is anything praiseworthy - meditate on these things." ~ Phil. 4:8

Prayer:

O Lord, I turn to Your for guidance. Help me to put You first in my life. Amen.

11

On Passing a Test

One small boy moved from a city in the North to a small southern town. The urban/rural shock was great for the lad and left him a little confused. The teacher in the small town tried to find out the boy's grade level so she gave him a quiz in math. She centered on the multiplication table. She began with the multiplication of numbers times two. In her southern accent she asked the boy, "What is *two'tums* nine?"

"I don't know," the boy replied.

"What is *two'tums* four?"

"I don't know," the boy responded.

"What is *two'tums* five?"

"I don't know!" the boy answered in frustration.

The teacher chastised her new student, "I don't believe you don't know the multiplication table."

"No, Ma'am, I don't know that, and I don't know what 'tootums' is either!"

Two times was lost in translation.

When I was preaching in Indonesia, I used this illustration. "When I return home, I could try to save money by attempting to cross the Pacific Ocean in a bathtub, but if it was possible, it would be foolish for me to try."

My interpreter interrupted, "Bathtub won't translate. Nobody here has a bathtub. They have a hole in the floor and pour water on themselves."

My illustration of using a bathtub for a boat was not only an example of a poor unworkable choice, but a confused idea for people who didn't take a bath in a tub.

Of course, the idea of substituting something else to cross the wide Pacific Ocean would be a foolish choice - you see I had a ticket on a 747 Jet. The fare had already been paid. All I had to do was board the plane and trust the pilot to take me home.

Jesus Christ died on the cross for you and me. He is the Way, the Truth and the Life. He paid for all our sins. He is our ticket home. It is through Jesus that we are transported to our heavenly home. There is no substitute for Christ our Savior. Jesus is our pilot. Climb aboard and enjoy the journey.

Scripture:

"A furious squall came up and the waves broke over the boat, so it was nearly swamped. Jesus was in the stern, sleeping on a cushion. The disciples woke him and said to him, 'Teacher, don't you care if we drown?' He got up, rebuked the wind and said to the waves, 'Quiet! Be Still!' Then the wind died down and it was completely calm."~ Matt. 14:30-32

Prayer:

O Lord, calm the storm in my life. Please bring peace to my spirit. Amen.

12

An Old Dyer County Tale

Vern Forcum, a prominent Tennessee businessman, use to tell the story of a character who lived in a neighboring small town in West Tennessee. The fellow's name was Theron. One day, Vern Forcum was in this town on business when he saw Theron pulling a heavy log chain. A log chain is a heavy thick chain to hold logs together to transport them. He asked, "Theron, why are you pulling that heavy chain?"

"Mr. Forcum," he asked, "did you every try to push one?"

Theron had a point. Pushing a log chain doesn't make much sense. It doesn't take a rocket scientist long to figure that out. Whatever purpose Thoreau had for the log chain was never known. But he was going about the correct method to move the chain.

There is a correct method for most things. Dropping a bad habit is the best way to break one. It would seem that a person could figure this out. Frequently, we hold on to our established method of behavior because we can operate by habit easier than by thought. Thinking can be hard work. Thinking is in danger of being replaced by the computer. It's quicker to push a button. Do we have more confidence in the computer than we have in ourselves? Are we doing a better job improving the computer than we are in improving the human mind?

Thinking is creative and productive. It is essential for life on earth. Mental laziness destroys our ability to think.

Scripture and Prayer:

The following is St. Paul's great prayer to know and express the love of Christ –

" For this reason I fall on my knees before the Father, from whom every family in heaven and on earth receives its true name. I ask God from the wealth of His glory to give you power through His Spirit to be strong in your inner selves, and I pray that Christ will make His home in your hearts through faith. I pray that you may have your roots and foundation in love, so that you together with all God's people may have the power to understand how broad and long, how high and deep, is Christ's love. Yes, may you come to know His love - although it can never be fully known - and so be completely filled with the very nature of God.

"To Him who by means of His power working in us is able to do so much more than we can ever ask for, or even think of - to God be the glory in the church and in Christ Jesus for all time, forever and ever!" Amen. ~ Ephesians 3:14-21 TEV

13

A Questionable Salesman

Fact or fiction, there's an old story of a certain man who sold cars in Dyer County, Tennessee. Some of his cars were good and some of his cars were questionable. But, usually the price was affordable, so he had many customers.

One day, a man with a mean reputation bought a previously owned automobile from this used car dealer. To sell this particular car, the dealer made a lot of good claims about this car. The car did not live up to the claims of the dealer. The man who bought the car put out the word that when he saw the dealer he was going to shoot him. Everywhere the salesman went, people reminded him of how angry and mad this fellow was.

Then one day it happened! Unexpectedly, the two ran into each other on the street corner. Quickly the salesman blurted out, "I heard about how mad you were about the automobile you bought from me. None of this is my fault."

"What do you mean that none of this is your fault?" the man asked the dealer.

"Well," said the used car dealer, "it's all your fault. You knew when you bought this car from me that I was the biggest liar in West Tennessee, and you bought it anyway."

The two started laughing and walked away at peace with one another.

There have been plenty of times when a soft answer and a humble confession have defused an explosive situation. When our position has been questioned, an honest answer and a quick response saying, "I don't know," may clear the air of unnecessary strife and conflict.

It is no threat to our self-confidence to admit that we are mistaken. Human error that is not the result of our unwillingness to put forth our very best effort is after all just human. We all make mistakes. Hopefully, they can be corrected without undue stress. If we forgive others of their mistakes, we can usually find those who will forgive us of ours. When I was in seminary, I stood before the school cashier. She stood behind a counter that had bars that would make some banks envious. This elderly woman wore a sunshade and produced an atmosphere that revealed the long years she had spent in this office.

"What's your name?" she abruptly asked.

"Henry E. Russell," I replied.

She opened a cash drawer and pulled out a large clump of dollar bills. She briefly counted out some of them and pushed them under the cage in front of her with a sheet of paper for me to sign.

"Sign here!" she instructed.

"What is this?" I asked.

"Money for a scholarship!"

"I know nothing about a scholarship. Perhaps this is a mistake."

She looked at me with a sense of disgust and declared, "I never make mistakes."

"Thank you," I said. I took the money and left and gave thanks to God for people I did not know who out of their generosity gave money for a scholarship.

Scripture:

St. Paul in his long journey to Rome, after three months at sea, finally landed at Puteoli. He then went on to Rome where good friends met him. "At the sight of these men Paul thanked God and was encouraged." ~ Acts 28-15 NIV

Prayer:

O Lord, we thank You for encouraging friends and for the Presence of Your Holy Spirit who gives us daily courage. May we be more like You and them. Amen.

14

Fiction, Fact, and Reality

The jailer came with the keys and unlocked the cell door An attractive woman stepped out. She was escorted to the front desk where she was given her purse, the key to her automobile and all her personal belongings.

The officer apologized and explained, "You were in a lineup of three cars. The auto in front of you was not moving. You were in your car blowing your horn, cursing the driver in front of you, and demanding that the person move on. Behind you was an unmarked police car. Your behavior became almost violent. The officer observed that on the back of your car were a few emblems. A bumper sticker read, 'Honk if you love Jesus.' There was a sign of a fish with a cross on it. A church sicker invited people to attend church. The officer in the car behind you looked at you and your car and arrested you because he thought you had stolen the car."

This story may or may not be fiction. It may have been passed around, and you may have heard it. But it is a fact that our behavior on the road may not represent who we really want to be. Not putting Christian symbols on the back of our car may protect us from exposing the fact that we are one person on the road and an opposite individual in church.

Some preachers are unique. They may have scared the Hell out of more people by their driving than by their preaching. I guess that scaring the Hell out of people may be one means of salvation, but it is not my favorite means of deliverance.

Jesus taught the disciples to preach. At Capernaum, Mark records this message about Jesus - "He preached the word unto them." What was the word that Jesus preached? It was this:

The word of *healing*
The word of *forgiveness*
The word of *repentance*
The word of *redemption*
The word of *faith*
The word of *love*
The word of *heaven*
The word of *eternal life*
The word of the *resurrection*

Scripture:

"In the beginning was the Word, and the Word was with God, and the Word was God." ~ John 1:1

Prayer:

O Lord, when You speak Your word, help me to listen and be glad. Amen.

15

Guidance

A young couple took their small boy to their family doctor with a problem.

"Our son has a problem. He sees green spots, yellow spots, red spots and black spots."

"Has he seen a psychiatrist?" asked the doctor.

"No, just green spots, yellow spots, and red and black spots," replied the father.

Communication can be a problem. Lots of people don't communicate. Frequently, there are people who do not look at their problems in the eye. They live under the misconception that if they do not look at their problem, it will go away. So they look the other way.

The late Pierre Harris was a famous Methodist preacher. He was pastor of First Methodist Church in Atlanta. He was a much sought after dinner speaker. He could entertain people and make them laugh and cry at the same time. One of his favorite comments was, "I'd rather have a person say, 'I seen' and really see something than to have him say, 'I see' - and not see anything."

It is possible to use good English and be able to have a vision for your life, your community, and your faith. Life is a journey. I recently went on a deep sea fishing trip with some of my family. For a while, I was on the verge of almost being seasick. I have sympathy with those who really get seasick. A pessimist is a person who has been seasick all the voyage of his life.

After Jesus had been crucified, John records the following story: "That evening, on the first day of the week, the disciples were meeting behind locked doors because they were afraid of the Jewish leaders. Suddenly, Jesus was standing there among them!

'Peace be with you,' He said. As He spoke, He held out His hands for them to see, and He showed them His side. They were filled with joy when they saw their Lord! As He spoke, He held out His hands for them to see, and He showed them His side. They were filled with joy when they saw their Lord!" (John 20:19-20)

How does God act? He reveals Himself to us. The Bible is full of acts of revelation. God shows Himself through the Scriptures. God shows Himself through prayer. God reveals Himself through the Presence of His Holy Spirit. Have you ever felt in prayer that you could reach out and touch God? Such an experience brings joy to your life. God reveals Himself through Providence. Looking back upon the yesterdays of our life, we can see God at work. Also with a developed and trained faith, we can see God at work in our life today; therefore, with assurance, we can see God in the our tomorrows.

Scripture:

"Jesus Christ the same yesterday, today, and forever." ~ Hebrews 13:8

Prayer:

O Lord, I can always count on You to be here for me. I want You to count on me to be here for You. Amen.

16

The Need to Be a New Man

Ed was a very successful man. He became an executive with his firm. But the experience of life made him bitter, negative, cynical, and at times abrasive. A cloud of gloom and despair seem to hover over him. You could almost see it follow him around.

Ed was an early riser. On one morning, he ran into his fellow merchant on the courthouse square. Ed proceeded to dump all his negative garbage on Homer. After Ed had thrown all his negative, bitter views and opinions on Homer, there was a pause. Then Homer responded, "Ed, I wouldn't have run into you today for a $100 dollars, as much as I would have like to have had the money."

With some people, being unpleasant is a work of art. I can't believe that they enjoy it. I once heard a man declare, "I'm a mean old man, and I aim to get meaner." This is not a good philosophy of life. This attitude will take you nowhere and cause you to drink from the fountain of bitterness.

Sometimes people do change. It all depends on how God works in their lives. Let us encourage people to surrender to God's Presence in their lives.

Paul reminds us, "As for you brothers, never tire of doing what is right" (2 Thes. 3:16).

I think we have a problem in the struggle between good and evil - the good people get tired of being good before the evil people get tired of being evil. Let us continue to keep our commitment strong and alive so that our faith and character will be productive for our lifetime and beyond.

Scripture:

"Put off the old man, who is corrupt. Be renewed in the spirit of your mind." ~ Ephesians 4:22

Prayer:

O Lord, help me maintain my faith and trust in You. I can do this with the help of Your Holy Spirit. Amen.

17

Garbage

In New York City a few years ago, the garbage workers went on strike. The stuff was piled high. In the middle of all of this, I heard about a man who had no trouble getting rid of his garbage. How did he do it? He said, "I wrapped all my garbage in beautiful paper and left it on the front seat of my car. I left the car unlocked and went to work. Someone stole it!"

I don't care how attractive it is or how beautiful it appears to be if once you steal something and it turns out to be garbage. When a person surrenders to dishonesty, the loss of being an honest person is not worth the price of whatever you were able to steal.

A "political" definition of an honest man is "Once you have bought him, he stays bought." However, being loyal to dishonesty is not a commendable characteristic. Honor among thieves might keep you from getting killed, but it doesn't matter very much in the long run since you have already committed spiritual suicide. The Bible says, "The wages of sin is death, but the gift of God is eternal life." You are blessed because you can enjoy God's greatest gift, eternal life.

Every TV should have an extra button that reads, "Garbage in – garbage out." Why? Because most of the programs are garbage. Why let TV bring people into your home that you would never invite. There is garbage in my home, but I take it out and dispose of it in the trash can. It is not piped into my living room.

A friend of mine received a call from her mother who lived in a nursing home. "Reva," she said to her daughter, "Will you please come over here and fix my television? I enjoy it sometimes, but now it won't work."

Reva, wonderful daughter that she was, went to the nursing home and turned on the TV and moved through the channels. "Mother, your TV seems to be fine. What do you think is wrong with it?"

"Why, Reva, the programs are awful!"

That is so true. That is what's wrong with TV. Who can fix it? Are the elderly who can't read because of poor eyesight the victims of TV?

Scripture:

On May 24, 1738, John Wesley read these words at 5 a.m. on the day of his "Aldersgate Experience." The passage was 2 Peter 1: 1-8. You will be blessed if you read it. Here is a portion of it:

"His divine power has given to us all things that pertain to life and godliness...

Make every effort to add to your faith goodness,
    and to goodness knowledge,
    and to knowledge, self-control,
    and to self-control, perseverance,
    and to perseverance, godliness,
    and to godliness, brotherly kindness;
    and to brotherly kindness, love.

"For if you possess these qualities in increasing measure, they will keep you from being ineffective and unproductive in your knowledge of our Lord Jesus Christ." ~ 1 Peter 1:5-8

Prayer:

O Lord, help me to keep my ability to think and make healthy decisions. Amen.

18

Slap Stick Fun

At the close of the Second World War, Grace and I were completing the final phase of our education. We were at Southern Methodist University. She was an art major at the school of Fine Arts and Sciences, and I was in the final days at the School of Theology named for Mr. and Mrs. Joe Perkins, who had given a considerable amount of money to the school in 1945. Two million dollars and more is a lot of money now, but in those days that was an enormous pile of cash.

At this time, Grace and I were living in a beautiful garage apartment that was equipped with an icebox. I was very familiar with iceboxes. Before the days of refrigerators, I grew up on our farm in West Kentucky. We had an icebox, and when our neighbors had emergencies, they came to my dad and mother for ice. For the benefit of younger people, the icebox is an insulated box that holds ice that helps keep food cold. However, the ice always melts. There is a hole in the bottom of the box for the water to flow through and a pan under the box to catch the water.

One night, Grace and I went to see an Abbot and Lou Costello movie - two comedians of our era. All I remember about the movie is an unforgettable scene with an icebox. Abbot and Lou were trying to empty the drip pan from under the icebox, which was completely full of water. They struggled to get the pan out that was stuck.

I was certain that they were going to spill the water all over the place. Finally, they successfully emptied the pan of water. What made this scene amusing was that instead of putting the empty pan under the icebox to catch the dripping ice water, they filled the pan with fresh water and put it back under the box.

At various times over the years of my life, I have felt that all I was doing was changing the water under the icebox. Many of the activities of life do not make sense. We are frequently caught in a task or job that seems to have no more meaning than changing the water under the icebox. We have some choices. We can change jobs, knowing when to change a job is a sign of wisdom. If that is impossible, what we bring to our job can give it meaning and purpose. With imagination and applied psychology, we can add to the purpose of our job.

We can see our meaningless tasks as an opportunity to serve others and our community. We can bring hope and good cheer to the work place. We may be able to add fun and fellowship to the place where we work. Suddenly, we can say to ourselves, "I didn't know that changing the water pan under the icebox could be such fun."

When we are involved in what seems to be a useless task, we can dedicate this job to the Lord; we can ask Him to show us meaning here.

Scripture:

"And we know that all things work together for good to those who love God to those who are the called according to His purpose."~ Romans 8:28

Prayer:

O Lord, we surrender this boring task to You. Will You breathe life into these dead dry embers? Help me find the best way to perform this task. Please bless it with Your joy and Presence. Amen.

19

To Your Health

One of the many places that Grace and I lived was Dyersburg, Tennessee, a beautiful town about eighty miles northwest of Memphis. Tom Curry was owner and director of Curry Funeral Home in Dyersburg. He was a World War II captain and served in the European arena. Tom was a member of my church where I served for seven years. He was a good friend of mine, and we had a good time together.

He once told me a story of one of the rural residents who had poor health and finally decided to go Arizona where he lived for a couple of years and then died. The family shipped his body back to Dyersburg to be buried. Two of his friends came by Curry's funeral home to pay their respects and offer condolences to the family. As they went up to the casket to view the body, one of them said, "Doesn't he look great?"

"Yeah," the other friend replied, "those two years in Arizona sure did him good."

Looking good and being alive are two different things. Sometimes a considerable amount of money and time is spent in looking good. Outward appearance can show signs of a great life, but all the while we can be dying within. An old sage I can remember from my youth said, "The greatest conflicts are not always fought on the battlefields of the world, but often within the hearts of men." Inner strife can destroy our peace of mind. Peace will bring inner calm and assurance.

An old Indian bought an article from the company store. A nickel got caught in the wrappings, and in a few days the Indian came to the store and returned the nickel. Times were hard on the reservation and someone asked him, "Why didn't you just keep the nickel?"

"Well," said the old Indian, "I thought about it." But there are two men inside of me. They kept talking in the night. One of them said, 'Keep it. It's only a nickel.'

'But it's not mine,' the other answered.

'True but no one will ever know.'

'Take it back,' the other voice persisted.

"The conversation went on all night long. I couldn't get any sleep. So I brought back the nickel."

Inner peace comes from doing the right thing. The rewards of being honest to myself and to God is peace of mind. Confessing my faults and my shortcomings to God brings a marvelous sense of forgiveness. There is no shortcut to God's grace - to His unmerited favor - except by way of confession. Confession to others may or may not bring results, but confession to God always brings joy, peace, and best of all His forgiveness.

Scripture:

Some of the last words of Jesus were: " Peace I leave with you. My peace I give to you. I do not give to you as the world gives. Do not let your hearts be troubled and do not be afraid." ~ John 14:27

Prayer:

O Lord, please come into my life and bring Your Presence, Your peace, and Your power. Amen.

20

Theological Confusion

A minister received a telephone call in the wee hours of the morning. The man at the other end was crying. He was obviously under the influence of alcohol.

"Pastor, I don't know whether I'm a conservative or a liberal."

"You are drunk," the pastor said. "Come by my office in the morning when you are sober, and I'll explain it to you."

The drunk continued to cry over the phone and finally stuttered out, "Pastor when I am sober, I don't give a damn."

Sobriety is more than being free from alcohol. It is possible to be drunk on religion. People who are under the influence of distorted dogma can be offensive and dangerous.

I remember people in the county seat of a small town who would sit around in the summer time and discuss the Bible. They had opinions about a book they had never read. They were certain they were right, and everybody else was wrong. I am certain that God is not found at the end of an argument. There is no such thing as a final argument. There is always one more point.

God is found in a great adventure, an adventure of faith that leads one to confession and commitment to Jesus Christ as the Son of God. Avoid any argument that separates, divides, and brings strife to others.

God alone has the last word, and it is not argumentative in nature. God's latest and last word is love. John 3:16 is worth remembering, "God so loved the world that He gave His only Son that whosoever believes in Him might have everlasting life." Accept God's personal love for you and be blessed.

Scripture:

"Be clear-minded and self-controlled so that you can pray. Above all, love each other deeply because love covers a multitude of sins. Humble yourselves, therefore, under God's mighty hand, that He may lift you up in due time. Cast all your anxiety on Him because He cared for you." ~ 1 Peter 4: 7, 5:6-9

Prayer:

Receive God's blessing: "And the God of all grace, who called you to His eternal glory in Christ, after you have suffered a little while will Himself restore you and make you strong and firm and steadfast. To Him be power forever and ever." Amen. ~ 1 Peter 5: 10-11

21

An Old, Old Country Story

At a country store in the 1920's, there was an unusual display of a little red hen setting on a nest. A customer came to buy groceries and noticed the real barnyard hen in the store on the nest.

"Why do you have this hen in here?"

"Lift her up and see," said the merchant.

The customer lifted up the hen from her nest and saw two baby kittens. The kittens eyes were almost open.

The grocer said, "The old hen was trying to hatch out some eggs. The eggs got broken, but the hen remained on the empty nest determined to hatch out some chicks. I tried to get her to leave the nest but she wouldn't do it. This morning a mother cat was crossing the road, and a passing car killed her. I didn't know what to do with the baby kittens, so I placed them under the hen on her nest. This seemed to satisfy the frustrated hen, and it quieted the kittens. So I left them there until I could decide what to do with the old hen and the kittens."

When people came in the store and asked about the hen on the nest the storeowner told them to lift up the hen. When they saw the kittens, the owner would explain.

After a while, the village idiot came into the store and inquired about the hen sitting on the nest. He was told to lift up the hen from the nest and see. When he picked up the hen and saw the baby kittens in the nest, he dropped the hen back on the nest and said, "Oh my gosh, I'll never eat another egg!"

I can appreciate the village idiot's reaction. He thought something had changed in the food cycle. Small towns usually have a village idiot. These people were usually treated with respect. They were a part of the town. Sometimes, they rode the fire truck, they frequently led the parade, and people loved them and treated them with kindness. I grew up in a small, small community. Our town was too small to have a village idiot, so all of us took turns being one.

We are not all smart all the time. Love and compassion goes out for a person who has difficulties. Usually these people have a good disposition and are happy. We can learn a lesson about joy from them. They are childlike and don't realize they are supposed to worry. They are very accepting and loving. Those who have problems relating to others can live miserable lives.

In Dallas, Texas, a church found a family living near the city dump. The house was more than inadequate. It did not keep out the cold air of winter. The family had little furniture; in fact, they used wooden crates for a table and chairs. This church had compassion on this family and decided to start helping them by putting real furniture in their home.

The social worker came back sometime later to find all the furniture gone and the family was living again with boxes. When the social worker asked what happened, the wife replied, "We sold them! My husband wanted a better car, and I always wanted a new hair do. Don't you think my new hair looks great?"

It's hard to make responsible decisions when you mentally lack something in your life. Like most people, my heart goes out to people whose life style is filled with unnecessary hardships, who try and try again, but always seem to fail.

Failure is no respecter of persons. At some time, we all fail. Many of us shoot ourselves in the foot. Careless living can bring injury to any of us. We all need to learn what to do when we fail. We can get to our feet with God's help and more than recover our losses.

Scripture:

"Fear not for I am with you; be not dismayed, for I am your God. I will strengthen you. Yes, I will help you, I will uphold you with My righteous right hand." ~ Isaiah 41:10

Prayer:

O Lord, thank You for giving us another chance. It's great to know You never run out of chances for us. You are a God of the second chance, the third chance, and beyond. Thank You for being patient with us. Amen.

22

Not Far from the Frontier

I was born in Paducah, Kentucky, but my parents moved to the country - a decision my mother never liked. She grew up in her teens in Paducah. My dad was in the dairy business. He produced and bottled milk. His father was in the same business. In fact, my grandfather, Claude Caesar Russell, came to Paducah from Russellville, Kentucky. He and my grandmother, Annie Maria Ewell Russell, were fifth cousins. Her grandfather was General Russell and Russellville, Kentucky, was named for him.

In 1918, my grandfather had one of the first dairies in Paducah. To deliver milk, he would drive a wagon down the street and would ring a bell. People would come out from their homes with a pitcher or some kind of a container and my grandfather would ladle out the milk. My father took over the dairy, and later he sold bottled milk. His bottling plant was a building in the back yard on North 6th Street.

Major Charles Ewell, my great, great grandfather, received several thousand acres of land in West McCracken County when he was discharged from the Revolutionary War. He moved from Virginia in a covered wagon.

One of the pieces of furniture he brought with him was a beautiful spooled cherry bed. It previously contained ropes, and then later it had slats. How I hated that bed. I believe it was the most uncomfortable bed I ever slept on. I guess it was Providential that I had to sleep on that bed. It prepared me for the beds I slept on in the early years of parsonage living as a young Methodist minister.

I heard about a family who finally made a lot of money. The lady in the family spent $100 to have her family tree looked up.

This was a lot of money at that time when one dollar was worth $30. After she discovered her family history, she spent $500 to have it hushed up.

Another lady spent money on her family tree only to discover that one of her great, great, grandfathers was electrocuted in the state pen. She was terribly embarrassed, but the historian fixed it up. He wrote about her ancestor, "He held the chair of applied electricity in one of our great state institutions."

What do birthdays mean? I'm getting older, but am I wiser? Birthdays usually mean that the calendar is still in action. It's a good habit to live outside of yourself. Stay interested in the community, the church, your friends, and things that are going on outside your home.

Remember people, avoid too much TV, and limit the intake of news, especially if you can do nothing about. Pray prayers of thanksgiving, and continue to recognize God as your Heavenly Father. This will remind you that you belong to a dynamic and eternal family.

Never forget that we are close to this eternal family on earth and in heaven. Those family members are still close to us, even though they may have moved to their heavenly home long ago.

Scripture:

Remember the words of Jesus to Mary at the tomb of her brother Lazarus: "I am the resurrection and the life: He who believes in Me will live, even though he dies; and whoever lives and believes in Me, will never die. Do you believe this?" ~ John 11:25

Prayer:

O Lord, I believe, help my unbelief. Amen.

23

A Ghost Story

I grew up in the Western end of Kentucky where the Tennessee River empties into the Ohio River in the tri-cities of Grahamville, Heath, and Future City, just outside Paducah, Kentucky, where I now live. The tri-cities at that time had a population of 400 or 500, if you counted the chickens. I grew up on a dairy farm on Russell Road named for my grandmother, my grandfather, and my father, who operated a dairy for a lifetime at the spot. Our farm was at the end of two school districts - Grahamville and Palestine. It was two and a half miles to either school from our farm. Since my parents had friends at Grahamville, I went to a two-room school there.

One night, a cowboy movie was scheduled at Palestine School. The admission was five cents. This was in 1930 in the heart of the great depression. I was 9 years old. A crowd of about ten of us left a little before dark to go to the movie. Our journey was down a long dirt road that I was unfamiliar with since I attended the other school. This road was the only route to Palestine School where the movie was being shown. There were two great obstacles we had to pass. One was a vacant house, and the second was a family cemetery beside the road.

There were many stories about the house. On the way to see the movie, it was still daylight when we passed the old house where "ghosts" were said to live. One of the boys reminded me about the ghost and said that it was about to get dark and the ghost would soon begin to appear. He picked up a rock and threw it on the roof of the house. When he did this, the silence of the twilight was broken, not only by the sound of the rock hitting the roof, but also by the sound of the moving of tiny feet. Such activity in the vacant house was proof enough to all of us that the house was haunted.

We saw the movie, but it did not have our full attention because we knew in the back of our minds we would have to journey home in the dark, which meant passing the old cemetery and the haunted house. The movie was over, and the night was dark, but we were grateful for the beautiful harvest moon that lit up the sky and gave an eerie atmosphere to the empty countryside. Before we knew it, we had walked to the old haunted house in the abandoned cemetery.

Somebody threw a rock on the roof, and the vacant house became alive with more ghosts than we had heard in the twilight. Oh man, the ghosts were out tonight. We could hear the shuffling of feet as the trees over the cemetery began to shake and move, but there was no wind. Everyone took off running. After we caught our breath and stopped a moment, I wanted to go back and get another look at the ghost. I was scared and tried to enlist somebody to go back with me.

Nobody would go, but they all agreed that they would stay a good distance down the road and wait for me to take another look at the ghost. With my heart in my mouth and my legs trembling, I returned to the scene of the haunted house, the abandoned cemetery, and the moving trees above it. I was more afraid than I could possibly describe here.

As I looked over the haunted house, I could see that the tree above the cemetery was still moving. There in the middle of the cemetery was a big white object. The moon came out from behind a cloud and in one excited moment the light from it fell on the big moving ghost. The moonlight revealed a tall white horse that was standing there. She was eating the leaves of a vine that had grown into the trees over the limestone tombstones. Every time she pulled a leaf off the vine, the tree would shake. The horse was the ghost in the moonlight, and she had made believers out of all of us. I understood what was going on, but I was still scared, so it was no trouble for me to run and yell, "Ghost, ghost, big, white, and moving."

I thought it would be fun to substantiate their fears by scaring them. The consequences of doing this was that they all ran off and left me to walk home alone. Fear and imagination can produce hysteria. The Bible says, "Perfect love casts out fear." Our love is not perfect; we are flawed by sin. But we are forgiven and loved by God anyway. As we put our faith in God, the ghosts of the past can give way to God's redemptive love. We can approach tomorrow without fear and uncertainty when we know that God has His hand on tomorrow.

When I was growing up, I had a good home and wonderful Christian parents who loved me. Like most children in the great depression days, I had only the generosity of my folks who were working hard to make a living. I needed little and had more than I deserved. I had to have several operations on my ear. It bothered me that I cost my folks so much money for medical expenses. Three operations on my right ear were painful to them and to me personally.

As a young person, it amused me to find in the marriage ceremony of the *English Book of Common Prayer* (a beautiful book) the solemnization of matrimony in which the groom was to repeat to the church and to his bride, "With all my worldly goods, I thee endow." Most of the young men I knew didn't have "goods."

At one wedding, when the minister had reached this part of the ceremony, the sister of the groom commented, "There goes his motor scooter!"

Youth comes to us with limited financial resources, but blesses us with time, energy, and good health.

Scripture:

The Bible is full of exhortations to "fear not." Look them up and meditate on God's promises. Here are a few of them:

" Fear not, for I am with you; Be not dismayed, for I am your God. I will strengthen you, Yes, I will help you, I will uphold you with My righteous right hand."~ Isa. 41:10

"Fear not therefore, you are of more value than many sparrows." ~ Matt. 10:31

"God is our refuge and strength, always ready to help in times of trouble. So we will not fear, even if earthquakes come and the mountains crumble into the sea." ~ Ps. 46:1-2

"Those who live in the shelter of the Most High will find rest in the shadow of the Almighty. He will shield you with his wings. He will shelter you with his feathers. His faithful promises are your armor and protection. Do not be afraid of the terrors of the night, nor fear the dangers of the day. If you make the LORD your refuge, if you make the Most High your shelter, no evil will conquer you; no plague will come near your dwelling." ~ Portions of Psalm 91

Prayer:

O, Lord, help me establish goals and objectives for my life at the age I am. Amen.

24

A Good Question

Andy Capp by Reggie Smith is an enjoyable English cartoon. Some years ago, Andy came out of a pub and staggered into a light pole. He tried to get his bearings, only to fall into the gutter. He continued to have a few unhappy moments with an upset stomach. Finally, he commented, "I don't understand it. Why is it that something I love so much treats me so bad?"

Alcohol has never been a means of real support. Just a little drink to lift me up can do a good job of letting me down. A lady said to her husband, "I am going over night to visit my mother. While I am gone don't you go to the pub."

She left and her husband went around the corner to the neighborhood pub. In fact, he spent most of the evening there. Just before he left, he went to the barkeep and ordered another drink. The bartender said, "You have had too much to drink."

"But I want one more for the road."

"That is ridiculous, you just live next door."

He insisted on another drink, and when he finished, he immediately fell to the floor. He pulled himself up and said, "I'll be okay as soon as I get outside. The fresh air will revive me." He managed to hold on to the front door, but when he took the first step he fell down again. He finally crawled around the corner and pulled himself up to the front door of his own house. But inside, he still could not walk. He finally undressed and crawled into bed.

Late the next morning, his wife came home and woke him up and said, "You went to the pub last night!"

"No, no. I was here all night. How do you know I went to the pub?"

"Well, they called this morning and said you left your wheelchair there."

Is it possible that a person could be so drunk that he didn't know he was crippled? I have known sober people who were so developed and active that we did not think of these people as being crippled. Some of the most brilliant people have been handicapped and have had to be confined to a wheelchair, including the late President of the U.S., Franklin D. Roosevelt.

Any average person can be mentally handicapped. He can develop a warped mind, a negative spirit, an uncontrollable temper, a selfish and self-centered ego, and so on it goes.

Scripture:

" I can do all things through Christ who strengthens me." ~ Phil. 4:13

Prayer:

O Lord, I am sorry for who I am, but I'm thankful that I'm not what I used to be. Amen.

25

Replace Criticism with Love

A certain couple was in an earnest and frank discussion. The husband said, "Do you mind if I point out two or three minor flaws in your personality?"

"No," said his wife, "I am aware of those minor flaws you are talking about. They kept me from getting a better husband!"

Just As I Am is a great hymn. I appreciate this great song. Billy Graham uses it as the closing hymn in of all his crusades. Really, the only way we can come to God is *Just As I am*. God does not ask us to make changes and improve ourselves before we come to Him.

Since God takes us just as we are, should we not accept one another in this manner? When we surrender to God, we do not stay just as we are. Coming to God is an act of surrender to Him. Surrendering to God:

1. Gives us access to His power.
2. Gives us the ability to see ourselves as we really are.
3. Gives us the company of His Presence.
4. Enables us to receive His guidance.

Can you believe that God has a plan for your life? In spite of all the things God is doing, He still has time and a purpose for you. God can show you His plan. It could happen at church, or on your way to work, anytime you are willing, God is available.

There's always room for self-improvement. But usually, we do not work very much in this room. It gets crowded with excuses and fights to defend our ego. When self-improvement is the lowest thing on your "to do list," it is probably the thing that is most needed. Making room for God in our life can help us get ahead of ourselves and prevent unhappy moments. Prayer is the key to a better life, especially when we ask God to show us what we cannot see in our lives. Prayer is simply talking and listening to God. The more we give God credit for what happens good in our lives, the easier it is to see Him at work.

Scripture:

"For I know the plans I have for you," says the Lord. "They are plans for good and not for disaster, to give you a future and a hope."~ Jeremiah 29:11

Prayer:

O Lord, let me begin with praise and thanksgiving to You for all You have done in my life. Create a new spirit in my life. Help me enjoy Your Presence and submit to Your power. Amen.

26

Is Being Number One Worth It?

A certain man took great pride in his age. When he finally reached one hundred years of age, he shared this information with any one who would listen. He attended a graveside service for a man he knew. At the cemetery, he met a man that he thought was near his age. Not being certain, he asked the old fellow his age so he could top him with his one hundred.

"How old are you?" he asked the stranger.

"One hundred and one," was the surprised answer.

"It would hardly pay you to go home," was his disappointed reply.

If our self-esteem depends on being smarter, older, or possessing more money than someone else, we are riding for a fall, increasing age does not automatically bring us wisdom or fame. There is always someone who can be victorious over us. "Competition is the life of trade," but it does not increase our popularity. Christians get their worth from God. A good healthy case of self-esteem is always accompanied by a spirit of humility and thanksgiving.

A fine, old gentlemen spent his life being thankful and positive. He experienced a serious illness, and when it was over a friend met him and asked, "Did you find anything positive to be thankful about during your illness?"

"Yes," replied the old positive person.

"What were you thankful about during your sickness?"

"Well, I was thankful for the fever that warmed me up, and the chills that cooled me off!"

I'm not sure any of us can achieve this level of optimism, but I know all of us can do a better job of being positive and thankful, even for the difficult experiences of life. In old age, we can be blessed with good memories, and we can find new friends. We must not be mad about past experiences. We must forgive everybody. This contributes to our mental and physical health.

Here is the one sermon of my life. I repeat it like the chorus of a beautiful and meaningful song. It's recorded in Luke 6:37-38 in the *Good News Bible, Today's English Version*:

> Do not judge others, and God will not judge you.
> Do not condemn others, and God will not condemn you;
> Forgive others, and God will forgive you.
> Give to others, and God will give to you.
> Indeed, you will receive a full measure,
> A generous helping poured into your hands –
> All that you can hold.
> *The measure you use for others*
> *Is the one that God will use for you.*

Think about this. If I think that all I can give for others is a thimble full, then the thimble is the size of my measure, and I use it to dip into my resources and give to others. After I have given my thimble's worth, I lay aside my thimble measure and rest. Then in time of need, I call upon God to help me, He takes my measure, the thimble, and drops into His great resources, and all I get is a thimble's worth. Would it not be smart for me to consider enlarging the size of my measure?

PS – This is not my sermon, it is Jesus' sermon, and He let me use it.

Scripture:

"Do for others what you would like them to do for you. This is a summary of all that is taught in the law and the prophets." ~ Matthew 7:12

Prayer:

O Lord, help me to increase my measure of blessing to others, so that I may be blessed by You in return. Amen.

27

Scriptural Support

A preacher was famous for his ability to offer a scripture of guidance and support for all the experiences of life. At one of his public speaking events, he accidentally swallowed a bug. He coughed and turned red in the face. He finally recovered, and a man in the congregation said, "Preacher, you always are able to come up with a scripture for every experience of life. Give us one for swallowing a bug."

"He was a stranger and I took him in," the preacher quipped. This scripture was not intended for this purpose. Neither was it intended to suggest that we are to take advantage of people who are not at home in our culture or land. Hospitality and good will make the world a better place to live. We can't get too much of this because there are a lot of timid and unsure people who will not get out of themselves long enough to serve others even with a handshake or an act of kindness.

Times have changed. It used to be common knowledge that the "the fleas come with the dog." But today, a lot more comes with the dog than fleas. The responsibilities today of dog ownership are extensive. It would make us wish for fleas only.

We were sitting outside at the beach and a friend walked his dog into our circle. The dog eagerly came up to us, but his owner said, "He is not being friendly. He is looking for treats. When he finds out you don't have any, he will leave."

In our friendship with others, what are we looking for? Their approval? A needed compliment? Someone to listen and agree with us? Is it okay to be like the modern dog, to be friendly expecting a treat? The best way to be a friend might be to be sincerely interested in someone else, care what happens to him or her, and listen as much as he or she needs you to listen.

Friendship means a lot to us. A great minister friend of mine, Dr. Si Matheson, was an outstanding preacher and a more than able pastor. He could lead the singing and help people enjoy taking part in the song service. Everywhere Si went people loved him. After retirement, Si preached at a small church for over 15 years. He raised money for a retirement home and saw it to completion. He was chaplain at a hospital in Panama City Beach, Florida. Si and his wife Mary were great role models and good friends of ours. Here is one of the stories Si told me.

After serving one church for a very long time, the conference moved Si to a larger church. At the last service, the church lay-leader stood and said, "Jesus brought Brother Si to us, Jesus sent him to another church, let us stand and sing, *What a Friend We Have in Jesus.*" Change comes to all of us, but it is important to always remember that God is with us.

Scripture:

"Jesus Christ the same yesterday, today, and forever." ~ Hebrews 13:8

Prayer:

O Lord, we thank You that through the bitter sweet experiences of life, You are there to season life with Your peace. Amen.

28

A Risky Assignment

An officer commanded a submarine in World War II. One night, it was necessary for the submarine to surface to charge the batteries. The enemy was on the shore of an island. He posted a guard to be a lookout during the night. The man was a new draftee, so the officer felt he should impress upon him the significance of his nighttime duty.

"Young man," he said, "this is a big job I'm giving you. It is important that you stay awake and alert. All the men on this sub are depending on you to keep watch so the enemy will not take us by surprise. As commander of this sub, I'm depending on you. The President of the United States is depending on you! All the folks back home are depending on you to do a good job!"

The man gave the officer a salute and said, "Sir, that's right, all those people are depending on me; I'm depending on me, too."

He was correct to add himself to the list. Others are looking and watching our conduct and behavior - how we do our job; how we deal with temptation. It is absolutely correct to include ourselves in our effort to behave. Self-disappointment is the greatest blow we can receive. Let us avoid it at all cost. Being on guard against ourselves can prevent trouble later.

Scripture:

One of the beautiful and tragic stories in the Bible is found in Acts 7:51-60. In any translation, the message comes through. Stephen's message was critical of the leading religious leaders of his day. Stephen let them know that they had treated Jesus in a horrible way. These people became so angry that they drug Stephen outside the city and began to stone him. Stephen had a vision of Jesus standing at the right hand of the Father. In other scriptures, Jesus is sitting at the right hand of God. However, in Stephen's vision, Jesus was standing at the right hand of God.

When a person stands, he is getting ready to receive someone, so Jesus was standing to receive Stephen into heaven. Perhaps minutes later, after Stephen's vision, he was stoned to death. It is interesting that Stephen died with the same anointing from the Holy Spirit that Jesus had on the cross. Listen to Stephen's words, "Lord Jesus, receive my spirit." He knelt down and cried out in a loud voice, "Lord! Do not remember this sin against them." He said this and died.

The scripture specifically mentions the presence of Saul – who later would be called Paul – at Stephen's stoning: "They dragged him out of the city and began to stone him. The official witnesses took off their coats and laid them at the feet of a young man named Saul." Saul approved of his murder. He continued to persecute the church until the day on the road to Damascus when God overtook Saul, and Jesus, through the power of the Holy Spirit and with the help of courageous Ananias, transformed Saul into Paul. When we witness for Christ and forgive others, God can transform our world.

Prayer:

Can we take a moment and dedicate ourselves and say as Ananias did, "Here I am Lord." Amen.

29

A Guiding Light

It's amazing how our forefathers crossed the great oceans of the world. The sea was awesome and the storms were able to make great waves. The water was trackless. Once you left shore, the roads disappeared and the landscape was lost on the horizon.

A woman was on her first sea voyage, and after the land disappeared, she went to the captain and asked, "How far are we from land?"

"Only a mile and a half," replied the captain.

She left with a sense of calm, but she wanted more information, so she inquired of the officer, "In what direction is it a mile and half to land?'

"Straight down, madam, straight down."

Security is not always found in being near the shore. Launching out into the deep is important, if we are to reach the other shore. The stars were guides for the ancient sailors, especially the North Star. Many a course was fixed on the North Star. While they were steering by the North Star, nobody in his right mind ever planned to reach the North Star. But many a sailor and traveler charted his course by the North Star; he planned to get home by the North Star.

God has given us many *North Stars* in the Bible, by which we can guide our lives. Some guiding lights in the darkness are:

Be perfect, even as Your Father in heaven in perfect
This is a goal to work for. It's our guiding light, our spiritual North Star.

Love one another.
This is the North Star of peace on earth.

Love you enemies.
This is the North Star of human relations.

Forgive others, even your enemies.
This is the North Star of health and healing.

Give to others.
This is the North Star of faith, hope, and good will.

Do unto others as you would like them to do unto you.
This is a simple, but profound practice that can be universally applied, bringing great results

Scripture:

Hear Jesus' Sermon: "You are the light for the whole world. A city built on a hill cannot be hidden. No one lights a lamp and puts it under a bowl. Instead, he puts it on a lamp stand, where it gives light to everyone who is in the house. In the same way your light must shine before people, so they will see the good things you do and praise your Father in heaven." ~ Matt. 5: 14 TEV

Prayer:

Lord, help me stay plugged into Your power supply so my light will not go out. Amen.

30

A Compliment?

A missionary taught English in an African village. She was loved for her wonderful spirit. Her skills and talents enabled her young students to read and write in another language. Learning English opened a new world for many people and especially for these young boys and girls. She was scheduled to return to the states for a year. So she said goodbye to her students. She received many gifts. There was a note written in English from one of her young students, "Dear Teacher, Thank you for everything. You are like the flowers. You smell forever!"

Perhaps we all leave behind an aroma of some sort. This young boy was kind and meant to complement his teacher. I would agree with him that some people do "smell forever." Frequently, their behavior stinks. Sometimes they leave behind a bad impression.

Nothing can be more obnoxious than a drunk whose alcohol has drugged his inhibitions and revealed to all the world what a miserable person he has become. Alcohol deadens a person's inhibitions and exposes his personal life to the entire world.

A drunk on a bus was crying and sadly saying to everyone, "I'm going to hell!" As the drug took over his behavior, he went up and down the bus saying to each passenger, "I'm gong to hell!"

Different people on the bus gave him their attention and concern only to discover how futile and useless it is to talk to a drunk. The man's voice became louder and louder. He kept repeating his theme song, "I'm going to hell!" He came upon a weary priest, and woke him up, "I'm going to hell!" he shouted in a very loud voice.

The irritated and disgusted priest said, "OK, go to hell, but be quiet about it!"

How many people may be quietly on the road to personal destruction? These people never let anyone know that they are living lives of quiet desperation. If they could open up to sober and serious conversation, they might be surprised to find out that these are people who care and who could be helpful.

Everybody needs a good listener. Talking can help people ventilate their anxiety. Words of assurance can give new direction and meaningful hope for troubled people.

Scripture:

"Don't worry about everyday life…can all your worries add a single moment to your life? Of course not. Why worry about your clothes?… Don't worry about having enough food, or drink, or clothing…Don't worry about tomorrow, for tomorrow will bring its own worries. Today's trouble is enough for today." ~ Portions of Matt. 6: 25-34

Jesus was saying trust God for these things. Worry and anxiety can dominate your life. Such behavior can produce fear and leave you miserable.

Prayer:

O Lord, help me trust and turn over everything to You and work as though it all depends on me. Amen.

31

Finding a New Home in a Crowded City

In September of 1943, I went to Dallas, Texas, to Southern Methodist University to attend the Perkins School of Theology. During WWII, the university was training military people. The school had military huts on the campus for training and housing. There was no place on campus for any more people and no place around SMU for student housing. Under these unexpected conditions, the question began to hit me, "Where am I going to spend the night?"

After I registered for class, I found a bulletin board in the hall with many messages posted for job opportunities on it. Finding people for jobs was indeed difficult. I pulled a notice on the board for employment, and after making a telephone call, I got on the street car, transferred to a bus, and finally arrived at Brewer Funeral Home on Ross Avenue. I inquired about the job opening, and they explained to me about their need for a part-time employee. I would have to work every other night and sleep in their dorm upstairs.

World War II was on and gas was difficult to come by. The city of Dallas did not have an ambulance service. So, consequently each funeral home had to provide transportation to the hospital for any of their customers that called for help.

"You mean I have to spend every other night being on call as a part time ambulance driver?" I asked.

"Yes," the director answered.

"Since I'm here every other night, why can't I spend every night here, and if you need me I'll be available."

They agreed, and I moved into the funeral home. It was the first night of an educational adventure in Dallas, Texas. I had no idea that I would live in the funeral home for eighteen months. It was here that I met many wonderful people on staff at the funeral home. Driving an ambulance on the streets of the city of Dallas at all hours of the night and day, plus going in and out of hospitals, gave me an education that no academic class could provide.

For a country boy from McCracken County in Paducah, Kentucky, sleeping at a funeral home was more than a new experience. I always thought you went to a funeral home when you were dead, so it was shocking to go there to spend the night and live there. The people who work in the funeral business have a very difficult job. They live with grief and sadness every day and night. Those whom I have known have been more than helpful, and there are many whom I do not know who are just as dedicated. Their main purpose is to serve the family in their time of need.

There was a teacher in the city school of Paducah who taught my mother and was a friend of my grandmother. I was the last person that was alive that she knew. She left word how she wanted her funeral conducted. I tried to follow her instructions, but she detailed who was to ride in the first car, the second car, and the third car that followed the hearse. When I got out to the funeral procession everybody was in different cars. I looked at all these elderly women and I said, "Miss Lucy, there's no way I'm going to move these women around. Please forgive me."

I had a friend named Tom who was in the funeral business in Dyersburg, Tennessee. The people lived in the boon docks of the county. Just before the funeral, one of the family came to Tom and said, "We found Paw's teeth. Will you put them in his mouth?"

They handed Tom the teeth in a sack. He opened the sack, and they were the original teeth that the deceased had lost one by one.

Just before the service they asked, "Did you put Paw's teeth in?"

"Yes," Tom replied.

This was an impossible task to put teeth in one at a time, but I actually saw Tom do it. He lifted up the pillow under the head of the man and put in the teeth sack and all.

Scripture:

"My God shall supply all your needs according to His riches in Christ Jesus." ~ Phil. 4:19

Prayer:

O Lord, thank You for giving us a new spiritual body after we have worn out this old one. Amen.

32

Carried Out

Broadway United Methodist Church is located at Seventh and Broadway in historic downtown Paducah, Kentucky, just seven blocks from the spot where the Tennessee River flows into the Ohio River, and together they make a mighty big splash.

In 1937, the church was located in midstream as the Tennessee River overflowed its banks and cut across town to meet itself, thus eliminating the traditional bend in the river.

Broadway is a great church full of interesting history. Vice President Barkley's funeral was there, and many people from Washington and other places in the USA attended it, but not many people from Broadway Church came to his funeral. It wasn't that they didn't like the VP, or that they were Republicans, it is just that traditionally the membership never liked to go to funerals.

Being a new minister and having worked my way through SMU with a good job at a funeral home, I could appreciate Broadway Church people not liking funerals and not attending them. In fact, confidently, I wouldn't go to my own, but that wouldn't be politically correct not to show up at one's own funeral.

A single lady died and left specific instructions concerning her funeral. She specified that she wanted absolutely no men pall bearers. It took some searching to find six women strong enough to carry her body to its last resting place, but her request was granted since she left a short note of explanation. "I want only women pall bearers. It is not because I'm a women-liber, but because I lived all my life as a single woman. No man sought the privilege of taking me out when I was alive, so I don't intend for them to do it when I'm dead."

When you die, it's proper for you to have the last word about your funeral. It's amazing what Jesus has done for funerals. He never appeared at any of them. The people of the day hired professional mourners. Further more, He said, "I'm the God of the living not the dead." He declared, "I am the resurrection and the life. He who believes is me, thought he were dead, yet shall he live, and whosoever believes in me shall never die."

Scripture:

Jesus had a great word for all of us when He said to his disciples, "Now is your time of grief, but I will see you again and you will rejoice, and no one will take away your joy." ~ John 16:22 NIV

Prayer:

O Lord, help me work through my grief. Heal my sorrow day by day. When my sorrow comes over me like an ocean wave, help me know I will not drown, for faith has taught me how to swim. Amen.

33

Frustration Can Be a Lasting Experience

A certain minister achieved success as a leader. He was well thought of by his peers. In his earlier years, he was a pastor of a fine church in a small West Tennessee town. In the spring of the Easter season, the choir of his church worked hard and produced a beautiful anthem. The Sunday crowd was small, but the next Sunday the crowd at the church was larger than usual. The pastor said, "Last Sunday our choir did a great job presenting a beautiful number. Many of you were not here to enjoy their hard work. So I'm going to ask them to sing for you again last Sunday's beautiful song."

There was an awkward pause. The pastor insisted that they repeat the number. The choir gave the musical number and it was a disaster. The strong voices were not there. The choir sat behind the preacher, and he was not aware of the absence of the supporting group of singers. After the embarrassing endeavor, was over the frustrated and embarrassed pastor tried to help the choir out of the failure.

"I'm sorry I did not know some of the leaders were absent," he explained. Then with a twist of his tongue he said, "I apologize, I did not mean to put the 'squire on the pot!'"

For many years, when ministers gathered in his district and got into heated discussions, this same minister would always have some strong opinions and insist that everybody see things his way. To bring him back into line, one of the contemporaries would always say, "Tell us about the Sunday when you put the 'squire on the pot.' " He would back down and laugh.

Slip of the tongue can be funny, especially in church. However, this pastor was successful enough for this funny trivia not to be a problem for him. It is best we identify with the strong positive moments of our lives. It is necessary that we laugh off our accidents and even our mistakes. Good men are remembered for who they were and what they did and not for what they accidentally spoke.

When I was in seminary back in 1944-46 in Dallas, Texas, one of the professors at southern Methodist University was teaching a course on public speaking. He reminded us to be careful about our illustrations.

A minister was conducting a funeral. He stood before the open casket, the beautiful flowers and the grieving family and friends. In order to be helpful, pointing to the body of the deceased, he said,

"Folks, don't be sad. This is just the shell. The nut has gone away."

What a terrible illustration. The words of Jesus offer hope, consolation and strength to His disciples. The words are for us today; they are both contemporary and eternal,"You now have sorrow, but I will see you again and your heart will rejoice, and your joy no one will take from you." ~ John 16:22

Scripture:

"I am not alone, because my Father is with me." ~ John 16: 32

Prayer:

O Lord, I know I will see again those I have loved. May Your joy be my strength. Amen.

34

Do You Like Your Name?

If we took a poll and asked people, "Do you like your name?" a lot of people would not. Over the years, they grow accustomed to their name. When students are asked to speak their names, some of them mumble their names in embarrassment. A friend of mine was named Steamboat Jones. His father named him "Steamboat." His father said he chose this name because as a baby, he reminded him of a steamboat. When my friend decided to buy a phone, the company refused to list his name "Steamboat" in the directory. "Surely you have another given name besides this name," the company insisted.

When Steamboat tried to open a bank account he had the same problem. The banker said, "We do not take nicknames."

"But, Steamboat is my real name," he said emphatically, "and here is my birth certificate to prove it!"

I was in my banker's office when a merchant friend of mine came in and confirmed the following story. Folks this one is real. I changed the last name a little so that I would not be sued should someone ever find their name connected with one of these rambling. You may find it hard to believe that a person could get sued for telling the truth, but tradition has it that some messengers have gotten shot by people who didn't like their message.

There was a certain lady named Wilston who refused to name her children at their birth. She waited until her children got old enough to pick the name they liked. There is a lot of wisdom in this decision. In many cases, the kids called themselves by the name they liked for years before making that name legal. Her ten-year-old son named himself with the initials B.G. He used these two letters B.G., and he was officially named B.G. Wilston. Years later, he was asked if B.G. stood for anything or if he just liked the sound of the letters. He proudly declared that he liked the sound of the two letters that he had chosen for his name and that they did stand for two words – "Billy Goat."

This also reminds me that a man was so embarrassed about his name that he went before a judge and asked to receive permission to change his name.

The judge asked, "What is your full name that you find offensive?"

"Johnny Stinks," was the response.

"Well, I could see how such a name could be embarrassing," the judge said. "We can arrange for a court order to get your name changed. What new name have you selected to replace, Johnny Stinks?"

"Sir," the man answered, "I would like to be called 'Charlie Stinks.' "

We all have legal names, but we also have another name that identifies us; it is called *reputation*.

Scripture:

"To the angel of the church in Sardis write, 'I know your deeds, you have a reputation of being alive, but you are dead.'" ~ Rev. 3:1

Prayer:

O Lord, help me to wake up and pay attention to my reputation. Help me close the gap between who I am and who people think I am. Amen.

35

Loyalty

There is no substitute for believing in yourself. Taking a serious inventory of your ability is personally reassuring.

Some small boys were playing baseball in a park when a stranger walked by and said to one of the players, "What is the score?"

"They are ten, and we are nothing."

"I am sorry you are losing," replied the stranger.

"We aren't losing," one of the boys replied.

"Ten to your nothing looks like you've lost," the stranger reasoned.

"No," said the boy, "we aren't loosing. We haven't come to bat yet."

This represents ultimate optimism.

I can appreciate Texas pride. Texas is a big state. Their resources are tremendous. Before joining the Union, the state of Texas had its own army. Texans' self-confidence expresses itself in many words of appreciation for its citizens. The story is told of a cowboy who spent longer than usual at the bar one night. On his walk home, he cut across the cemetery. Workers had opened a new grave and the Texan, who had too much to drink, stumbled and fell into the open grave. He made several attempts to get out of the grave but failed. The drug made him so sleepy he took a long nap.

Early the next morning, he was awakened by the rising sun. He was confused and did not know where he was. He felt the side of the grave, stood up, raised up on his toes and looked up out over the edge. The morning sunrise reflected off of the dew sprinkled tombstone. Then he realized that he was in a cemetery, and thinking that he had somehow died and been buried, he let out a shout, "Glory Hallelujah! It's resurrection morning and a Texan is the first to rise."

This reminds me of a poor fellow who had too much "cool aid," and under the influence, took a short cut across the cemetery to get to his home. During the day, a grave had been dug in anticipation of a funeral the next day. As this old guy was walking along, he fell into the grave. He tried to get out, and in the process, he woke up the other drunk who had fallen in the grave before him. He said to the new arrival, "Don't bother trying, you can't get out of here!" But he did! Fear can cause us to sober up and put forth a great effort to do the impossible.

When I was a boy in Western Kentucky, I lived on a dairy farm. On the other side of the road from our farm was a house people rented. It was in 1932, during the Great Depression. A man was repairing an old car. He had the rear-end out of the auto. It was lifted off the ground and placed on blocks of wood so he could lie under the vehicle and work freely. He accidentally kicked over one of the supports, and the Model-T fell on him.

He yelled out in pain. His wife came running out of the house and saw him trapped. She picked up the rear-end of the car, and he crawled out. The lady was not very large. I couldn't believe it. The old car was lighter than usual because the heaviest part had been removed, but it still took two big men to put the car back on the blocks. By the time, I got over there the man became sick at his stomach, and I was afraid he had been severely injured. However, I found out later that he had been chewing tobacco and had swallowed some of it.

In times of fear and excitement, some people find they have more strength than normal. For the Christian, God is the resource for our help and strength.

Scripture:

"What else do I have in heaven but you? Since I have You, what else could I want on earth? My mind and my body may grow weak, but God is my strength. He is all I ever need." ~ Psalm 73: 23-26 TEV

Prayer:

O Lord, I look to You. Your Presence in my life and the strength You give is sufficient for abundant life now. Amen.

36

A Questionable Trade

A clergyman was riding his bicycle down the street when he passed a house having a yard sale. On sale was a fairly decent lawn mower. A little boy standing beside the mower declared that it belonged to him. The minister said to the young man, "I'll trade you my bicycle for your lawn mower. Will it run?"

"Yes," said the young boy. "I would like a bicycle." So they agreed on the exchange.

However, the young boy said, "Preacher, I need to warn you that sometimes in order to get this lawn mower started you have to cuss it."

The preacher took the mower and ignored the comment of the young boy. Much later, he was mowing his yard when the thing stopped and wouldn't start again. After cranking on the mower without any results, he remembered that the boy said something about starting the mower so he got the kid on the phone.

"Son, the mower I traded for my bicycle won't start, and I remember you said something about starting it, but I forgot exactly what you said."

"Sir," the boy said, "I said that sometimes in order to start this mower you had to cuss it."

"Oh, I wouldn't do that," the minister responded. "In fact, I don't remember any cuss words. It's been many years since I even thought of such words."

"Preacher, if you'll keep on cranking that mower those words will come back to you!"

In moments of frustration, we are tempted to curse the source of our unhappiness. Job, a Biblical figure with more problems than any human has ever endured, was tempted by his wife when all his problems seemed to overwhelm him.

"Why don't you curse God and die?" she asked.

But Job replied, "Shall we indeed accept good from God, and shall we not accept adversity?"

Cursing can be also an act of fear. When Peter was in the courtyard after the arrest of Jesus, a maid said to him, "You must be one of them, your accent is like his."

To disguise himself, Peter cursed and lied, "I never knew the man."

Never use God's name in a curse word. Such misuse of God's name destroys your ability to use God's name when you are in prayer or in times of distress. It is much more effective to go to the source of the problem and seek a solution.

Scripture:

"Let the word of Christ dwell in you richly in all wisdom." ~ Cols. 3:16

Prayer:

O Lord, when I am frustrated, let me turn to You in prayer so I may receive peace from stress. Amen.

37

High Finance

A certain person struggled, and at last, made the final payment on his house. He then put a new mortgage on his house so he could buy a new car. He did not want his new expensive car to sit out in the weather, so he went to the bank to borrow money on the car so he could build a garage.

"If I do let you have the loan, how will you buy gas for your new car?" asked the banker.

"Well, that's simple. A person who owns his own house, car, and garage, shouldn't have any trouble obtaining a credit card for gas."

The easy payment plan has made life difficult for many people. My English friends refer to the installment plan as the "high buy plan." It is important to control spending. Avoid impulsive decisions about spending.

When a husband asked his wife, "Why is our budget out of control?" She replied, "The neighbors buy so many things we can't afford!"

A lady said to her husband, "If it wasn't for my money, you wouldn't be living in this beautiful practical house! If it wasn't for my money you wouldn't be driving that expensive sports car parked in the driveway!"

The husband straightened up and said, "If it wasn't for your money, I wouldn't be here." The real reason for marriage is for love and companionship. If you marry for beauty, it can fade.

If you marry for money and wealth, you can lose it. Marry a person with good character and a fine disposition, and your chance for happiness will be more than good. Marriage is almost never a 50-50 proposition. Most of the time its 70-30 or 90-10 or whatever.

Jesus told the parable of the great banquet. Invitations were given, and the servant went and told three men that everything was ready. They began to make excuses. Here's my translation.

The first one said, "I just bought an expensive piece of real estate. Please excuse me. I need to go and see what it looks like." What a poor excuse, nobody would be so stupid to buy property they had not seen before.

The second one said, "I just bought a beautiful, expensive eighteen wheeler and I have never driven it. Please excuse me." Nobody would put that much money in a truck he had never driven.

The third one said, "I just got married and my wife wouldn't let me out of the house!" This was almost believable. When God invites us to enjoy being His guest, if we don't show up, God will replace us with somebody else.

Scripture:

Jesus replied, "All those who love me will do what I say. My Father will love them, and we will come to them and live with them." ~ John 14:23 NLT

Prayer:

O Lord, let me live in obedience to Your call so that I will not miss out on Your purpose for my life. Amen.

38

An Unusual Birth

Grace's uncle, Dr. Williams, lived in Greenville, Mississippi, where he practiced medicine for a lifetime. Once a young couple came to him because they were expecting their first baby.

"Dr. Williams, we have a problem," said the young mother to be. "I'm from Texas, and we now live in Mississippi. We would like our son to be born here, but my father is from Texas. His father was born in Texas, his grandfather was born in Texas, and needless to say my husband was born in Texas. He has caused a big scene over the fact that we will not go back to Texas for the birth of my baby. I don't know what to except from him when he comes to the birth of our child. We just wanted to warn you of his behavior."

The day arrived for the birth of her son. She was admitted to the labor room. Dr. Williams was asked to come to the waiting room. There he stood - a big Texan with a hat to prove it.

Dr. Williams said, "He went through the story explaining to me why he wanted his grandson to be born in Texas. He also admitted that his daughter was as hardheaded as he was and would not come back to Texas for the birth of the first grandson. Then he said to me, 'I wanted my grandson to be born on Texas soil. So, Doc, here is a plastic bag of Texas dirt. Will you put it under the delivery table just before he's born so my grandson can be born on Texas soil?' I agreed. The bag was sealed and clean so I threw it under the delivery table."

Loyalty and tradition can be a wonderful thing and to many people these values are worth saving. So why not be loyal to what you believe in if it enhances the experiences of your life and does no harm to others?

Having gone to SMU in Dallas, I can appreciate the Texas spirit. It made a great contribution to my life back in 1945-46. Believing in your heritage can make a difference in your behavior.

Being born again into the Christian faith makes you a citizen of both earth and heaven. Such an experience of believing and knowing that you are a native of the kingdom of God gives you both a confidence and an assurance that you are a person of dignity and worth. Such an inheritance keeps you from ever having an identity crisis.

A Pharisee named Nicodemus, a member of the Jewish ruling council, came to Jesus by night so he wouldn't be seen. Jesus said to him, "You must be born again!" "What do you mean?" exclaimed Nicodemus, "How can an old man go back into his mother's womb and be born again?" A Pharisee, who was an important leader, could not think outside the box.

Scripture:

"Flesh gives birth to flesh, but the Spirit gives birth to the spirit." ~ John 3:6

Prayer:

O Lord, help me start over again, make me a new person. Amen.

39

Too Many Meetings

A certain man was presiding at a meeting. A man in the audience, took over the floor, and would not stop talking. The presiding officer tried everything to get the boring dull speaker to stop. Finally in disgust and frustration, he threw his gavel at the irritating speaker. But the presiding officer's aim was not good, and instead of hitting the continuous speaker, he hit a man in the front row. Those near the injured person in the audience quickly revived the victim, however the boring man continued his tirade. Consequently, the injured person replied, "Hit me again, I can still hear him."

Some years ago, I was a student minister in Texas. The annual conference met, and retiring ministers were given the opportunity to speak before the conference. One clergyman was negative, bitter, cynical, and spoke for a long time. Finally, when he took a deep breath, the presiding bishop said, "Thank you brother."

"Wait a minute, Bishop, I'm not through," the preacher replied.

"Oh, I'm sorry I thought you came to a period."

"No, Bishop, just a semicolon."

It's frustrating when a person keeps on talking after he has run out of something to say. I have heard of people who buy a hundred shares of stock in a company and go to the meeting of the stockholders just to harass the administration.

Being negative beyond reason and being critical because you have over developed that part of your personality can cause you to self-destruct. Saying, "No," only stops something. There has to be a "Yes" along the way.

The drunk said to the alcoholic who attended AA, "The only difference between you and me is that I don't have to go to all those meetings." However, it was the meetings and the speeches that brought the former alcoholic sobriety.

In 1950, when I was establishing a church on a vacant lot in Memphis, I went to many meetings. There was a good man that I liked very much who was on the Finance Committee. The only problem was that he dominated the meeting and made a speech about every item and was always negative about it.

I decided to put a man on the Finance Committee who was in the building and loan business. He attended the first meeting where my negative friend had much to say. At the end of the long meeting, the new man asked if he could say a word. The chairman was glad for him to say something, and this is what he said: "I've never been on a church finance committee before. I didn't know what to do. But I learned tonight how to behave. Just be your own obnoxious self like Mr. Green here."

From that time on things changed. Mr. Green was quiet at the meetings.

Scripture:

"Be still and know that I am God." ~ Psalm 46:10.

Prayer:

O Lord, Help me to listen more and speak less.

40

Fact or Fiction

There is an interesting story of a scientist who invented a magic potion that when sprinkled on inanimate objects would bring them to life. He picked out the statue of a general mounted on his horse. The statue was very old, and the old stone military man and his beautiful horse had witnessed many events in the park. So the scientist decided to try out this magic potion on this statue of the old general. If it brought him to life for only a second, he would no doubt have words of wisdom to pass on to coming generations.

Finally, everything was in order. The scientist sprinkled the magic potion, and the great old general came to life and spoke one sentence, "Oh how I hate those awful pigeons!"

In this fictitious moment, his only utterance was a complaint. What do we remember about all our past experiences? Would we speak a word of appreciation or complaint, or would we utter a sentence of thanksgiving? An old native bought himself a new boomerang – the only problem, he spent the rest of his life trying to throw away the old one. Most of life comes back to us. We throw out our criticisms and complaints and they come back to us.

When we throw out appreciation of others these positive values have a way of returning to us. Perhaps life is more of a circle than we realize. Albert Einstein is reported to have said, "Evil is the absence of good, and good is the evidence of God." We all have a moment in time to declare our faith, speak our opinions, voice our concerns and reveal who we really are. That opportunity is called "Today." Today is caught between yesterday and tomorrow. One has gone forever and the other has not arrived yet.

Scripture:

"Elijah came to all the people and said, 'How long halt you between two opinions? If the Lord be God, follow him! But if Baal, then follow him.' And the people answered him not a word."
~ 1 Kings 18:21

Prayer:

O Lord, please be with me in the journey of life. I need Your guidance, for I have never lived tomorrow before.

41

What's In a Name?

In an effort to better serve people, churches have built rooms for babies and places for mothers to care for them. One minister came to me when I was a district superintendent and told me about a beautiful nursery they had constructed. He asked me if I had any suggestions about a name for the nursery.

"No," I said, "but I have a scripture in the 15th chapter of 1 Corinthians that Paul wrote. You could put this on a plaque on the outside of the room – 'We shall not all sleep, but we shall all be changed.' "

He didn't think this was funny; perhaps he didn't know a lot about babies.

I once took part in a cabinet meeting. It was a most distrustful meeting. A minister was the victim of a terrible and unhappy event. As a group, anything we did could only add to the disaster. We adjourned for the night, and the next morning there was an awful hangover from the sad experience of the day before. Everybody was unhappy and distrustful. The bishop asked me how I slept. I said, "Like a baby." They all looked at me with questionable doubt – I repeated, "I slept like a baby; I was up all night crying and going to the bathroom."

We can hurt for ourselves, but we can be equally sad for others. It's very painful and real distressing when we are unable to help others who are in need.

Prayer makes it possible for us to pass on to God our concerns for those whom we are unable to help. God can do what we cannot perform. That is why He is God, and we are mere humans.

The disciples experienced this when the man brought his son to them. The Bible says he was affected with a demon, and the father told Jesus that His disciples were unable to help. Jesus performed the miracle of healing.

Turn to Jesus and let Him give direction for your life. The Holy Spirit is God's great Helper, and He is available to all who turn to Him.

It is our duty to love others in the spirit and name of God. It is not our obligation to put our hands on them and change them. When we lift up those we love and turn them over to God, He will change them in his own time. It is difficult for us, but we must give up our job as being the person who is supposed to change everybody. God is still the Creator and Designer of human life. Let us step aside, and let Him do His work both in them and in us.

Scripture:

"We know that in all things God works for good with those who love him." ~ Romans 8:28 TEV

Prayer:

O Lord, I love you. My love mingles with Your love and this makes me a happy person. Amen.

42

Halloween

A Baptist minister told me this story that happened to one of his Baptist preacher friends. It was Halloween and the children of the town dressed in costume. It was a common practice to target this preacher who was well liked and a good sport in the community. A beautiful dark haired girl who was just barely able to talk was dressed like an angel. She rang his doorbell. When he answered the door, she looked up at him and said, "Trick or Treat!"

The minister who answered the door said, "I see you are dressed like an angel."

"Yes," the little girl replied.

"What kind of an angel are you?" asked the minister.

"I'm a Baptist angel," she said.

"That's great, I'm a Baptist minister. Wait right here. I want to get you something special."

He noticed that his wife had three beautiful apples on the dining room table. So he picked out the biggest and most beautiful one. He came back and said to the beautiful angel, "Open your sack wide." She did, and he dropped the big beautiful apple in her sack. She looked in the sack and said nothing. Hoping to increase her manners and get her to say thank you, he asked, "Now what do you say?"

She replied, "Your broke every damn cookie in the sack."

Some people dress up like angels, but when provocation or frustration arises, they talk like devils. "Hell" and "damn" are really theological words that are frequently misused by people who have a limited vocabulary. "Hell" is a slang word used to describe something or someone. My father would describe people he did not like in different way. I remember he described a person who had an abrasive personality by saying, "She looked like the devil before day!" I always wondered what the devil looked like later in the day, but I never asked.

Scripture:

"Jesus proclaimed us his followers as the light of the world, as the salt of the earth, and even as the bread of heaven. Has the light in us grown dim? If so, then darkness is gradually taking over our life. If the salt has lost its ability to be salt, then it is only a useless commodity of little value. In such a condition, we can no longer season life with spiritual power." ~ Matthew 5:13-14

Prayer:

O Lord, I take inventory of my character and in my faith in You. Along the way have I compromised, or diluted my faith in You? Please renew me with Your Presence now. Amen.

43

Child Guidance

A university professor and his wife, who was an English teacher, went to a well-know guidance professor. They said, "We are disturbed about our teen-age boys. They have started to use slang words like the "h" word and the "d" word. They think that's smart; we are embarrassed about them. We have tried everything. We gave up. I think they are trying to embarrass us."

The counselor said, "The next time they use one of these words hit them with the back of your hand. That will shock them and end their bad habit."

The next morning the mother was seated at the table, one of them on her right and the other on her left. She asked the one on the right, " What would you like for breakfast?"

He replied, "Give me some of those 'd' corn-flakes!"

The mother took the back of her right hand and hit him. The blow caused him to get off balance, and he fell backwards to the floor. She ignored the fallen boy and turned to her son on the left and asked, "What would you like for breakfast?"

The boy looked at his fallen brother on the floor and said to his mother, "Well, I sure as 'h' don't want any of those 'd' corn-flakes."

Actually, there was nothing wrong with the corn-flakes; the mother didn't like the way the boys talked. What is said is important along with the manner in which it is said. It is possible to be emphatic without being obnoxious. Much of life is spent in not getting the point. This is especially true where discipline is concerned. Punishment is administered to get the message about human behavior across. This usually happens after all else has failed. Striking a child is not a good practice, and I do not recommend it, even though such a thing might help the parent.

I suggest spending more time with children at an early age. Such company establishes a line of communication between adult and child. Nothing can substitute for an absent parent. When children come into the world, they need a sign of warning carried around their neck, "Still under construction." A family job description is a great guide for family behavior; especially during the teen years.

Slang and cursing is the sign of a limited vocabulary. It is often a cover up for something else. Peter turned to cursing when he was faced with his fear and disappointment at the arrest of Jesus.

Scripture:

"A little later, those who stood by said to Peter again, 'Surely you re one of them, for you are a Galilean, and your speech shows it.' But he began to curse and swear, "I do not know this man of whom you speak." ~ Mark 14: 70-71

Prayer:

O Lord, forgive me when my life and speech has been in denial of my discipleship. Amen.

44

What About the Weather Tomorrow?

A certain movie producer was filming an outdoor epic in the West. Trying to figure out the weather was a problem. After consulting with local authorities, he sought the advice of an old Indian who was famous for weather predictions. He paid the old Indian well, and it was worth the price because the old sage was accurate. Everyday he talked to the Indian about tomorrow's weather - rainy, clear, windy, etc. One day, the producer asked his Indian guide for tomorrow's weather.

"Don't know," replied the Indian.

"Why don't you know?" demanded the movie producer.

"Radio broke," declared the Indian.

Being able to balance how much we depend on ourselves, and the amount we depend on others is an act of wisdom. Sometimes, we are right to be the lone ranger of our personal affairs, and at other times it is wise to seek advice and guidance from others. It is always a smart thing to believe in and practice prayer. Through prayer, we communicate with God, who offers His advice and council as well as the company of His Presence. Doing God's will is not always free, frequently it too comes with a price, but it is worth the cost.

Isaiah wrote this passage for us to ponder, "Watchman, what of the night?" The watchman said, "The morning will come" (Isa. 21:11-12). Time does not stand still for any of us. God encourages us to move on. Let us come alive in the pew. Our presence there is not to be only a consumer of the bread and the wine. The church pew is an exciting place of service. We stop looking at ourselves and see God's plan for our life. In the pew we share God's Presence with those around us. Nobody has yet measured the possibilities of pew power. The pew is the place where we worship and share God's presence with all those around us.

A great Methodist preacher by the name of Pierce Harris said many times, "I can take a bucket of water and a flash light and break up any Methodist meeting in Georgia!" Storms, lightning, and fear of flood can cut short our presence at church services.

Scripture:

"He who observes the wind will not sow, and he who regards the clouds will not reap." ~ Eccl. 11:4

Prayer:

O Lord, help me to be more than a fair-weather church member. Amen.

45

On Running Away from Home

At some time in our early childhood, many of us have thought about running away from home. I remember feeling unappreciated and thought I needed more attention. I shared my intention of running away from home. My Mother helped me pack my bag, and by the time we had done this I lost interest in leaving.

I can identify with a young lad who threatened to leave home and actually did so. Nobody tried to stop him. He stayed away for several hours, and then he began to get hungry. The day was about to end, and he had no place to go. So he returned for the evening meal and went in the house. He was ignored as though he had not left. To get the attention of the family, he said, "Well I see you still have the same old cat."

Feeling sorry for ourselves is one of the worst things we can do. Such an attitude weakens our ability to cope with our problems. We never get to the place where we can afford to feel sorry for ourselves. Problems and people go together. We can't afford to postpone being happy. Every day we need to be thankful. Let us take a lesson from the birds; the blue bird sings her song of joy while sitting on the garbage dump. Jesus said, "Not a sparrow falls to the ground that your heavenly Father doesn't notice it." He also concluded, "You are worth more than many sparrows. "

Feeling sorry for ourselves and being jealous of others can add up to misery for us. The elder brother in the story of the prodigal son says to his father on the return of his little brother, "Look, all these years I have worked for you like a slave, and I have never disobeyed your orders. What have you given me? Not even a goat for me to have a feast with my friends! But this son of yours wasted all your property on prostitutes, and when he comes back home, you kill the prize calf for him."

"My son," the father answered, "you are always here with me, and everything I have is yours. But we had to celebrate and be happy because your brother was dead, but now he is alive, he was lost, but now he has been found."

The elder brother had an unresolved problem. He did not like his little brother. The family thought he was cute, they spoiled him, and he learned early how to manage his father and mother. The older boy saw through this unruly kid. He even had the nerve to ask his father to give him what he was going to receive when his father died. Besides, the brat had never worked a day in his life! So the elder brother was glad to see the guy leave and sorry to see him return.

A child once prayed, "O Lord, I could be a better Christian if it wasn't for Charles."

He was asked, "Who is Charles?"

He replied, "Charles is my brother."

Life is at its best when we love a brother or sister and trust the father to change them.

Scripture:

"Love each other with genuine affection, and take delight in honoring each other. When God's children are in need, be the one to help them out. And get into the habit of inviting guests home for dinner or, if they need lodging, for the night. When others are happy, be happy with them. If they are sad, share their sorrow. Live in harmony with each other. Don't try to act important, but enjoy the company of ordinary people. And don't think you know it all! Do your part to live in peace with everyone, as much as possible." ~ Portions of Romans 12 NLT

Prayer:

Lord, fill my heart with Your love and compassion for others, so I can love others with Your love. Amen.

46

The Joy of Meeting Others

In 1957, I went to Cuba on a mission trip. This was two years before Castro took power. My presence was part of an Island-wide revival all across the Methodist Church in Cuba. During those revival meetings, many young people came to Christ all over the island. It was an interesting experience. The Cuban people were wonderful.

The Methodist Church was composed of children and young people, not many adults. I flew to Havana and then down to Cienfeagous (that is Spanish for 100 fires). I stayed in a hotel, and a bus took me out to a little town called Lemus. There I spent the day. I visited from house to house in the little village. At every house we picked up more children. Nobody could speak English, and I could not speak Spanish, so we had a great time calling out words.

For example, a child would hold up a dog, they would give me the Spanish word, and I would give them the English word. I could not eat their food. One day, I had spiced beans and rice. I sat at the table with the family and beneath the table on the dirt floor, a little pig ran around hoping for some scraps from the table. I was doing a pretty good job of eating, when I remembered one of Jerry Clowers' stories about a situation like this. Jerry related that he was eating at the table, and a little pig was hovering around his feet.

"Nice pig!" Jerry said. "He sure seems to like me."

"Yes," his hosts replied. "You are eating out of his bowl."

After remembering these words, I lost my appetite.

In the evening, I preached on the porch of a house that was vacant. The sister of a young man I knew at Lambuth College was my interpreter. We had one big light bulb. The people sat in the yard. Many young people became Christians during those meetings. Each evening at 11 p.m., the bus came for me, and I went back to the hotel to spend the night.

The people in the church there asked me to talk to a man who had some property, who they said liked Americans. He offered to sell a lot to the church. When I left, the wonderful people gave me a bowl; they carried my luggage on the plane so they could see what one looked like on the inside.

I went back to Fulton First Methodist Church where I was pastor and raised enough money to buy the lot for the Cuban church. I have never forgotten my Methodist friends there. I would like to go back someday. I loved them. I wanted to return to Cuba, see my friends, and take Grace with me, but it was one of those things that never happened.

Sometimes that's life for you. That was in 1957, and we were like ships that pass in the night. But that little village, that small church, and those wonderful people will be on the TV screen of my mind forever. The past all flows into the present and runs over into the future. Praise God!

Scripture:

"You are my friends..." ~ John 15:14 TEV

Prayer:

O Lord, thanks for all the people I have known. I ask that You Bless them all and I look forward to meeting them in heaven. Amen.

47

What Makes a Good Choice?

A minister had finished his theological education. He wanted to marry the right young woman. He had a long list of qualifications, but he had a problem. He could not sing. He knew very little about music so he felt that he needed to marry a lady who could sing and be able to help him balance out his ministry.

Finally, he found a young woman. She could sing, in fact she had the most beautiful voice he had ever heard. However, here was one problem. She was the ugliest woman he had ever seen. After going with her, he decided that her musical talent and her ability to sing was more important than her ugly appearance. They were married and went on their honeymoon.

The next morning, he was awakened by a loud noise. He discovered that the irritating noise was coming from the woman he had married the night before. He took one look at her sleeping. Her mouth was open, her face was covered with a white cream, and her hair was filled with big curlers. This was a shocking experience for him. He had trouble adjusting to her nighttime appearance. Finally, he could take it no more, he shook her and said, "Wake up! Wake up! Wake up and sing!!!"

Abraham Lincoln's advice about marriage was, "If you make a bad bargain, hug it all the more tightly." Physical appearance is not the best of choices in marriage. Sometimes beauty queens fade more quickly than less attractive people. Character, love, and a good disposition are more important than physical characteristics. Being able to accept others and to love and forgive one another makes for happy living.

A minister I knew had a beautiful wife and a lovely daughter who won a lot of beauty contests. I was with a group where his daughter was present. This preacher was a little on the ugly side. But he was truly an outstanding person. He said to me, "Go over and tease my daughter and tell her she looks like me and see what she will say. So I went over and said, "I'm glad to meet you. I would have known you anywhere. You look just like your father."

This beautiful young lady said,"I love my father, he's the greatest man I know, but you know I don't look like him." This young lady knew this was a joke, but she did not look like her father. Not in physical appearance, but she did look like him. She had his out-going personality, his interest in people, his strong moral character and good disposition.

Marriage is not just for young people. When you get old and your physical appearance begins to go downhill, you still have someone who loves you. This describes a meaningful marriage. Some peoples' commitment span is not very long. These people have trouble maintaining their relationship for a long time especially a lifetime. It is dangerous for us to treat God the way we treat our friends and those close to us.

In the 15th chapter of St. Luke, there is the story of the lost sheep. How did the sheep get lost? It was looking for greener pastures. So it wandered away a little at a time just one or two pastures away. Then night came, and the sheep was far from its home. It had wandered so far that it was out of range from the Shepherd's call. This is the way people get lost. They are searching for greener pastures - places where they can make a better living, buy more stuff. They have moved away from the church. Their prayer life is not functional. They think little of God. They become lost in the Urban Jungle. Who will look for the lost person? Where is the good shepherd who will bring the lost sheep home and make heaven rejoice?

Scripture:

"I say to you that likewise there will be more joy in heaven over one sinner who repents than over ninety-nine just persons who need no repentance." ~ Luke 15:7

Prayer:

O Lord, help me learn how to look for the lost in the world around me, and help me bring them home. Amen.

48

Get Close to the Fire

A certain man who was an official in his church had three sons. He lived in the mountains, and he had strong feelings about his boys. All three were grown now. One was the pastor of a large city church. The other son, who was also a minister, was president of a church college. The third son was a bum.

The father asked his sons to come back to the old log cabin and spend Thanksgiving Day and night with him. The two ministers agreed, but the third one, who was a delinquent bum didn't want to come. After much persuasion, the bum said he would attend. The father wanted all three of them to spend the night and sleep in the three upstairs bedrooms like they used to do when they were all at home. The three men arrived and after a visit, they all retired to their childhood rooms.

The father wanted to show his love for them so he got up early and built a roaring fire in the big fireplace. He was very proud of his two preacher sons, but he wanted to reach out to his third son who seemed to be content to be a bum. After the fire was warm and inviting, the father fixed a big breakfast. He let the boys sleep and come down when they woke up. The first one to arrive downstairs was the president of the church college.

His father asked, "How did you sleep, son?"

"Great, Dad. I dreamed I was in heaven."

"What was heaven like?" his father asked.

"Just like home, Father," the minister replied as he took a cup of coffee and went and stood before the fire.

The second to arrive was the minister of the large city church. His father asked,

"How did you sleep, son?"

"Great, Dad. I dreamed I was in heaven!"

"What was heaven like, son?" his father asked.

"Just like home, Father," his second minister son replied. He poured himself a cup of coffee and went and stood in front of the fire with his brother.

Finally, the third son who was a bum staggered down the steps. He blinked and saw his two brothers already dressed and standing before the warm fire.

His father asked, "How did you sleep, son?"

"Awful, Dad. I dreamed I was in hell."

"Oh my, what was hell like?" his father asked.

"Just like home, Father," the son who was a bum replied. "I couldn't get to the fire for all the preachers."

Jealousy, opinionated people, and judgmental behavior can destroy brotherhood. Acceptance and appreciation can pave the way for understanding. What we have done in life makes the world a better place and gives us personal satisfaction. But it is not our accomplishments that earn us a place in our Father's house. We are at home there because we were born there or were adopted into the family of God. Jesus said to Nicodemus, "You must be born again" (John 3:7).

A friend asked me to take part in a project and I said, "I can't do, it my parents won't let me." They looked puzzled and I said, "Father Time and Mother Nature."

Scripture:

"So teach us to number our days, that we may gain a heart of wisdom." ~ Psalm 90:2

Prayer:

O Lord, there are things I can no longer do, but I can always love You and Your people. Amen.

49

Warning!

A visiting minister was trying to stir up the local congregation who had a name for being indifferent and lukewarm. There was a group in the congregation who was not paying attention. In fact, some of them were talking and seemed to be indifferent to the visiting preachers. Their behavior frustrated the minister. Finally he said, "If you people around here don't pay attention and repent, you are going to go to hell."

The words of waning went unheeded by this group of people. This made the preacher angry so he repeated, "If you people around here don't pay attention and repent, you are going to go to hell!"

After the church service, he confronted these people who ignored his warning, "Why are you people around here unwilling to listen?"

The people replied, "We aren't from around here."

Some people don't realize that the message of change and redemption is for everyone. God's Word is eternal. God's Word is for all of us. One word from God fits all people in all the circumstances of life. "God so loved the world that He gave His only Son that whosoever believes in Him should not perish, but have everlasting life" (John 3:16). An old hymn says it this way, "It's not my brother, not my sister, but its me, oh Lord, standing in the need of prayer."

Here's where it all began. One size fits all. God's message of love and redemption fits all people wherever they live. Long ago Jonah learned that God is everywhere, and we cannot escape from His presence and call upon our life.

The Bible is full of God's eternal messages. My approach to the Bible verse has been, what did this mean in the day that it was written? How does it apply to my life today? This enables me to enjoy my FAITH today.

Scripture:

"My word shall not pass away," Jesus. ~ Matthew 24:35

Prayer:

O Lord, I thank You for Your Eternal Word. Upon it I can act, and by it I can live. Amen.

50

Tell Me About Your Dog

A certain man was sitting on a bench in the park. Beside him sat a beautiful dog. A man passed by and asked the man on the bench, "Does your dog bite?"

The man hesitated for a moment and said, "No, my dog does not bite."

The stranger reached over to pet the dog. But the dog responded by biting his hand. The fellow drew back his hand and said, "I thought you said your dog didn't bite."

"That's not my dog," the man replied.

Sometimes, we get into trouble because we assume something that may not be so. Let us be certain that we have all the fats before we act. It is not always wise to involve ourselves in strange situations we know nothing about.

In 1972, I went to St. Luke's United Methodist Church. At that time, it was the largest church in our conference. They had two morning services, so people did not know everyone who belonged to the church. The sanctuary had four exit doors so a lot of people left without knowing one another. I got in front of the line out one of the doors. I saw a single lady that I had met a few weeks before. I remembered her name, and as I shook her hand, I said, "Good morning, Dorothy. I like your new hair style!"

She looked at me with a sour expression on her face and said, "You mean you didn't like it the way it was before?"

Some people do not like others to get in their space and make comments about their personal appearance. After that, I never said anything more to her than, "Hello, Dorothy."

Beware of people who get their exercise by jumping to conclusions. A human being is a very complex creation. This creation, though male or female, is able to growl like a bear, behave like a bull, be as stubborn as a donkey, walk like a duck, sing like a bird, eat like a pig, behave like a chicken - so the comparison goes on. Human behavior cannot always be predicted, and it can rarely, if ever, change by itself. The concern and helpful guidance of other people can help, but the person himself must cooperate with the forces that produce change.

God will help you. The Holy Spirit can change the life of a person, but the individual must do His part. I have seldom known God to act by Himself in a person's life. Be patient with God. "You have heard of the patience of Job," and how things ultimately turn out for the good. (James 5:11)

Scripture:

"Wait on the Lord; be of good courage, and He shall strengthen your heart; wait, I say, on the Lord." ~ Psalm 27:14

Prayer:

O Lord, I wait to serve You in the name of Jesus. Amen.

51

Bumper Stickers

I saw a bumper sticker that I would like to put on the back of my car. The sticker showed a little boy who had fallen down and acquired a knot on his head. He was rubbing the lump, and the message read, "Praise God anyhow."

It is really true we can get more from a spirit of praise and thanksgiving than from criticism and complaint. Another bumper sticker that I have on my old car reads, "As long as there are tests there will always be prayer in the public schools."

Life tests us everywhere, not just in the public school, but in all the experiences of life. Passing life's tests calls for personal preparation. The motto of the Boy Scouts is "Be Prepared." The unprepared are an accident about to happen. The bumper sticker I like the best, I saw many years ago on a passing car. It read, "For a taste of religion, bite a preacher!"

I think this is hilarious. Lots of people never experience the length, the heights, the depths, or the width of faith in Christ. Their Christian behavior and spiritual experience consist of nothing more than biting and snapping at moral leadership. Here is my personal prayer for you:

> Our kind heavenly Father,
> In our great effort to get money
> And the material things of life,
> Help us, as we live, to acquire
> An acceptable character approved by God,
> A sense of personal responsibility,
> And a genuine love for one another.
> AMEN!

We are not fully prepared for life until we develop our ability to go to God in prayer!

Scripture:

St. Paul wrote: "I have complete confidence in the gospel: it is God's power to save all who believe, first the Jews and now the Gentiles. For that gospel reveals how God put people right with Himself: it is through faith from beginning to end. As the scripture says, "The person who is put right with God through faith shall live." Rom. 1:17

Prayer:

O Lord, I do my good works because I want to share with others what God has done for me through Jesus Christ. My works are an expression of my love for You, nothing more and nothing less. Amen.

52

Can You Believe It?

Two men were in a boat on lake fishing. It was Sunday morning. On the other side of the lake, a church bell began to ring. One of the men said, "Don't you feel ashamed? Here we are fishing on Sunday morning. It's time for church. Other people are going to worship. We should be in church!"

The other man replied, "Oh, if I were home I couldn't go to church. My wife is sick."

It was acceptable to him to leave his sick wife and go fishing, but her illness would keep him from attending church if he were home. Amazing logic. I don't think we listen to what we say.

Early in my ministry I moved to a town in Kentucky. I visited a banker who said to me, "I don't go to church. I have lost my hair. I sit on the back row and when they open the door the draft blowing on my head gives me a cold." This man died many years ago. It would shock him to know that he was remembered for this one excuse.

A man stood up in a church meeting and confessed to a lifetime of unacceptable and shocking behavior. Finally, he concluded his long confession of personal sins with this word, "Thank God, in all of these experiences, I never lost my religion." I'll let you provide your own comment about this person's witness.

In all these cases, religion had become static. *Static*, when used as an *adjective*, means *stationary, unmovable. Static*, when used as a *noun*, means an *irregular, disturbing noise*. The word *static*, describes the *condition of a dried up faith*.

Here are three thoughts worth remembering:

1. God hears prayer.
2. God forgives sin.
3. God provides strength for the journey of life.

Faith comes alive when you place it in the hands of the Living Christ. Surrendering to Christ gives you access to the Holy Spirit who becomes your Guide and Helper. The Holy Spirit performs spiritual surgery on us. Static religion is removed from our lives and a dynamic faith is placed at the center of our being. This is described as heart felt faith.

Religion for a Christian is a person to person affair. The person of God encounters the person called you; and a new person is born. Keep your life open and alive to the living Christ and there is a new you coming every day.

Scripture:

"Faith is the substance of things hoped for…" ~Hebrew 11:1

Prayer:

O Lord, I surrender to You all over again. Through Your Holy Presence, I become a new person to face a new day. Amen.

53

What Day Is It?

Andy Holt, one of the great presidents of the University of Tennessee, said that one morning as he was reading the newspaper, his wife asked him a question.

"Andy, do you know what day this is?"

Half-listening he stated, "Yes, I know what day this is."

His wife said, "I don't believe you know what day this is."

Suddenly, I realized that I didn't know what day it was. Fearing that I had missed an important day, I hurried off to the office. I got there before my secretary, and she was surprised to see me so early. I confessed to her my dilemma, "I told my wife that I knew what day it was, and now I have forgotten an important event." My secretary got out the calendar and went through all the dates she kept for me. Anniversary? No. Birthday? No.

Then we went through a long list of personal events that my secretary helped me remember. None of these were today. I had my secretary make a reservation at the nicest restaurant in town. She called my wife and told her that I would pick her up. On the way home, I bought her a flower to wear since she loves flowers. We had a great evening together, and she never mentioned the special day again. I heaved a sign of relief, let her out of the car and put it in the garage. She met me at the door and said, "Andy, I want to thank you for the wonderful evening. This is the best Ground Hog Day I have ever had."

An ad in a popular magazine caught my attention. I saved it over the years. It described a piece of furniture. It read, "Too bad it won't stay new forever, but just think what that means. By the time it's not contemporary any more, you'll have a beautiful antique."

This is exactly what has happened to the faith of many Christians. Their faith and experience will not stay new forever. Faith in God is kept up to date through renewal, reform, and recommitment of ourselves to God as we know Him today. Belief in God as a system of ideas, teachings, or a source of spiritual facts may be contemporary, but only temporally.

We must keep faith in God alive within us. If our personal faith is left to itself, it can become outdated, outmoded, and out of power. Christianity must become and remain a part of our personal and social structure. If Christianity is removed from the people of God and left to exist by itself, it becomes a beautiful antique, an item housed in a dated building, a reminder of the past that does not fit into the present and certainly has no place in the future.

Every believer has a job taking the word of God from the pages of the Bible and translating it into a life of service in the community. The Good News of the Bible also develops character. Furthermore, it expresses itself in words of character and words of kindness and acts of love and good will.

A man held up a telephone book and said, "This is a great book, it contains a lot of characters but not much of a plot." You may know God's name and address, but you get to know Him personally through Jesus Christ.

Scripture:

St. Paul described the word of faith, "If you confess with your mouth, 'Jesus is Lord,' and believe in your heart that God raised him from the dead, you will be saved." ~Romans 10:8-9 (NIV)

Prayer:

O Lord, thank You for the Living Christ who brings me to life. Amen.

54

An Attention Getting Parable

A priest and a rabbi were returning from a golf match. A rabbit ran out in front of the priest's car. He hit the animal and both the priest and the rabbi cringed. The priest stopped his car, reached in the glove compartment and pulled out a bottle of liquid. He went back and sprinkled the contents on the rabbit. The rabbit instantly jumped up and ran off.

The rabbi witnessed this procedure and was amazed. "What was that you sprinkled on the rabbit, Holy Water?"

The priest replied, "No. It was hair restorer."

Here is a parable to get your attention. Wouldn't it be great to have a magic potion to sprinkle on your fallen hair, or hare, however you spell it? It is frustrating that with all our technology we cannot redo the accidents of life. Only on film or in a movie are we able to replay or turn back the experiences of lie.

In the nursery rhyme *Humpty Dumpy*, "All the king's horses and all the king's men couldn't put Humpty Dumpty together again." Like all the king's horses and men, we can't put together the good eggs or the bad eggs of life once they have fallen. The bad eggs make a terrible stink when they fall. It is a fact that no arrangement of rotten eggs can make a good omelet. Yet, there are always people who want to make money out of the bad eggs that fall.

In fact, the king's men and some of his horses today sell the broken, fallen mess of human tragedy to magazines, TV producers, and moviemakers. Why is there a market for the obscene, the bizarre, and the buzzard droppings of delinquent humanity?

There are people who are bored with the regularity of life. The leftover jerks and obsolete hippies are living lives empty of purpose and meaningless desperation. These lazy misfits feed on human garbage. As a leader and a reader, we are called to do something about child pornography. We can begin by exposing this as a horrible personal and social illness. It continues to live because people make money selling its germs. The public must destroy the market for such sexual illness. Keeping this sickness alive doesn't make sense.

Good health requires that everyone take a regular dose of moral responsibility. *Right* is a wonderful substitute for *wrong*. Labeling such sexual delinquency as wrong enables people to know that embracing the wrong way leads to disaster. Anybody who goes the wrong way on a one-way street is headed for a horrible collision.

The city of Paris, France, has over three thousand one-way streets. Any Frenchman knows the result of going the wrong way. Life has one-way streets. They lead somewhere. This is very simple, yet also very profound. Find the good way, the healthy path that leads us to a heavenly home on earth. If you are an egg who has been broken there is Good News. What the king's horses and men cannot do, God can do. He can put your broken pieces together again if you will turn everything over to Him

Scripture:

"When anyone is joined in Christ, he is a new being: the old is gone, the new has come." ~ 2 Corinthians 5:17

Prayer:

O Lord, save me from going the wrong way on a one-way street. Amen.

55

Can a Dog Be Smarter than a Man?

An ambitious young man took a job in a men's clothing store. The owner was getting older and was looking for a manager to give him some help. The shopkeeper challenged a certain young man who wanted to be manger, "I'm going on vacation. You see that sport coat on the manikin in the show window. While I'm gone, if you sell that sport coat, you can have the job of store manager. However, if you don't you are fired!"

"But sir," the employee responded, "that coat has been in the show window since I've been working here. You have reduced the price. It's the most hideous coat I have ever seen. Everything about that coat is awful."

The storeowner said, "That may be true, but the deal is, sell the coat and you become manager. Fail to sell it while I'm gone, and you are fired."

The owner went on a long happy, restful vacation. When he returned, he went to his store. He looked in the window and the sport coat was gone. The empty manikin was still in the window suggesting to him that the sport coat had just been sold. The owner couldn't find his employee anywhere. He searched the store and finally found the young man on the floor behind the counter. As the owner was helping him up he said, "I sold the coat! I sold the coat!"

"You sure did, and I am proud of you," said the owner. "But your clothes are torn, your face is scratched, and your right hand is bleeding. What happened?"

"Well, Sir," the employee replied, "I sold the coat to a blind man. It fit him perfectly, but when his seeing–eye dog saw the coat he attacked me."

Are dogs ever wiser than men? Are they more discriminating than men? Do they not know the difference between male and female dogs? Do only a few dogs bite the hand that feeds them?

For the most part, dogs are loving and loyal to the person who is their master. As a Christian, I proclaim Christ as my Master. Gladly I show my loyalty and devotion to Him. As a human, I can be blinded by sin. I can be and usually I am in need of God, who sees life like it is and what it could be if I move in the direction that He would have me go.

In today's world, politicians who hold public office are advised to get a dog. That way, there will be someone in town who likes them. Dogs can be great companions because they can usually be trusted. This reminds me of a story:

Ole Jake got him a new dog. He took the canine with him duck hunting. Jake shot a duck, and it fell in the lake. His dog walked on the water and picked up the duck and brought it to him. Jake was amazed. Every time he shot a duck, the dog walked on the water and picked up the duck.

Jake was excited. He picked up the dog and headed for the country store to tell all the fellows, but then he remembered that he had frequently enlarged on the truth; therefore his friends would probably not believe him. So he went by and picked up honest John. Everybody believed honest John. He took honest John to the lake to watch. Jake shot a duck, it fell into the lake, and his dog walked out on the water and picked up the duck. Jake and his dog did this over and over again. Honest John was silent; Jake could stand it no longer so he said, "Honest John did you notice anything different about my dog."

"Yeah," said honest John, "he can't swim!"

A good laugh is a healthy experience any way you can get it. As a farm boy, I grew up with animals. I found that they had personalities and habits that were similar to our own. I guess it helped me understand people a little better. Animals can only act like themselves. But man can act like a bear, a dog, a donkey, a chicken, or a small rooster. Of course sheep and goats are included.

Scripture:

"All we like sheep have gone astray. We have turned, everyone, to his own way. And the Lord has laid on Him the iniquity of us all." ~ Isaiah 53: 6

Prayer:

O Lord, help us who live in an urban society to learn about sheep and the need for a shepherd. Amen.

56

One of My Favorite Stories

Adam was in the Garden of Eden. After the experience of just being placed here, he was somewhat bewildered by everything and especially by a woman named Eve. He said, "Lord, I thank you for everything, especially the beautiful, wonderful woman you have given me! Lord she is so thoughtful, kind, and considerate."

"Yes, I know Adam. I made her that way so you would like her."

"But Lord in many ways she is smarter than I am, but every now and then she does dumb things. Why?"

"I know Adam, I made her that way so she would like you."

Men and women are different in thought, in behavior, in almost all of life. How do we feel about the differences that exist between us? Do we try to reform one another? Do we try to exert power over the other one? Do we react more than we respond in our relationship? Do we have expectations that the other person can't fulfill? Do we want our own way, always remembering the time we didn't get our way and promptly forgetting the times when things went our way?

Have we divided our relationship into a 50-50 affair, forgetting that life is never 50-50? Frequently it is 90-10 or 20-80, on and on it goes. Let us stop and appreciate one another. Let us build each other up in love. Let us keep no records except a reminder that the greatest joy in life is the opportunity to love one another. Read again 1 Corinthians 13. Here is a great pattern for all kinds of love and practice in marriage if it is to be blessed:

Love
Bears all things,
Believes all things,
Endures all things.

Love
Never fails!

Love
Does not keep records of wrong –
In the end as in the beginning:
There is health,
There is wealth,

There is success,
There is failure,
There is hope,
There is despair.

Life is a mixture of many powerful and great experiences,
But the greatest of these is Love!

There is nothing better than a good marriage, and there is nothing worse than a bad marriage. In the movie, *It's a Wonderful Life*, Jimmy Stewart plays the role of George Bailey. Over the years, my children have watched it many times. I have enjoyed the movie, but I was always half listening reading a book, answering the phone, etc. I thought that I knew the story well. Then one day I heard something for the first time.

To review the story quickly, a deposit was misplaced and ended in the hands of the greedy land developer. The bank was short, there was a run on the bank, and the depositors started to take out their money for fear they would lose it. After they were convinced that the bank was okay, in their love and appreciation they began to return their money.

One woman brought back her money and put it back in the bank. She explained, "I was saving this money for a divorce in case I got married." This is more than a funny line. Some people carelessly enter marriage believing that if it doesn't work out, I can always get a divorce. Well you can, but there are only a few divorces that are not very painful. Marriage has a better chance if both people do more than their best to keep it alive.

Good people suffer when marriage fails. When people come out of a bad or impossible marriage, they need encouragement and the helpful understanding of their friends, their church and their community. My suggestion is to turn to God and know that He still loves you and will see you through.

Scripture:

"But as it is written: 'Eye has not seen, nor ear heard, Nor have entered into the heart of man The things which God has prepared for those who love Him.' " ~ 1 Cor. 2:9

Prayer:

O Lord, save me from blaming others when events go wrong. There is always more than enough blame and guilt to go around. I ask for Your forgiveness and freedom from guilt, and having received this I am glad to pass it on to others. Amen.

57

A New View for Review

I love the Atlantic Ocean, the Gulf of Mexico, and the Pacific Ocean. As a person who lived in the interiors of the USA, I did not get to personally see the ocean until I was grown. I will never forget the first time I saw it. I didn't stop and test it. I didn't take a glass beaker and analyze a cup of its water to see if it contained the correct amount of salt and oxygen. I just looked at the ocean, and my heart was overwhelmed by what I saw.

A certain minister made a trip to the Pacific Ocean with some friends. When he saw the Pacific Ocean for the first time he said, "Boy, isn't she a success!" I never thought about the Pacific Ocean as a success. But if you define success as a great power, adequate amount of water, the home for millions of creatures, vast unbelievable beauty, then I'm sure that the Pacific Ocean is more than a success at being an ocean.

In his book *Love, Medicine, and Miracles*, Dr. Bernie S. Siegel, MD quotes a message by Teilhard de Charin, "Someday, after we have mastered the winds, the waves, the tides, and gravity, we shall harness for God the energies of love. Then for the second time in the history of the world man will have discovered fire."

I don't want to put it off. I want to harness for God the energies of love. I want to do it NOW. I want to solve the drug problem and the emptiness of the human experience. Remember NOW spelled backwards is WON. Together all of us with God's help can turn NOW into WON. The Bible says, "Today is the day of salvation – Now is the accepted time. Now has Christ risen from the dead."

Scripture:

"The Lord will command His loving kindness in the daytime, and in the night His song shall be with me, and my prayer unto the God of my life."

"Why am I so sad? Why am I so troubled? I will put my hope in God and once again I will praise Him, my Savior and my God." ~ Psalm 42:8-12

Here's a lasting answer to moodiness. Through the Holy Spirit, Jesus comes to us during our stress and says again, "Be of good cheer." ~ John 16:33

Prayer:

O Lord, I claim this day for You. Today, I'm going to put my faith in action. Today, I want You to help me change my life. Amen.

58

A Wedding to Remember

This is a true story that happened in Dyersburg, Tennessee, sometime in the early 1900's. There was a big wedding at the First Methodist Church. The people getting married were well known and guests were invited and attended from all over the South. A prominent lawyer and his wife were invited to sit in the ribbons. It was wintertime, and the lawyer had a furnace that he had to stoke. Many houses were built on hills in this town, so it was easy to install a furnace beneath your home. The lawyer was baldheaded, and he wore a red baseball cap when he fired the furnace, this kept the soot off his bald head.

They were in a hurry, so the last thing he did was to fire the furnace so the house would be warm when they returned. This well-known couple made it to the wedding. It was a formal affair. The man had on his frock-tail coat, and his wife was dressed in an evening gown. They sat near the front, and when he was seated there was a quiet ripple of laughter that went over the wedding guests.

After a few moments, an usher appeared and said to the lawyer, "Sir, do you know that you have on your red baseball cap?" Embarrassed the attorney quickly grabbed the red cap off his head. He had forgotten to take it off when he went down to fire the furnace. He elbowed his wife and out of the side of his mouth he said to her, "Why didn't you tell me I had on my red baseball cap?"

His wife replied, "I didn't notice!"

"Didn't notice!" the lawyer replied. "Can't you see how ridiculous I looked in this frock-tail coat and red baseball cap?"

"I didn't see it," his wife insisted.

"Why you didn't see it?" the lawyer demanded.

His wife whispered, "I haven't looked at you in twenty years!"

Twenty years is a long time to not look at your husband or wife. Perhaps the last time we looked at the one we live with, we didn't like what we saw. Criticism expressed or unexpressed can be damaging to a longtime relationship. Of course, if we are critical but keep our mouth shut about it, we avoid 50% of the trouble.

However, unspoken negative, critical feelings can be very destructive. We bury these destructive feelings deep in our subconscious. Such opinions left in our minds is like sweeping the trash under the rug. After a while, the rug becomes lumpy. If this practice continues with the rug, its beautiful appearance is destroyed. For the Christian, there is the redemptive act of prayer.

1. Confess to God in silence the exact nature of your problems.
2. Replace criticism with acts of appreciation and thanksgiving.
3. Let your attention be acts of building up one another with kindness.

Scripture and Prayer:

"I am weak and poor, O Lord, but you have not forgotten me, You are my Savior and my God, hurry to my aid!" ~ Psalm 40:17

59

Changing Our Point of View

Two men were working on the street in front of a tavern. In a little while, a priest came walking down the street and went into the tavern.

One of the repair men said, "Look at that priest going into a saloon!"

"Yea, that is awful," said the other.

Later, a Rabbi came down the sidewalk and entered the bar.

"Look, there goes a Rabbi," said one of the men. "What happened to morals?"

A little later one of the workmen saw their own minister go into the same bar. He turned and said to his friend, "There must be somebody mighty sick in that place."

Loyalty can lead to prejudice. Prejudice can lead to opinionated remarks about others. Such behavior can divide a crowd into "them and us." Self-examination can reveal two sets of values - one set of values for us and one for them. In the New Testament, Jesus says, "Do not judge others, and God will not judge you" (Matt. 7:1-2).

Scripture:

"For with what judgment you judge, you will be judged; and with the measure you use, it will be measured back to you. And why do you look at the speck in your brother's eye, but do not consider the plank in your own eye? Or how can you say to your brother, 'Let me remove the speck from your eye'; and look, a plank is in your own eye? "Hypocrite! First remove the plank from your own eye, and then you will see clearly to remove the speck from your brother's eye." ~ Matt. 7:2-

Prayer:

O Lord, help me to take a second look at myself before I rush out to judge others. Amen.

60

A Medical Observation

A friend of mine was a surgeon. I was his pastor many years ago in Dyersburg, Tennessee. Dr. Moore had a good habit of attending church. If his professional duties carried him out of town on the weekend, he always made it a habit to attend Sunday morning worship. He was at a medical convention in New England one Sunday so he sought out a church. The building was almost empty and the service was very formal. He walked into the large building and noticed that there were plenty of places to sit. He chose a long pew that was empty except for a dried up elderly lady who was sitting at the far end.

After sitting there for a few minutes, an usher dressed in formal clothes stood beside him. On a silver plate, he presented Dr. More with a piece of paper that looked like a note. The usher used his grey-gloved hand to point to the lady dressed in black at the end of the pew. Dr. Moore opened the note and it red, "This is my pew you are sitting on. I paid $10,000 for this pew!"

When Dr. Moore finished reading the note, he wrote on it and handed it back to the waiting usher. His reply was, "You paid too d--n much for it!"

Many years ago, some church hit upon the idea of renting or selling the pew. The idea was to raise money for the church. If a person owned or rented a pew, they would feel more obligated to attend. This may have worked, but in most cases owning or paying rent for a pew was a good excuse not to attend.

Others see trying to fill empty pews as a great opportunity to witness to their faith. Those attending church realize that they are not the audience. God is the unseen audience who listens to our prayers, receives our gifts, our music, and our sermons. It is to God we offer our praise and thanksgiving. It is from God that we receive assurance of His forgiveness and love. From God, we learn that when we say *our* church, the word *our* does not mean it belongs to us, but rather we belong to it.

Scripture:

"I would rather be a doorkeeper in the house of my God, than dwell in the tents of wickedness." ~ Ps 84:10

Prayer:

O Lord, help me to see the church for what it is. Criticizing her members, demanding that she serve me - all these expectations will not help my church or me. Please help me be more thankful for her. Amen!

Remember, the church is the place where I can serve God and have an effective ministry. I never thought about that.

61

Be Careful What You Look For

After the morning worship service, a wife quizzed her husband, "Did you see that stupid dress that the woman had on who sat in front of us?"

"No," replied the husband.

"Did you hear the preacher announce the wrong hymn?"

"No," replied the husband.

"Didn't you hear the soloist in the choir get off key?"

"No," replied the husband.

"Why didn't you observe these things?"

"Well," said the husband, "I fell asleep."

"How disgusting! A lot of good it did you to go to church!"

There was a day when a lot of people who attended church had this attitude, but that day has passed. People who attend church today are there because they want to be present. They want to see God's face, hear His voice, and experience His assurance that He still loves them.

Prayer has replaced criticism; the critics have faded away. They may come back, but their presence is periodic, and their criticism is used to cover their absence. I'm not saying that there is not criticism in the church. There will always be things that people will not like, there will be changes that some people find unacceptable, but what I am saying is that people who attend every Sunday are not there because of these experiences. The core of the church is the people of faith who are serious about their activity at the church.

A friend of mine was in the Navy in World War II. He was given the job of cleaning the kitchen for a white glove inspection. He said, "The lieutenant came in and with his white glove and began to look for grease and dirt. He ran his glove over the door trim, but I was not worried because I had cleaned it. He tried the floor, but the glove came out clean.

Finally, he took the stove apart, but I was not worried because I had cleaned it completely. His glove remained clean and white. Then he took his white glove and stuck it up the exhaust vent. Still clean, but he reached up as high as he could and when he pulled his glove out, there was a dark spot on one finger. He held it up and rated my kitchen as dirty.

I thought to myself the next time he comes in I'm going to have some soot ready to put on his glove. This will save him the time and energy of looking for dirt."

What are we looking for? If we keep searching we can find it. May our search be positive and rewarding because our mission is one of appreciation. Here is my thought about the church - Over the years and toward the end of life, I never had anybody say to me, "I joined the church because the people who criticize the church and complained about her people inspired me and led me to her Christ." I never heard this, and I never will. A negative attitude about the body of Christ will never produce positive results.

Scripture:

"Looking unto Jesus, the author and finisher of our faith." ~ Hebrews 12:1-2

Prayer:

O Lord, Help me look for the good in others. It's possible to find what I'm looking for.

62

On Trial!

A certain minister was invited to preach a trial sermon at a strong rural church. This minister was a perfectionist. He wanted everything to be in order. He did not like distractions when he delivered the sermon. The minister had just begun his sermon when an old dog wandered down the isle and lay down in front of the pulpit. The dog started scratching himself, and his behavior caught the attention of the congregation. The dog distracted everybody. The congregation paid so much attention to the dog, the sermon was ignored.

Finally, the mutt settled down for a nap. About mid way in the sermon the dog began to snore. This got louder and then he began to dream he was chasing a rabbit. The dog's legs moved rapidly, and he let out a bark. This was too much for the fastidious clergyman to take. He stepped down from the pulpit and woke up the dog and gave the mongrel a swift kick that sent him yelping from the church building. The minister got back in the pulpit, got back on track with his sermon, and finished with a long climax. He thought, "That will make up for the dog's interference."

A person in the congregation came up to the minister and said, "Parson, you know that dog you just kicked and drove out of the church belonged to the chairman of the pulpit committee! He thinks more of that dog than he does of his wife."

The preacher went over to the chairman of the committee who was going to vote on calling him to the church and apologized. "I didn't know that dog was yours. I thought he was a stray animal. I'm sorry!"

"That's alright, Preacher. Think nothing of it. I'm glad you ran him out of the church. I wouldn't have had my dog hear that sermon for any amount of money!"

There is an old adage that makes sense, "Let sleeping dogs lie." When I was a young student, I went with my parents to a school board meeting. There was a large crowd, and most of them were against the movement to enlarge the school building. One man was very much against the idea. He gave as his reasons:

1. It would cost money.
2. He didn't like change.
3. It was a new idea that had never been tried.
4. It was not needed.

On and on he went. After he finished, the chairman called upon the county superintendent for a word. I'll never forget his remark. "The more I see of some people, the better I like my old hound dog." With that he got up and left. This is not a good way to end a meeting.

Scripture:

"We love Him, because He first loves us." ~ 1 John 4:19

Prayer:

Dear Lord help us to love people with your love regardless of the things they do that irritate us. O Lord, thank You for Your love, Your mercy and Your grace. Amen.

63

Railroad Problem

A certain hillbilly applied for a job on the railroad. He was given a hypothetical oral test. A clerk sat down to examine him and asked, "If you saw two trains going sixty miles an hour and they were headed for one another, and you were the only one who knew this, how would you stop or warn them?"

"I would blow my whistle!" the hillbilly answered.

"But the noise of the engine would drown our your whistle," said his examiner.

"I would get out my red bandana handkerchief and flag them down," the hillbilly replied.

"But suppose it was at night and they couldn't see you. What else would you do?" the examiner questioned.

"I'd get out my lantern and signal them," the hillbilly replied.

"But suppose your lantern was out of oil and would not light. What else would you do?" asked the examiner.

"I'd call my sister," said the hillbilly.

"Why would you call your sister?" he questioned,

"Well, she has never seen a train wreck!"

The lives of many prominent beauty queens and movie stars' have been described as train wrecks. Too many drugs, long hours, multiple lovers, an over abundance of attention, plus access to an unlimited supply of alcohol have proven to be too much for super stars.

The influence of Hollywood and movies did a great job helping win World War II. They glamorized the men and women of the armed services. They presented the U.S.A as a great nation. They supported the cause of freedom. But times have changed. Hollywood and American movies have been a horrible influence on our culture. The movies and movie producers have given a bad image of American people to the world.

Movie and TV stars have read their own exaggerated press releases telling how great they are. They believe this stuff. Silly people have made these people rich and famous, but their bad reputations are a disgrace. Movie producers and TV writers have abused their freedom. These sick ideas have produced social germs that are evil and destructive. Our society has had more than enough violence, destruction, and death.

A lesson in true humility can be learned from history. F.D. Roosevelt selected Harry Truman to be his Vice President. Mr. Truman was a vote getter but not a competitor to the great F. D. R. When F. D. R. died, Harry Truman said he felt that a great weight had been dropped on him. His long time friend Sam Rayburn came by to see him and said, "They'll tell you what a great man you are, Harry, but you and I both know it ain't so."

History has labeled Harry Truman greater and wiser than any of us living at that time thought that he was. Contrary to what anybody says, he ended the War with Japan, saving millions of lives, and he brought into being the atomic age. How the world handles atomic knowledge is still to be spelled out. It happened on his watch. What is happening on our watch? Harry Truman signed a register while he was in the White House. Under his name he put his address as 1600 Pennsylvania Avenue. On second thought, he wrote beneath the words, "Temporary Address."

Leaders come and go. Their appearance is temporary in the light of the long span of history. Most Presidents of the U.S. who serve a second term have a concern about how history will judge them. Do we have a concern about how history will judge the way we have lived?

Scripture:

"Send out your light and your truth; let them guide me. Let them lead me to your holy mountain, to the place where you live." Psalm 43:3

Prayer:

May freedom and responsibility walk together under the canopy of Your beauty and truth. May the love of God and love for each other be our guiding light. Amen.

64

Learning to Say "No"

Years ago, a certain man was driving through the country. He came to a place where the roads crossed. There was nothing else there but one lonely country store. The man decided to stop and go in and see what the store was like. He opened the door and the four walls of the store were full of shelves. All the shelves - front, back, and sides - were filled with jars of pickles. After looking at all the pickles, he saw one man working quietly among the shelves and asked him,

"Do you sell a lot of pickles here?"

"Nope," was the reply, "but the man who calls on me does."

Obviously, the merchant was overloaded with pickles. His supply was much greater than his demand. The salesman who called on the country grocery man was only interested in unloading his pickles. He was not concerned about how the grocery man was going to get rid of what he had sold him. The merchant did not know how to say, "No."

"No" is a great word. It will never start anything, but it is important to end or prevent something from happening. Every drug addict would be living a better and freer life if he had learned to say, "No." Every alcoholic would be living a sober life if he had leaned how to say, "No."

Saying, "No," to evil is a healthy way to live. We cannot make friends with evil. Learning how to identify what is good for you is a wise way to live. Life calls for a firm "Yes" and a strong "No." For a Christian, there is no such thing as moral neutrality. Using correctly the words "Yes" and "No" as major words with true meaning can save us from minor difficulties.

Scripture:

"Let your *yes* be *yes* and your *no* be *no*. Anything else is evil." – Jesus ~ Matt. 5:37

Prayer:

O Lord, thank You for forgiving me of my sin. Help me to forgive. Amen!

65

Out of Touch with Reality

In this story, two fishermen spent a lifetime competing with each other. Time had taken away their opportunity to fish, but they continued to tell fishing tales. Of course, no person believed them, but that did not hinder their effort to outdo each other. It did not make any difference that both of these old fellows had lost touch with reality. It was fun to see who could tell the biggest fish story that never happened.

At a picnic, these guys were entertaining a group of kids who were listening to their fish stories. "I caught a fish so big that I couldn't get it into my boat. It must have been twenty feet long."

Not to be outdone, the other guy said, "I was fishing one day off the coast of South America, and I pulled up a lantern. On the bottom of it was a date showing the year. The date was 1492. The amazing thing was that the lamp was still burning!"

An adult overhearing these exaggerated lies said, "You fellows need to stop lying about your fishing."

"Okay," one fisherman said to the other. "If you will take 10 feet off the size of your fish, I will blow out my lantern."

A lie will always remain a lie. Reforming it will not change it into a truth. Some stories have been made ridiculous for the sake of fun. They were so far from the truth that they were funny. These lies are easy to identify for what they are.

The world's greatest liar was one of Adolph Hitler's generals. I won't identify him, but I will quote his philosophy of life: "If you tell a lie often enough and long enough, finally somebody will believe it to be true." Political lies are excused as campaign rhetoric. Half-truths told as the truth to get someone elected to office is unacceptable behavior. The voter is on the verge of not believing anything people say who are running for public office.

A practical mystery- in the form of a political question - is, "Why would someone spend a million dollars or more to elect themselves to an office that will never pay that much money in his or her lifetime?"

A politician asked a man to vote for him.

"I wouldn't vote for you if you were St. Peter!"

The seeker of a political office said, "If I were St. Peter, you wouldn't be in my precinct!"

Pilate was a masterful political leader. He found no fault with Jesus. His job was to keep the peace, but the crowd was more than determined to destroy Jesus. Finally, Pilate came up with what he thought was a sure fire solution. The custom was to release one prisoner at the time of the Passover. Pilate would let the crowd decide. He picked out Barabbas, a prisoner that no one liked. Barabbas was evil - a habitual criminal. Pilate put Jesus and Barabbas side by side. Here was a clear-cut decision, and Pilate was sure the people would choose Jesus above Barabbas.

"Whom will you choose, Barabbas or Jesus the Christ?"

The crowd shouted, "Give us Barabbas!"

Pilate's questioned, "What shall I do, then, with Jesus, who is called Christ?"

"Let him be crucified!" yelled the crowd.

Pilate asked the most profound question that has ever been asked, "What shall I do with Jesus?" (John 19, Matthew 27:22). Pilate had Jesus on his hands and did not know what to do with him.

God has entered our life through Jesus Christ. What will the world do with Him?

Crucify him? - Unthinkable.

Neglect Him?

Ignore Him?

Marginalize Him?

As a believer, you have Jesus on our hands. What will you do with Him?

Accept Him?

Surrender to Him?

Love Him?

Serve Him?

Scripture:

"Open the gates, that the righteous nation which keeps the truth may enter in." ~ Isa. 62:2

Prayer:

O Lord, we choose today as always to love Him and serve Him. We give thanks to Him for our salvation and peace. Amen.

66

Fear

F.D.R., President of the U.S., said to the people of America, "We have nothing to fear except fear itself." I have lived long enough to know that fear by itself can be more than a person can handle. As a very small child, I had an ear infection that turned into a staff infection, which has lasted a lifetime.

After three painful operations without a cure, I was told in 1931, when I was going on ten years old, that I needed to have a radical mastoid operation. There might be a chance that the surgical procedure could leave me with a twisted mouth and slurred speech. However, the doctor said such a chance should be taken because if the ear infection was left alone, it would eat a hole in the partition between my ear and my brain and I would die. My mother, a wonderful woman, said that I could make the decision. I said, "No more surgery!"

The competent, outstanding surgeon explained to me what would happen. If this were not done, I would not live to be 18 years of age. The contentious doctor explained to me how I would die. I believed him, but something within me said, "No."

I became a Christian at an early age. When I was twelve years old, I accepted the call of God on my life to become a preacher. I kept this to myself. I knew I was not worthy to be a minister. Fear was in my life – fear of not being able to speak, fear of not living long, fear of continued suffering.

Accepting the Presence of God in my life offset some of the fear of dying. It was the fear of living and not being able to measure up to what God expected of me that set up the struggle. Uncertainty became a part of my life. My impression of the doctor's words was, "You are not going to make it anyhow." When I met Grace in 1942, and we later became engaged, I took a chance and told her the doctor's diagnosis that I could die at any time. She wanted to marry me anyway.

One of my fears was overcome by faith. God Himself laid my fear of being unacceptable and not good enough to be a minister to rest. I never forgot His words. They were not audible, but so very real: "I am calling you to preach the Gospel. I am not calling you because you are worthy, or capable. I am calling you because you are willing! If you are willing, come follow Me!"

Are Ye Able Said the Master was the hymn of my youth. Earl Marlett wrote the hymn. I had the privilege of meeting him at Perkins School of Theology in Dallas, Texas, years later. But before meeting Dr. Marlett, I had already met the Master.

Fear continued to fight a battle with faith in my life. In 1960, gall bladder surgery saved my life. Wonderful doctors who were members of my church did the necessary things to save my life. God did His part and healed me.

In 1978, my second son, Steve, went to medical school. When he took the course module on the ear, he asked his professor to examine my ear and the infection. The professor told me the risk involved and that I could die anytime. My son was disturbed, but when the kind professor left, I told my son, "Don't worry about what he said. The doctor told me that in 1931." Interestingly, in 1988, I was on prednisone for something else, and it totally healed my ear as a side effect.

Fear rose up to try to dominate my life again in 2000, with bladder cancer. By that time, Steve was practicing medicine. He talked to Dr. Hiet who performed the surgery, and the Lord healed me again. My wonderful wife Grace gave me strength. In the same year, Dr. Polly Le Beuhn discovered colon cancer, a Paducah doctor operated on me, and God healed me again. Five years later, liver cancer was discovered, and the doctor at Vanderbilt Hospital took out half my liver, and God healed me again.

I say all this to say fear is strong, but great medical help and guidance plus faith in God healed me again and again. My goal is to die well, and not to die sick. I want to go home to be with the Lord when I have fulfilled His calling and purpose for me here.

Scripture:

"I sought the Lord, and He heard me, and delivered me from all my fears. And when Jesus went out He saw a great multitude; and He was moved with compassion for them, and healed their sick."~ Ps. 34:4; Matt. 14:14

Prayer:

O Lord, thank You for Christian assurance. Thank You for forgiving me of my sins and loving me. I am grateful to You for Your unmerited favor, which I never deserved. Such a blessing is a gift from You through Your Son Jesus Christ. Amen!

67

Finding the Right Medicine

The telephone rang in the drug store of a small southern town. The drug store was closed, and everybody was gone except the man who was cleaning up the place. The phone kept ringing. Finally, the man laid down his mop and went over to the phone and answered, "City Drug Store!"

The voice at the other end asked many questions. The caller gave a long list of drugs with long difficult names without a pause. The lady continued and at last she wanted to know what each item cost. When she paused to get her breath, the cleaning man spoke up, "Madam, after I told you 'City Drug Store' that's all I know."

It's useless to keep on talking after you have run out of anything to say. Remember laughter is one of life's greatest medicines. A person needs to laugh twelve times a day. Learn to laugh when there is no joke. If you can't find anything to laugh about, look in the mirror. Laugh at yourself. Most of us take ourselves too seriously. Balanced living is a combination of laughter and serious response.

Putting yourself down is the devil's job. Are you going to do his work for him? Let God enter your life though prayer. Let the Holy Spirit give you guidance, purpose, and power. Jesus identified the

Holy Spirit as God's Helper. Find out the help He has for you. Are you exercising your body? Are you feeding your mind with healthy ideas? Are you entertaining joyful and positive thoughts? Are you a friend to strangers?

Everybody likes to talk about himself. Are you a good listener? While someone is talking to you, are you hearing what that person is saying? Many people use the time they are listening to others as an opportunity to organize what they are planning to say when the other person stops talking.

Good listeners keep their mind free from their own thoughts. They are careful to focus their mind on the person who is talking to them. We may start out with good intentions, but as the years pass, we develop habits of listening, hearing, and thinking that take over our previous acts toward others. In other words, we treat everybody the same.

We are all alike, but we are all different! One opinion or evaluation, like one size that is supposed to fit all, can frequently end up fitting nobody. Every person is a unique experience and should be accepted and treated as such. This is the way to bless others.

Scripture:

"A merry heart does good like a medicine; but a broken spirit dries up the bones." ~ Proverbs 17:22

Prayer:

O Lord, help me to go to the website of forgiveness, love, hope, and assurance that has been established by Christ on the cross. Amen.

68

Misunderstanding

Ears are funny looking things that stick out on the side of our head. They keep our hats from falling over our eyes when we wear one, but they also serve other purposes as well. Mainly, ears are meant to help us hear. Jesus said, "He that has ears, let him hear." Sometimes, we don't hear because we are only half listening. Some people have genuine hearing problems. I can identify with this since I have been without the use of my right ear all my life.

A certain minister was speaking in a new town. His wife was with him, and he wanted to recognize her, so he said to the congregation, "My wife is with me, and I want to acknowledge her presence. We have been married for 35 years, and I want to say she has been tried and true."

His wife who was standing by his side said, "What did you say?"

I said, "We've been married for 35 years, and I've found you to be tried and true." She took the mike from his hand and said, "I've been married to you for 35 years, and I'm tired of you too."

Misunderstanding happens because people hear things the wrong way. Communication is a real problem, even when people speak the same language. The same word can have a different meaning, depending on how the word is spoken.

A 911 call came from a distraught man whose wife was in the process of delivering a baby.

The caller said, "Her pains are five minutes apart!"

From the 911 operator, there was a question, "Is this her second baby?"

"No, this is her husband."

It is an exciting experience when a baby is to be born. I drove an ambulance in Dallas, while I was going to SMU in 1944. I learned a lot about people. I carried a lot of pregnant women to the hospital in the middle of the night. One young man came to work at the funeral home, and the very first night we were called to take an expectant mother to the hospital. During WWII, people did not have enough cars and gasoline was rationed, so they called an ambulance. The new young man and I got to the home, picked up the lady, and put her in the ambulance.

The *new grandmother to be* said to the *new father to be*, "I think you should ride in the ambulance with your wife."

"But," the husband said, "You are her mother you should go with her."

The woman in labor said, "Shut the door. Neither of them want to ride. I'm having this baby now, let's go without them."

I put the new man in the small seat beside her and I said as I shut the door, "As soon as we got out of this subdivision, I'm going to turn this into an emergency." Out on Ross Avenue, I turned on the siren and the red light. When all this happened, the young man in the back went berserk.

"Preacher, she is having this baby now," he said, as he opened the sliding window behind me.

"I know that's why they called us, go sit down," I said.

"But, Preacher, what can I do?"

I realized he was more trouble than the lady, so I told him to tell her to put her knees together. This would keep him busy, even though it would not stop her delivery.

I cut off the siren as we approached the hospital. Just as I stopped, the medic came out and took her and my cot into the delivery room. When I got out of the ambulance, I saw that my new helper was about to faint. I went over to him and he began to speak.

"I'm quitting," he said, "I'm quitting now. I called my mother, and she is coming to get me. I didn't know what this job was like."

I went back to the dormitory at the funeral home without him.

Dr. Clovis Chappell was a national preacher and an excellent author who wrote many books that helped people. I heard him tell about checking into a hotel room in a small town. As his custom was, he got up early and jogged. He had not been to this place before so he saw a man on the street waiting for a bus, and he asked him, "Are the people around here enjoying their religion?"

The individual responded, "Yes sir, those that got it do!"

It is possible to be inoculated with a small portion of *dead* religion, which prevents you from having a case of *real* religion. "Religion that God our Father accepts as pure and faultless is this: to look after orphans and widows in their distress and to keep oneself from being polluted by the world." ~ James 1:27

Scripture:

"The entrance of Your words gives light; It gives understanding to the simple."~ Ps. 119:130

Prayer:

O, Lord, increase our insight and understanding. Amen.

69

Finding the Responsible

When I was a student at SMU, Perkins School of Theology, I had a friend who was from Kansas. He was an FBI agent and a lawyer and decided to go to seminary and study for the ministry. Loyal was married, and as a lawyer, he and his wife had a saying when things would go wrong, "Let's sue them." It was a joke with them.

When they had their first baby and his wife was waking up, she said, "I want to sue somebody, and that's not a joke!"

I'm sure after childbirth most women would feel like that. But when they see the baby and hold it in their arms, they feel differently about it. Being parents is not an easy time, whatever the circumstances.

A couple was discussing the problems they were having with their teenage son. Finally, the father said, "Let's buy him a bicycle."

"Do you think it will help" his wife asked.

"No," said the father, "but it will spread his meanness over a wider territory."

Getting rid of problem people is not found in moving them from place to place. Penetrating the mind and emotions of a person with the leadership of the Holy Spirit is the best way to make new people. The people of Jesus' day dwelt on health problems by washing and cleaning of the hands. Careful preparation of food was essential. But Jesus reminded them that not only what goes into a person's mouth is important. It is equally worth remembering that what comes out of a person's mouth is also worth watching.

Words can describe the inner contents of one's life. Not only do such words reveal an inner bitterness, but also they are misleading to those who listen. Giving inferior or wrong directions to those who are lost will not help them get back on the highway. We can be misled by asking people for directions who do not know the way, but who do not want to admit lack of knowledge.

Words of appreciation and hope are always welcomed by the discouraged and frustrated. Such positive guidance can make life a joyful journey. When I was preaching in the Philippines, I quickly learned not to ask someone I did not know for directions. You could never be sure if the people you met were sending you on a wild goose chase. For some reason, these people did not want to admit that they did not know the way, so they would give you some kind of an answer.

In early American history when the West was being developed, a wagon train hired an old Indian to guide them over the threatening Davis Mountains in what is now West Texas. The leader of the wagon train asked the Indian, "Are you sure you know the way?"

The Indian replied, "I am the way."

Scripture:

Jesus declared, "I am the way, the truth and the life." ~ John 14:6

Prayer:

O Lord, help me to follow Your Son, Jesus Christ. May I always check with the manual and road map You gave me, the Bible and Your Holy Spirit. Amen.

70

Why Can't We Balance Our Budget?

A cartoon shows a husband and wife pouring over a sheet of paper full of figures. The husband asks his wife, "Why can't we balance our budget?"

"Why, it's no mystery!" she exclaimed. "The neighbors buy too many things that we can't afford!"

Keeping up with others can be frustrating and difficult to manage. Why are we competitive with others? Why do we buy bumper stickers and put them on the back of our car saying, "Our child won more marbles than anyone else!"

Where is the borderline between being rightfully proud of those we love and using their success to make us look good? We are called to be ourselves. This is not an excuse to be obnoxious. It is a guideline to healthy living. A few moments of self-examination can remind us who we are.

Some of the world defines us by what we own. Physical appearance is a description of who we are. But there is an invisible thing called character that is our real frame of reference. Knowing ourselves is a key to abundant living. Learning how to live within our limits and challenging our limits when necessary is important. Asking questions like, "Is it worth the cost?" "When we achieve our goal what then?"

When I was kid, we had a very small dog with a loud bark and a desire to attack anything. One day a big oil truck drove up to deliver gas at our farm. This dog ran out barking and growling. How ridiculous! Suppose she won and took possession of the oil truck. What could she do with it? Some of the things we go after may be impossible to keep once we get them. Possession of them would make us look foolish.

Sometimes, life is just a struggle to keep teeth in and hair from falling out. My friend said that his wife was at the beauty parlor trying to stop Father Time. Some of the things that keep us young is to act our age. It is not easy to be ourselves when we are not sure of our identity.

Scripture:

"Those who are led by the Spirit of God are the sons of God. For you did not receive a spirit that makes you a slave again to fear, but you received the Spirit who makes you sons." (And daughters) And by Him we cry "Abba" (Aramaic for Father) Father. The Spirit

Himself testifies with our spirit that we are God's children. Now if we are children, then we are heirs, heirs of God, and co-heirs with Christ." ~ Romans 8:14-17.

Prayer:

O Lord, we thank You for the wonderful good news. We belong to You and Your family. Help us to enjoy our eternal family. Amen.

71

Mary!

How many "Marys" are there in the world? Who knows, countless thousands I'm sure. There were many queens by this name. Of all the people named "Mary" I wonder if they have been influenced by their name?

If it were possible to list and analyze the people who were given the name "Mary," what do you think would be the results? Perhaps "Mary" was the name of a relative or a friend. The most famous of all people named "Mary" was Mary the mother of Jesus Christ.

What I am about to say concerning the name "Mary" could apply to any person by another name. The great frustration is if your name is "Mary." What have you done to that name? Have you been faithful to that name?

As I am writing this, I am sitting in the waiting room of a beauty parlor in Panama City Beach, Florida, waiting for my wife. The lady who owns this shop is named "Mary." Her shop is attractive. She decorates it to celebrate every season of the year. Ladies who come to her shop arrive tired, weary, and all washed out. Mary washes their hair and gives them a fresh new look. She hugs everybody, and they all leave with a smile. She is doing a good job living up to her name "Mary."

I read in the paper of an account of a man who had committed a horrible crime. His name was John Wesley. I am sure that when he was born and was given the name John Wesley, his parents had high hopes for him by giving him a meaningful name. However, he did not live up to his name.

A paperboy stopped by a house to collect from a customer. The man asked the boy's name.

"My name is Harry Truman."

The customer exclaimed, "That's a well-known name!"

The newspaper boy replied, "Well, it ought to be. I've been throwing papers in this neighborhood for six months."

He never knew that a former President of the United States had that name.

P.S. I once knew a fine Christian lady. She was a staff member that I inherited from the former administrator. It was a while before I learned that her name was spelled "Merry". What a great way to spell it.

Scripture:

Moses asked God for His name, and God said to Moses, "I am that I am. This is My name forever." ~ Exodus 3:13,14, 15

Prayer:

Dear Lord, help me to live in such a way that when people hear my name it gives them a sense of comfort and blessing and reminds them of a person who glorifies You. Amen.

72

Seeing Blind!

A bumper sticker on the back of the car in front of me read, "An eye for an eye will make the world blind!" Jealousy, revenge, harmful competition, and unnecessary criticism are destructive. Such behavior does not build good relationships. I never liked people who said to me, "I have a bone to pick with you." As far as I was concerned, such a comment reduces our behavior to the level of the buzzard. The buzzard is not my favorite bird.

Years ago, when I was preaching in Cuba, I spoke for a week in a little town called Lemanoes. A bus from a large church dropped me off at this beautiful little place. The children and the people were great.

In the little town of Lemanoes, I got a new perspective on the bird called the buzzard. At sunset each evening, the buzzards would come and land in the palm trees. These birds were so big that they would weigh down the branches of the trees. The people there welcomed every one of these birds because they picked up the garbage.

As far as I am concerned, bone picking and buzzards go hand in hand. I have known people who developed the abrasive part of their personality. It was uncomfortable to be in their presence for very long.

Thankfulness, appreciation, and a cheerful attitude is a happy and healthy way to live. Leave the garbage to the buzzards; try to be a songbird or a bird of paradise. Forgive everybody and God will forgive you and open the door to happiness in your life. I noticed that the blue bird sings her song of joy while standing on the garbage dump.

Blessed are those who have eyes to see, ears to hear, and tongues to speak, especially if those parts of their body have been dedicated to the Lord. Such people are able to amplify the message of Gods' love and power to change human nature.

Prayer and Scripture:

One of the great prayers of the Bible is found in the last chapter of the book of Hebrews 13:20:

"May the God of peace who through the blood of the eternal covenant brought back from the dead our Lord Jesus the Great Shepherd of the sheep, equip you with every good thing for doing His will, and may He work in us what is pleasing to Him, through Jesus Christ, to whom be glory forever and ever." Amen.

73

A Startling Sight

An airplane landed and the pilot explained that there was going to be a delay in the flight before the plane would take off again for its next destination. He suggested that the passengers might like to get off the plane and stretch their legs. All the passengers except a blind lady got off. The pilot knew her as a frequent passenger so he asked her, "Would you like to get off the plane. We'll be here for a while?"

"No, thank you," she replied, "but if you would walk my dog I would appreciate it."

So the pilot put on his dark sunglasses and took the blind lady's dog for a walk. In just a little while, he encountered the passengers of his plane. They saw him with dark glasses and a Seeing Eye dog.

They were shocked, believing that the plane they just rode was piloted by a blind man.

Appearances are not always what they seem to be. The Bible warns us to shun all appearances of evil.

News broke that a New York governor was linked to a prostitution ring. The question is, why would an intelligent and highly skilled person get involved in such an affair. This is a common question. Why do we shoot ourselves in the foot?

Leon Hoffman, a psychoanalyst in New York, attempted to unravel this complex question. Dr. Hoffman ventured a guess by saying, "We are all human." Just about everyone would agree. He went on to say that power seems to give privilege; at least those in power seem to think so. Interestingly enough, Dr. Steven Cohen a professor of public administration at Columbia University raised the question of double standards. Should different people because of their position and power be held to different standards? Dr. Cohen seemed to think that there were different standards for different people.

These learned men discussed the psychology of exception and the adolescent belief, "I won't get caught."

Let me put in my two cents worth. There is the experience of temptation that is no respecter of persons. Temptation came to Jesus many times. He was not exempt from temptation. Jesus said, "Get behind me, Satan."

We need to identify the source of temptation. Evil is real, doing business with evil will give it a foothold in your life. Evil, like a dream, will remain in a person's life, as long as it is supported by a sin. The presence of a long-standing sin gives evil a reason to abide in the person.

Surrendering to God gives the Holy Spirit the permission to cast the sin out of life.

Just because the airplane pilot was walking a Seeing Eye dog did not mean that he was blind.

Scripture:

"But now you are free from the power of sin and have become slaves of God. Now you do those things that lead to holiness, things that end in everlasting life." ~ Rom. 6:22 NLT

Prayer:

O Lord, help me to do the things that build people up. Break the negative and critical habit that doesn't do any of us any good. Amen.

74

Not Everybody Can Be Funny!

A group of prisoners were in a very controlled environment. Conversation at mealtime was almost prohibited. However, one prisoner brought laughter to the group by calling out numbers. For example, he called out number 44 and everybody laughed. Later, he spoke the number 65 and loud laughter followed.

A new prisoner seeing this done also wanted to be a comic and help people laugh. So later, he asked the prisoner who called out the numbers how he was able to get the unhappy inmates to laugh just by calling out a number. The prisoner explained, "We have a lot of jokes listed by numbers, and the list is distributed to all the prisoners. They memorize the jokes by numbers, so when I called out 44, 65, they know the numbers of the jokes and respond by laughter."

The eager prisoner asked for the numbered list, and at the next meal he called out 51 - no laughter. Next he called out 22 - the number was followed by silence. Finally desperate, the prisoner shouted out 44, 65, which were the same numbers they had all laughed at before, but there was no response.

Later, he asked the man who had given him the list of jokes, "Why didn't the men respond with laughter when I called out the numbers of the jokes?"

"Well," his fellow cell mate said, "some people can tell jokes and others can't."

Time and circumstance set the stage for human action. Knowing when to speak and when to be silent is an art of human behavior. Sometimes we get it right, and often we don't. This is the risk we take and the cost involved in helping people laugh.

Not long ago, my friend Dr. George Mathison, senior minister of the First United Methodist Church in Auburn, Alabama, began a delightful speech by quoting a movie star. "She said to her seventh husband, 'I won't keep you long.' " The quality of a speech is determined not so much by its length, but by its content. The delivery, the relevance of its subject matter, all go to make the address moving and inspiring. Greater than our speech is the cause we represent.

Jesus said of his enemies, "They hated me without a cause" (John 15:25b). Hatred is like that. It doesn't make sense. Fear can cause us to loose our joy. There is nothing that is funny when we are facing disaster. Peter lost his cool in the garden after Jesus was arrested. A young girl in the garden said to Peter, "You are bound to be one of them, your accent is like theirs." Fear caused Peter to deny Jesus three times, and during one of these denials, Peter cursed to show that he was not a disciple. Then Peter remembered the words of Jesus, "Before the rooster crows twice you will deny Me three times."

The crow of the rooster came at the beginning of the dawn. After hearing the rooster, Peter wept bitterly because he was disappointed that he had let down Jesus, who he loved so dearly. At the resurrection of Jesus, the angelic word was, "He is not here; He is risen. Go tell His disciples and PETER" (Mark 16:6-7).

How thoughtful of Jesus to remember Peter after he had cursed and denied Him.

Scripture:

"Then were the disciples glad, when they saw the Lord."~ John 20:20

Prayer:

O Lord, we are glad when we see You working in our lives. Amen.

75

Signs and What They Say

One of the pastorates that I remember with delight was time St. Luke's United Methodist Church in Memphis, Tennessee. It was a joy to know and live with a variety of talented and exciting people. One lady who was on the faculty of the university next door to the church was visiting in my study planning to go with us on another trip to an interesting part of the world.

At the time of her visit, I was working on a series of sermons and had my desk covered with several commentaries and reference books. There was also a lot of paper scattered across my desk. As she got ready to leave, she looked at my desk and jokingly said, "A cluttered desk resembles a cluttered mind."

I agreed with her remark and asked, "If a cluttered desk resembles a cluttered mind, what does an empty desk stand for?" She laughed and left the room.

We have to watch and read our symbols very carefully. I simply believe that too much judgment is placed on the meaning of body language. Because a person stands or sits a certain way does not imply that he or she is experiencing fear, doubt, or uncertainty.

In his Sermon on the Mount, Jesus warned us about being too judgmental of others. Such attitudes promote criticism that can be hurtful, unjustified and most likely untrue. Such behavior turns us into negative people. It causes us to develop the dark side of our personality. While my friend was being funny and meant no harm, there are others who try to put down people with their caustic remarks.

Let's be careful what we look for in life, lest when we see and find it, such a view may turn upon us and devour us. Tomorrow, we may become what we are today, but everyday gives us a chance to change that. Being able to laugh at ourselves is not practiced very much; however it is a healthy experience. Maintaining such a personal view requires common sense. Everyone should decide for himself when to take himself seriously and when not to. Worry can be devastating because we take our own thoughts seriously. These complaints and unhappy concerns are mine. If they were somebody else's, I could dismiss them completely.

I have never heard anybody say, "I'm a happy person because people criticized me. I am enjoying life because some people found fault with me." The truth of the matter is that we all know our shortcomings and our failures. It's true that the biggest room in the world is the room for self-improvement. We find change to be painful. We plan to do something about it, but not today.

Years ago, *Life Magazine* published letters to the editor. Some readers wrote in and criticized Winston Churchill for ending his sentences with a preposition. Mr. Churchill's letter of response caught my eye. His reply: "That's the kind of thing up with which I will not put!"*

A hammer has long been a great tool for the human race, but in the hand of a person who sees everything as a nail, it becomes a destructive weapon.

Scripture:

"Sharp tongues are the swords they wield; bitter words are the arrows they aim." ~ Psalm 64:5

"Some people make cutting remarks, but the words of the wise bring healing."~ Prov. 12:18

Prayer:

O Lord, let me encourage all who seek to follow God through Jesus Christ. Amen.

* The only thing funny about Churchill's sentence is the way he was making fun of those who criticized his "wrongful" use of prepositions.

76

An Unusual Request

It was Sunday and Christmas Day. I lived in Brownsville, Tennessee. As district superintendent of the Brownsville district, there was in my territory a large penal farm. The inmates worked the farm and supplied their own food and groceries for other institutes run by the state. Some of the troubled people had life sentences. The state encouraged ministers to come to the chapel and offer worship services for those who were placed there.

Because Sunday was Christmas Day, there were no clergymen available. I was asked to take part of my Christmas and go for an afternoon service. I agreed, and when I went to the chapel at the farm, I was approached by a trustee who said, "Preacher, will you preach a long sermon, perhaps the longest you have ever preached?"

"Why do you want a long sermon. This is Christmas, does that have anything to do with the request for a long service?"

"No sir," said the trustee. "The reason we would like for the service to be long is that there is no heat in the cells, only in this place."

Is there really a warm place where we can take refuge from the cold? Is there a place where we can receive strength for our weakness? Guidance for our behavior? Yes, there is! The path of forgiveness leads to a warm heart. Full forgiveness is extended to all who confess, repent, and turn to God.

We can accept this forgiveness and pass it on to others. Complete forgiveness for everybody, including ourselves, those who have injured us, even our enemies, can bring lasting peace to our spirits. Forgiveness is good for our wellness, but it's even better for those who do not deserve it. It is better for me than it is for them.

A friend of mine who is an ex-governor said to one of his enemies, "I want you to forgive me for the way I feel about you."

What a wonderful way to say, "I know what is going on, but I forgive you anyway."

The world is a crowded place, and it's easy for us to bump into one another. Our ideas clash, our purposes compete with each other. Winston Churchill did not like John Foster Dullas, and it is reported that Churchill once said of him, "He is a bull that carries his own china shop with him wherever he goes."

If we live long enough, we will all at sometime or other put our foot in our mouth. Saying the wrong thing even at the right time can be an uncomfortable and embarrassing experience. Someone said, "A clear conscience can be the result of a bad memory."

Let us identify with our best thoughts, our good behavior, and our positive motives. We can thank God for His wonderful forgiveness; His great grace is undeserved, but deeply appreciated.

Scripture:

In the parable of the talents, the Master said, "Well done, good and faithful servant. You have been faithful with a few things; I will put you in charge of many things…" ~ Matt. 25:21

Faithfulness in small things is one of the keys to success.

Prayer:

O Lord, when I remember You and Your love to me, even though I don't deserve it, it brings peace to my soul.

77

New Life Secret

Warren Boyd gave his witness and told how he endured 26 drug rehabs without any lasting change. However, at age 32, he experienced being a father with redemptive results. He said this about his daughter: "When the nurse placed her in my arms, I knew it was all over."

With great effort and commitment to become sober, he overcame his drug habit. Now, he works to help others get delivered. "This whole thing of hitting rock bottom is a farce," Boyd said. "Rock bottom always has a trap door!'

Being a new parent can have a defining moment, which enables a person to come out of a moral slump.

Scripture:

"Come now, and let us reason together," says the LORD, "Though your sins are like scarlet, they shall be as white as snow; though they are red like crimson, they shall be as wool." ~ Isa. 1:18

Prayer:

> In an act of surrender, we can sing and pray:
> Change my heart O God; Make it ever true.
> Change my heart, O God; May I be like You.
> You are the Potter; I am the clay,
> Mold me and make me; This is what I pray.
> Change my heart, O God; make it ever true.
> Change my heart, O God; may I be like You. Amen.

78

Olympics 1988

Twenty years ago in Olympic history, Grace and I were in Australia. We had been on a preaching mission in the Orient. We were eating dinner in the home of a Christian in Australia and had gathered around the TV to watch the swim meet for the gold medal. Australia won the gold and the coach was beside himself with joy. He hugged everybody in sight, and his emotions got out of control. The Australians gathered around the TV and commented about the excited coach. "Look at him! He's gone wild! He acts like an American."

I told this story at Broadway United Methodist Church in Paducah, Kentucky, one Sunday morning after the Olympics. After the service, a man and woman came up to me and in an excited accent said, "We are from Australia."

We never are sure who is listening. It would be nice to know. For every speaker there may be an unknown listener. Jesus said, "Everyone who has ears let him hear." That is correct, that is what ears are for. Is God listening? We hope so. We believe He hears our prayers and answers them the way we want, especially when they are in our best interest. We can trust God to take care of us after we have put forth our best effort.

Not every experience has a conclusion. A hillbilly in Eastern Tennessee, left his mountain home. He went to Chicago, and finally to New York City. When he landed a seat on the stock exchange, he never returned to his mountain home. One day, he received a service call saying, "Papa is dying, can you come home?"

He replied, "I am sorry; I cannot leave. I am about to close a big deal. Give Papa a great funeral. Don't be cheap about it. Send me the bill for the expenses and I'll pay it."

About a week later. he heard from his family, "Paw died. We gave him the greatest funeral this mountain community ever saw. Here's the bill, $10,017.38." The out of town son cut a check for $10,017.38. The next month, he received a bill for $17. 38. He paid this bill, but another bill for $17.38 came in the mail the following month. For the next six months he received a bill for $17.38. After this, he called one of his brothers and asked, "Why do I get a bill each moth for $17.38 listed as funeral expenses?"

"Well, you said bury Paw and don't be cheap about it. We spent 10,000 for the funeral. The $17.38 a month is for the rented tuxedo we buried him in."

Scripture:

"Let the words of my mouth and the meditation of my heart be acceptable in Your sight, O Lord, my Strength and my Redeemer." ~ Ps. 19:14

Prayer:

Dear Lord, let my words be a blessing and encouragement to those who hear them. Amen.

79

An Exciting Story of a Church

This incident happened in a church that was in the process of calling a new preacher. The preacher was asked to go before the congregation and preach a trial sermon. This would give the congregation a good sample of his ability to make a talk. It would also reveal his ideas of ministry and what he expected from the congregation.

This was an exciting and participating congregation whose custom was to respond to the minister's messages with a frequent "Amen! That's right!"

The new preacher began his sermon. "If I am to be the pastor of the church, it has got to get up and WALK!"

"Amen!"

"Yes, let her WALK!" the congregation shouted back.

"Furthermore," the preacher exhorted, "this church when I am pastor has got to do more than WALK. It has to RUN."

"AMEN!"

"Let her run."

"This church has got to fly," retorted the preacher.

"That's right Pastor, let her FLY!"

"If this church is gonna fly," the pastor continued, "it means all of you are going to have to attend all the time, work hard, and give at least a tenth of your money."

The shouts rang back, "Let her walk, Pastor."

"Amen!"

When it comes to our part in an effective endeavor, are we upset over changes and need for participation and money?

I once knew a small church that received an enormous amount of money from a deceased member. Finally, the reaction of the congregation was to reduce the budget of the church to the amount of the income that the trust produced.

A church that does not reach out will eventually pass out. Pretty good is not good enough. We must not be satisfied until we give God our best.

Scripture:

"About the ninth hour of the day (about 3:00 p.m.) he saw clearly in a vision an angel of God entering and saying to him, "Cornelius!" And he, gazing intently at him, became frightened and said, 'What is it, Lord?' And the angel said to him, 'Your prayers and your generous gifts to the poor have come up as a sacrifice to God and have been remembered by Him.' " ~Acts 10:3-4

Prayer:

O Lord, help me to serve You in Your church. Together let's make it a dynamic and powerful witness in the world. Amen.

80

A Summary of Faith

The most outstanding theological mind of the 20th century was probably Carl Barth. He was asked to sum up in a short statement the meaning of the Christian faith. To this question, he answered, "Jesus loves me, this I know, for the Bible tells me so!"

When I was pastor of St. Luke's United Methodist Church in Memphis, in the 1970's, there was a wonderful couple that had a cute baby boy. They brought him to the morning worship service and kept him in the balcony. It was there they fed and attended to his personal needs. They attended every worship service with him. He literally grew up in the church service, and they shared him with the entire church.

When he was four years old, I was preaching, and in the middle of my message I quoted Carl Barth's statement, "Jesus loves me this I know, for the Bible tells me so!" At this point, this four-year-old boy spoke up with an excited and loud voice, "I know that! I know that!" This statement bought down the house with laughter and love for one of their favorite sons.

"I know that!" Can you say this? "I know that!" You certainly know the song, but do you really know and believe that "Jesus loves me!" All this makes a profound difference in our lives. Such knowledge gives us assurance and hope. It offers power for personal living. Be sure you can say, "I know that!" There is nothing better than Christian assurance. For example:

Praying to God with praise and thanksgiving;
Following after His leadership;
Reading His word; loving all the people of God;
Forgiving everybody, as we want God to forgive us;

Dedicating our resources to His church;
Sharing with those who need us;
Singing God's praises.

All these and many more acts of faith add up to Christian assurance.

Scripture:

"But be doers of the word, and not hearers only, deceiving yourselves. For if you just listen and don't obey, it is like looking at your face in a mirror but doing nothing to improve your appearance." ~ James 1:22-23NLT

Prayer:

O Lord, help me to be faithful to myself, to others, to those whom I love, and to You. Amen.

81

Are You a Member of God's Family?

"Those who are led by God's Spirit are God's sons. For the Spirit that God has given you does not make you slaves and cause you to be afraid; instead the spirit makes you God's children and by the Spirit, God joins himself to our spirit to declare that we are God's children. Since we are His children, we will possess the blessings He keeps for His people, and we will also possess with Christ what God has kept for Him." (Rom. 8:14-17 Good News Bible in Today's English)

When we turn to God and take Him seriously, then we discover that we have a spirit as well as a body and a mind. Such action introduces us to our Heavenly Father who is an Eternal Spirit.

How do we get into God's eternal family? The greatest way is to be born into the family. When we give ourselves to God as we understand Him and believe that He will receive us, then we can experience God's great love. When we surrender to God and acknowledge His Presence in our lives, we discover that we are now a family member.

This is an eternal family where God will always be our heavenly Father. His Son Jesus Christ will be our Savior. Our relationship with Jesus gives us status as a family member. We also know that God the Father and Jesus Christ are alive and present in our lives. This arrangement is made possible through the Holy Spirit who is our Helper, our Adviser, our Guide, and our Friend. So the family of God is ever present in our lives.

We are able to talk as a family member by praying to the family. This is what prayer is - talking to God and asking Him for help and guidance in your life. Trusting God with your life, enjoying His Presence, and thanking God for His blessings will make your life abundant and happy. You can always count on God and your family relationship to give you hope, peace, and personal strength. You can also discover that God has a plan for your life.

Jesus described heaven as a wonderful, exciting, enjoyable place. He said that there are no marriages in heaven. If you have had a good marriage, it's hard to believe that there could be anything better than that. However, if you have had a bad marriage, you are glad that you don't have to live in this marriage relationship for eternity.

On earth, one of the functions of marriage is to produce children. This is how not only the world is populated, but the way heaven is populated this way as well. Therefore, Heaven is my everlasting home, my future inheritance, and it belongs to my eternal family of which I am a part.

Scripture:

"And now we live in fellowship with the true God because we live in fellowship with his Son, Jesus Christ. He is the only true God, and He is eternal life."` 1 John 5:20

Prayer:

O Lord, I thank You that my future is in Your hands. Amen.

82

How to Get On Your Feet

On a car lot this sign appeared, "How to Get Back on Your Feet - Miss Three Car Payments."

Standing and walking are two human characteristics that are often taken for granted. Until we break a leg or experience a stroke, we don't appreciate the ability to stand or walk. The opposite of standing is falling. Falling is always a bad experience. Standing can mean taking a firm position and not being moved by the wind of circumstance. Paul had this advice to the Christians at Corinth: "Stand firm and steady. Keep busy always in your work for the Lord, since you know that nothing you do in the Lord's service is ever useless." (1 Cor. 15:58)

A small child had a confrontation with his mother. The mother wanted the little boy to sit in his chair. He was determined to stand up, but she was more determined for him to sit down. Finally after an exchange of heated conversation, the mother forced the boy to sit down. As he was seated in his chair, he firmly cried, "I'm sitting in this chair, but inside I'm standing up."

Life is a continuous challenge to stand for eternal values. Make a determined effort to stand up against rotten behavior. Keep healthy ideas in your mind. Paul reminds us, "Fill your mind with those things that are good and deserve praise; things that are true, noble, right, pure, lovely and honorable."(Phil 4)

Saint Paul goes on to say, "I have learned to be satisfied with what I have. I know what it is to be in need and what is to have more than enough. I have learned this secret so that anywhere I am, full or hungry, whether I have too much or too little, I have the strength to face all conditions by the power that Christ gives me." (Phil 4:13)

Scripture:

"Rise up in splendor. Your light has come. The glory of the Lord shines upon you."~ Isa. 60:1

Prayer:

O Lord, help me stand up for You, let me not fall for nothing. Amen.

83

Harness

In the 1930's, I lived with my family on a farm. We had a dairy, milked cows, and sold the milk to the plant that, in turn, pasteurized the milk and put it into bottles. Since we had over 50 cows, we had to take care of them. We fed them corn, and it was necessary to grow the corn for seed. Planting the seed required that land be broken and prepared. Planting the seed required that the land be broken and prepared. We used mules for this purpose.

It was necessary to catch the mules and prepare them for labor. We had to dress the mule first with a bridle placed on his head and bits placed in his mouth. A collar was fastened around his neck, and a harness was used to make the mule pull great loads and work the land. Seeds were then planted in the ground so corn could be grown to feed all the animals that lived on the farm. The harness enabled us to work the mule and produce food.

The poet talked about harnessing for God the energies of love. This is something all church members could do. How do you harness for God the energies of love? Love could be harnessed for God and put to work to produce a better and more productive land. Good will and friendship are the products of love. People who care about themselves and others can give new direction and purpose for the lives of all of us.

As I sit beside the Gulf of Mexico and watch the waves roll in and out, I am impressed with the tremendous energy that seems to go to waste. I am glad I don't have to push or pull the waves. One day, someone will harness the energy of the waves. I suppose it's left to the churches of all Christians and the Christians of all churches to harness the message of John 3:16.

Scripture:

"For God so loved the world that He gave His only begotten Son, that whoever believes in Him should not perish but have everlasting life." ~ John 3:16

Prayer:

O Lord, help me harness my energies for You. Amen.

84

Watching the Crowd at Wal-Mart

A young man sitting beside me at Wal-Mart had on a tee shirt that read, "I am out of bed and dressed, what more do you want?"

What I want from him and the shirt that he is wearing is not important. The real question is what does he want? Judging from his rumpled clothes, his dirty face and hair, there might be a lot more that he needs, whether he wants it or not.

Looking our best is the personal responsibility of all of us. Working is both a necessity and a rewarding experience. If we do not care about ourselves, how can we expect others to care about us?

Careful living includes giving attention to things beyond our dress. Being content with cheap and secondhand ideas is a very poor way to live and behave. There is little joy in being a carbon copy of somebody else. It may be worth it to be yourself and find out what this means.

You are a very special person. Even if you are a twin, you are still a person in you own right and different from birth. Have you ever done research to discover who you are? If you are reading this, you already know a lot about yourself. When you enter into a contract with God, you discover that you are wonderfully made and that God has a plan for your life.

Prayer is the act of asking God for direction for your life. When you acquire something, you first read the directions for how to put your new article together. Many difficulties that take place in your life happen because you failed to read all the directions.

The Bible is God's great set of directions for your life. It is a mistake to ignore such a storehouse of good news and advice.

Jesus put us on the spot when he summarized the Ten Commandments and concluded, "Love your neighbor as you love yourself." Self-love and self-respect should be healthy and can bring abundant life to us now. Joel 2:13 in the King James Version reads, "Rend your heart and not your garment." Tearing one's clothes was a sign of repentance.

Job's message is clearer in the *Today's English Version*, "Let your broken heart show your sorrow." Tearing your clothes is not enough. But do not leave your sadness there. Take it to the Lord, and leave it there. Jesus feels your pain; the Holy Sprit can heal your life. Jesus can cure your troubled heart.

Scripture:

Remember, Jesus said, "Let not your heart be troubled." ~ John 14

Prayer:

O Lord, give me Your peace, and I thank You for Your blessing. Amen.

85

Old Time Texas

A Texas winter in Dallas can be an unforgettable, shivering experience. In 1944, I was a student at SMU and had four churches about thirty-four miles from the school. One of these churches was a union church made up of several denominations that shared the same building.

The fourth Sunday was the Methodist Sunday, and it was my opportunity to preach to all the diverse groups that shared the same building. One woman who could play only four songs dominated the piano stool. She got the most out of the piano by playing frequently on all the keys, black and white, without any discrimination toward the tune of the hymn.

I picked this cold February to invite two music majors from the school of music to play and sing. Both of these young ladies had great talent and came at their own expense to bring two special numbers. After the first beautiful hymn, the soloist was scheduled to sing *The Lord's Prayer*.

This rural Texas church was a one-room affair. For heat, it had a coal-burning stove that sat in the end of the center aisle. The pulpit was above the stove. This stove had a pipe that went up to the high ceiling and was attached to the length of the ceiling and met the chimney, which was at the other end of the building. It was the job of one of the members to tend the stove and make sure it was keeping the church building warm. Just as the young lady began to sing the *Lord's Prayer*, the member in charge of the stove decided it needed tending.

He got down on his knees and looked at the bottom of the stove. Then he got up and took a poker and jammed it through the stove's open door. This made the coal fall down and burn a little faster. He then proceeded to shake the grate, getting rid of some of the ashes. When he shook the stove, the long pipe attached to the ceiling began to move and shake. I wondered if the pipe might fall and baptize us all with ashes and soot. But he was a professional; he knew what he was doing. He then took a bucket of coal and threw it into the burning coals in the stove. His last act was to stand on one foot and kick the door to the stove closed. He finished all this in concert with the closing "Amen" to *The Lord's Prayer*.

Why did this person choose to fire the stove during this musical presentation? Answer – his wife was the two finger piano player. This was his protest.

I never realized what I had done. It was not my intention to hurt the lady who was the pianist by bringing in these two young performers. I just thought the people would enjoy some good music for a change. As I have grown older, I have tried to think through my decisions.

In the novel *David Copperfield,* Charles Dickens wrote, "I ate humble pie with an appetite." ~ from Chapter 35

Prayer:

"That's me, O Lord!" Amen.

Scripture:

At Nazareth Jesus was at the synagogue and someone handed him the book of the prophet Isaiah. One of the lines Jesus read was, "He has sent me to heal the brokenhearted." Jesus can do that for you now! ~ Luke 4:18 KJV

86

Academic Jargon

A Cajun from Louisiana went to his banker and said, "Years ago I was really poor. My son got a scholarship at SMU in Dallas. He brought a crew from the University that made some tests and discovered oil on my property. They drilled, and many oil wells came in for me. I have never expressed my appreciation to SMU for discovering oil. So I have decided to give SMU at least a million dollars to show my appreciation."

The banker did not want that money to go out of Louisiana, so he said to the old Cajun, "Why don't you give that money to LSU?"

"Well," said the Cajun, "I never finished high school or attended college, so if it had not been for SMU, I wouldn't be rich today."

The banker had to stop the flow of money from Louisiana, so he decided to use academic jargon to persuade the man. "Before you give all that money to SMU, I think there are some things you need to know about that university. Do you know that the boys and girls that go there matriculate together."

The old Cajun was shocked, so he said, "They do?"

"Yes," said the banker. "Furthermore, they both use the same curriculum."

"Is that right," said the Cajun. "Hold up on that money."

A few months later, the old Cajun visited his banker again and said, "Go on and send that million dollars to SMU."

"Remember what I told you about the boys and girls and their behavior with matriculation and curriculum?" warned the banker.

"Yes, I remember," said the Cajun. "I understand this. I was young once myself."

The old Cajun was correct when he said, " I was young once," but he didn't have a clue about what it meant to be young.

Everybody can say, "I was young once." But nobody in all the world can say, "I was young twice. I was young three times. I was young four times." Nobody can ever say, "I will be young again; I will be young tomorrow; I will be young when I reduce; I will be young when I pay off my mortgage." Youth offers:

A fresh start.
A time to prepare.
Energy and strength.
Help from older people and a chance to learn.

The brother of my high school friend died a painful death at an early age. I took part in his funeral. Just before they closed his casket, a friend came forward and performed his last request. She placed two cigarettes and a pack of matches in his hand. He died of lung caner due to smoking. In his youth, it was fun to act like adults and smoke, but after his youth left, his habit remained to destroy his body.

In Chicago, in November 1879, a reunion was being held for soldiers who fought during the Civil War. President Grant and General Sherman were in attendance. Amid the fireworks, festivities, celebration, and oratorical speeches on the greatness of America and the honoring of the two great American heroes, Samuel S. Clemens (Mark Twain) was asked to end the ceremonies with a brief speech.

He stepped up to the podium and raised his glass in a toast, "To the babies, as they comfort us in our sorrow, let us not forget them in our festivities." Everyone wondered what babies had to do with all this. Twain continued, "We haven't all had the good fortune to be ladies: We haven't all been generals, or poets, or statesmen; but when the toast works down to the babies, we stand on common ground, for we've all been babies."

Once young, and then youth goes. Don't destroy or abuse your youth. Use it wisely. You'll never have it again. We are all too immature and not grown up enough to appreciate being young. "I was young once." For good or bad, I'll never get over it. Frequently, we can be our own worst enemy. Over the years, I have worked with people who had alcohol problems. I loved and appreciated these people. Sober, they were generous and enjoyable to know, but they were allergic to the drug of alcohol.

We all have inhibitions. Your inhibitions keep you courteous and polite. These traits keep you from calling me up and saying, "This is a stupid book. It's poorly written, full of mistakes, and I don't like it." You wouldn't do this. You are too kind. Instead, you say nothing and throw the thing in the wastebasket. But after you have had a few drinks, your inhibitions are drugged and you call me up and say, "This is a stupid and shallow book. I've heard all these stories before. Whatever possessed you to write this?"

And I reply, "You are right. You don't have to be drunk to realize this; you only have to be drunk to tell me this. I love you anyway. Thanks for buying the book. God bless you."

We all need to laugh and enjoy what we have left of life's blessings. After Jesus' horrible crucifixion, his death, and his resurrection, the Bible comments, "Then the disciples were glad when they saw the Savior."

We are truly glad when we experience Jesus in our life. The living Jesus comes to us as our Friend and Redeemer and His Presence makes us glad.

Scripture:

In great pain and uncertainty, Paul wrote, "I only want to finish the works that the Lord Jesus gave me with joy. "~ Acts 20:24 (My translation)

Prayer:

O Lord, help me to stay alive all my life. May I remain thankful and grateful to You to the end. Amen.

87

Feed My Sheep

A city boy spent the night with his country cousin. At the end of every day, the country boy would feed all the farm animals. The city boy watched a few times and then he said to the farm boy, "Let me feed the animals tonight."

"Okay," replied the farm boy, who was very glad to give him the chore. The boy went off alone and came back quickly, much to the astonishment of the country lad.

 "You were gone only a short time. Did you quit?" asked his country cousin.

"No, I finished. I fed them all."

The country boy thought he would check so he asked, "What did you feed the horses?"

"I gave them a bale of hay."

"What did you feed the cows?"

"I gave them a bale of hay."

"What did you feed the ducks?"

"I gave them a bale of hay."

"You did?" asked the farm boy in astonishment. "Did they eat it?"

"No, but they were talking about it when I left."

Not everyone is on the same diet. We like different things, events, and food. Response is better than reaction. We can treat everyone alike when we surrender to God's purpose for us and share what we have experienced with others. When we submit to God, He puts his hand on our shoulder and immediately the circumstances of life try to knock it off. A great prayer is, "Lord, would you put your hand back on my shoulder."

There are many experiences in life that challenge our mind and stretch our imagination. For example, there were a little over six and half billion people on earth in the year 2008. If all of them were to call on God at the same time, a true hypothetical question, but say that all God's children did cry out to Him, how could He hear them? I don't know that much about God to give you a strong positive answer. This I know, that God is much greater than man. I hold in my hand a computer chip the size of a quarter, which is capable of responding seven billion times to that many calls. Why should I not believe that God hears our prayers? I rest my case.

In 2 Corinthians 12, St. Paul talks about his thorn in the flesh. He said three times, I pleaded with the Lord to take it away. Verse 9, "But He said to me, My grace is sufficient for you, for my power is made perfect in weakness."

Scripture:

"Now this is the confidence that we have in Him, that if we ask anything according to His will, He hears us. And if we know that He hears us, whatever we ask, we know that we have the petitions that we have asked of Him." ~ 1 John 5:14-15

Prayer:

O Lord, thank You that You not only hear us when we pray, but that You also answer our prayers. We thank You for the answers in advance.

88

"Fire in the Hole!"

My great-grandson Preston went to the beach in Florida with his family. His grandfather and grandmother took him and his sister and cousins on a pirate ship in the Gulf of Mexico. One of the exciting things that happened on board the pirate ship was that at certain intervals one of the crew would yell out, "FIRE IN THE HOLE!" Then they would discharge a blank cannon that made a terrific noise.

After they returned from their vacation to Alabama, three-year-old Preston was playing with his cousin and yelled out, "FIRE IN THE HOLE!"

His playmates asked him, "Why are you yelling that?" Little Preston retorted, "Because I'm about to explode!"

We all give out warning signs that the pressure is too great or that we have had enough, and we are about to explode in a noise of anger. It is great when we can see this happening in other people and ease the tension before they call out, "FIRE IN THE HOLE!"

Such observations would make life easier for all concerned. Such behavior would be an intelligent act. It would be even smarter if we could anticipate the moment when we are about to explode and warn ourselves that we are filled with tension and things are about to explode. Laughter at the situation, or directed at ourselves, can be the equivalent to yelling, "FIRE IN THE HOLE!"

A new Christian became a member of a newly formed band. His job was to beat the drum. The leader of the band asked, "Why do you beat the drum with such vigor and power?"

The new band member answered, "Since I became a Christian and became aware of how much God loves me, and I realize He has forgive all my sins, I get so excited that I could burst this big drum!"

Scripture:

"And they said to one another, 'did not our heart burn within us while he talked with us by the way, and while He opened to us the scriptures?" ~ Luke 23: 32

Prayer:

O Lord, Thank you that Jesus the Risen Christ appeared to the men on the road to Emmaus. Help me to see You in my life today. Amen.

89

Cartoon Philosophy

Years ago as a child, I remember reading the *Collier's Magazine*. It was famous for its cartoons. One I recall was an old mountaineer and his wife who were dressed in rural clothes. She was pictured wearing a sunbonnet, and he had a long beard and his famous rifle. They were standing by the mailbox at the end of a very small lane in the mountain that connected it to a mountain road. They were looking for the postman. The old fellow held his pocket watch in his hand and remarked to his wife, "We will wait fifteen minutes more, and if the postman doesn't come, then today must be Sunday."

Rural people are not the only ones who are out of date and out of touch with the mainstream of life. However, those who are labeled as "out of touch" may not be unfortunate. A lot depends on those who are passing out the labels.

However, missing the mark can be disastrous, and plenty of people don't have a clue about what it means to live an abundant life. When is life truly abundant? Things do not bring abundant living. Ideas, causes, and experiences are sometimes overlooked events. Feelings are also influential and frequently are never forgotten for better or worse. What we give can be more important than what we receive. The way we feel about all of life colors it completely.

In Luke 8:41-48, there is a woman who had a sickness that she bore for 12 years, a bleeding condition that left her isolated and alone. Her sickness caused her to be out of touch with society.

As Jesus passed by on His way to respond to the request of a certain ruler, this woman said, "If I can touch the hem of

His garment, I can be healed." And immediately, her bleeding stopped.

As Jesus passed by on His way to respond to the request of a certain ruler, this woman said, "If I can touch the hem of His garment, I can be healed." And immediately, her bleeding stopped.

Jesus said, "Who touched me?"

In the great multitude, it was difficult to say. "Who touched me?" I am sure Peter said, "Somebody kicked me on the leg, another ran his elbow in my ribs. I don't know who the bloke was, but if I could find out, I would hit him in the stomach."

Jesus insisted, "Somebody touched me."

The woman came forward and confessed that she was the one and declared that she had been healed. Then Jesus said to her, "Daughter, your faith has healed you. Go in peace." Notice Jesus called her "daughter." This name acknowledged that she was a member of "God's Forever Family."

Scripture:

"If you abide in Me, and My words abide in you, you will ask what you desire, and it shall be done for you." ~ John 15:7

Prayer:

O Lord, help me to keep in touch with Jesus. He is the source of my power and strength forever. Amen.

90

What Can We Say?

A cartoon showed two American Indians sending smoke signals to one another. Without their knowledge, scientists discharged an atomic bomb on the desert behind the two men. It sent up a high cloud of smoke that caused one of the old Indians to look at it and say, "I wish I had said that!"

Making a big statement and getting the attention of everybody can be disastrous. It can show our emptiness to the world. Of course, if we have something of value to say, our statement can make a difference.

A word of goodwill that produces real friendship forms lasting relationship. These positive values seem to last. It's much easier to love forever than it is to hate for a lifetime and beyond.

Love produces the very best results. Love as active goodwill toward others is the best way to live.

A cartoon of my childhood was called *Andy Gump.* I remember one time when Andy's father was helping him to grow up. Every time Andy did something wrong, his father drove a nail in the post in their backyard. After a while, the post was almost full of nails. Andy looked at all the nails that stood for his errors and mistakes. He asked his father, "How can I get rid of these nails?"

His father said, "Every time you do something good, I'll pull out a nail." Andy worked hard doing good.

One by one, Andy's father pulled out the nails until there was only one nail left to be pulled out. Andy and his father had a little ceremony and pulled out the last nail. Andy looked at the clean post for a long while and then said, "But the holes are still there."

Our efforts to improve ourselves are to be applauded. But reformation, redemption, and restoration are not just a do-it-yourself program. Our reformation still leaves holes. God's love can fill these holes. We all need help from those who love us and especially from God himself. The work of the Holy Spirit can bring healing to our lives. Such a work is the grace of God. God's grace is a gift. We cannot earn his grace. Certainly we do not deserve it, but God gives His unmerited favor to us anyway! Our response to such love calls forth our profound gratitude. By this act of God, we are encouraged to live better lives.

Sometime ago, we were in Alaska with our family on a preaching mission. I was sitting in a chair and the house began to shake. I thought the washing machine had gotten out of balance while it was spinning dry clothes. Then as the walls began to shake, I realized that we were having an earthquake. All this happened and was over with before I could get out of my chair. When the plates move and the earth trembles, it can tear down buildings in a few seconds that it took years to construct.

Our job should be to rebuild and build up those whose lives have been shaken or destroyed.

Scripture:

"God has made everything beautiful for its own time. He has planted eternity in the human heart."~ Ecclesiastes 3:11

Prayer:

O Lord, thank You for giving me the chance to enjoy part of Your eternity today. Amen.

91

Life is What We Make It

A young actress, commenting about her 50 hour marriage to her long time friend said, "I do believe in the sanctity of marriage, I totally do. But I was in Vegas, and it took over me."

Have we become some kind of ethical and moral chameleon, changing values, philosophies and concepts of right and wrong wherever we go? The old saying, "When in Rome, do as the Romans do," has been around a long time. After this young actress becomes old and obsolete, marriage will still be around. Marriages suffer most not by laws, customs, or demand for changes, but by those who go into marriage as immature and ignorant about the definition of a marriage and how it functions.

Proper and healthy child guidance produces well-rounded and mature adults. Dysfunctional people seem to reproduce themselves in many different forms.

A grandfather took his grandson to the zoo. They passed many kinds of animals. They finally came to a cage of wild cats. The adult animals were unattractive, and the young boy looked at the beautiful baby kittens.

"Grandpa, these are cute kittens. They are pretty. What do you think they will grow up to be?"

"Wild cats," replied the grandpa.

"But they look so beautiful. Why do you say they will be wild cats?"

"Because their mothers and fathers are wild cats."

This is a safe prediction; but the human element can change. The influence of teachers and leaders can provide a child with the chance to change his heritage. A personal relationship with Jesus Christ and surrender to the Holy Spirit can produce wonders in any of us. Do we know how to give God a chance in our lives? Many times children of good, healthy, normal parents decide to react to their parental background and take a revolutionary position. Such a different behavior is the result of bad decisions.

A young daughter was helping her mother clean the house. There was a loud crash, and the daughter said, "Mother! You know that vase that has been handed down from generation to generation in our family?"

"Yes," was the reply.

"Well, this generation just dropped it!"

One of the oldest bits of writing in the world appears on a clay table in a museum in Constantinople. Translated it reads: "Alas, alas, times are not what they used to be, children no longer obey their parents, and everybody wants to write a book."

We can differ with our parents, but still love and respect them. I guess we all have a right to make our own mistakes, however, I used to tell my young kids, "Learn from other people's mistakes; you'll never live long enough to make all of them yourself."

Scripture:

"All those who are in Christ are a New Creation. What this means is that those who become Christians become new persons. They are not the same anymore, for the old life is gone. A new life has begun!"~ 2 Cor. 5:17 NLT

Prayer:

O Lord, help me to untie the apron strings without cutting the family ties. Amen.

92

Starting Over

A certain man and woman had a very large number of children. One of them came running in the house crying, "Mama come quickly, the baby has gotten in a mud hole." The mother went out in the yard to discover that the baby had been taking a mud bath. He had mud in his hair and all over him. About that time, her husband came out to see what all the excitement was about.

"That is the dirtiest kid I have ever seen," he told his wife.

She agreed, "You know, I believe it would be easier to get another one than to clean this one up."

Life can get so messed up with the dirt and filth of evil that the best plan is not just to clean up our act, but to become a new person. Taking on new life in Christ is the best procedure. Old promises can't do the job of making a person new. The new birth experience is what Jesus thought Nicodemus needed, and he hadn't even fallen in a mud hole. A new start from a different perspective can produce amazing results.

Years ago at a tent revival meeting, Brother Mayhaun called on a Christian leader to pray. This man tried to impress everybody with his vocabulary. In his prayer, he told God all the news. Then he gave God a long list of the things he wanted Him to do. He kept wandering around and around in his prayer, searching for a good ending. He could not think of the word "Amen," so he finally said, "I will call on Brother Mayhaun to finish my prayer.

Brother Mayhaun said, "I'll not do it. I'll have no part in such a mess. I'll start my own prayer."

Prayer is *praising God.*

Prayer is *confessing our sins.*

Prayer is *asking God to have mercy.*

Prayer is *seeking divine guidance.*

Prayer is *thanksgiving for what God has done for us through Christ Jesus.*

Prayer is *surrendering to God's will.*

Prayer is *expressing our love for God.*

Prayer is *conversation with God.*

Prayer is *spontaneous, from our heart, not off the top of our head.*

In 1963, Grace and I and all our family - Peggy, Rose, Rusty (Henry Ewell Russell, III), Stephen (Steve), and Betty Grace - went to England. I was an exchange minister, and the British Methodist Church assigned me to preach at the Albert Hall in Manchester.

We wanted our children to experience life at sea. The only ship available was a German vessel left over from WWII. It was a beautiful ship, but it was slow, and it took us nine days to cross the Atlantic. The ship had its own German band, a swimming pool, and we were requested to dress nicely for dinner. We were introduced to the German Band that sounded to us like "ump, paw, ump, paw, ump, paw."

Very, very few people could speak English. After a few days at sea and being exposed to German Band music, I asked the director if he could play the then popular song "The Tennessee Waltz."

"Yaw, Yaw," he said.

I went back to the table and told my family. The band began to play the Tennessee Waltz, and it came out "Ump, paw, ump, paw, ump, paw." Music is supposed to be a universal language, but in this case it came out with a German Band interpretation.

Much later, Grace and I were in China, and we went to an October Fest. At the close the German band played as a closing number, "Amazing Grace." It was beautiful. In the heart of "Red" China, we were blessed to hear this great song.

Scripture:

"Pray without ceasing." ~ 1 Thes. 5:17

Prayer:

O Lord, wherever I am, when I pray, I am at home with You. Amen.

93

Joshua

I went to a prayer breakfast, and one of the men who has a jail ministry spoke of three men by the name of Joshua. All three of them were in jail for crimes.

This reminded me of the story of a man who appeared before a judge.

"What is your name?" asked the judge.

"Joshua."

"There is a man in the Bible by the name of Joshua who made the sun stand still. Are you that man?"

"No, sir I'm the man that made the 'moon shine.' "

Some scientists tell us that the region of our universe visible from earth is 92 billion light years across. Most people accept this as accurate, even though none of us has really measured the universe. But if I put up a small sign that reads "Wet paint," a lot of people will stop to touch it to see if it is really wet. Some people believe that they can go around the law and not get caught.

Some people work hard to keep from working. These people think differently from others. In most cases, they don't do much thinking. Alcoholics Anonymous has a saying, "Our thinking is stinking, and it leads to our drinking." To some extent, we are what we think. Thinking produces ideas, and ideas form behavior patterns. Behavior patterns build highways in our minds, which are thought patterns on which all our experiences travel.

If I go to the bus station and take a bus and do not notice its destination, and much later I end up in Chicago, when I meant to go to Miami, it is obvious that I took the wrong bus. Frequently, new material is processed though the same old channel ending in the same conclusions. Wrong choices never produce right results. I grew up with Joshua's exhortation, "Choose you this day whom you will serve. But as for me and my house, we will serve the Lord" (Jos. 24:7). That's taking a real stand.

A woman had a problem. She frequently would pick up objects that did not belong to her. She did not need these items and they were of little value, but she would consistently steal them. Every member of the family tried to break her of the habit, and her husband tried to cover for her. One day, she was caught stealing a can of peaches. She was taken before the judge, and her husband went with her.

The judge asked, "Did you steal a can of peaches?"

"Yes, sir," she replied.

"Did you eat all the peaches?" he asked.

"Yes, sir."

"How many peaches were in the can?" he asked.

"Six," she said.

"You will spend six days in jail, one for each peach." Her husband looked as though he wanted to say something so the judge said to him, "Would you like to say something?"

"Yes, your honor, she also stole a can of peas."

The jury is still out on how much punishment breaks people from doing wrong.

Scripture:

In 1974, Grace and I attended the reopening of City Road Chapel, which was John Wesley's church in London, England. Queen Elizabeth attended. Lord Mountbatten read this scripture,

"You are a chosen people, a royal priesthood, a holy nation, people belonging to God, who are to declare the praises of Him who called you out of darkness into His wonderful light. Once you were not a people, but NOW you are the people of God; once you had not received mercy, but now you have received mercy." ~ Peter 2:9-10

Prayer:

O Lord, help me to live up to my spiritual heritage. Amen.

94

Surprise!

A lady reached her 90th birthday, and she wanted to celebrate by reclaiming her youth. Her daughter arranged for her to have a date with a family friend who was 95. He picked her up, and they went out for an evening on the town. A little after 10 o'clock, she returned home and her daughter asked, "How was your exciting evening?"

"Awful," she replied. "I had to slap him three times, and then I made him bring me home."

"Oh, my, why did you slap him? Was he fresh with you?"

"No, I had to keep him awake."

Time changes things and we are not always able to cope with them.

After the christening of his baby brother in church, Joey sobbed all the way home in the back seat of the car. His father asked him three times what was wrong. Finally, the boy replied, "That preacher said he wanted us to be brought up in a Christian home, and I wanted to stay with you guys."

Disaster struck the budget of a young couple. It was quite a struggle for them to pay their back bills and continue to meet their current obligations. One of their creditors turned over their account to a bill-collecting agency. This agency was known for the pressure they put on to collect the money.

After several nasty letters, the young couple sent a letter to them saying, "Let us explain to you our method of paying our bills. We get paid once a month, and we cash the check and put it in the bank. Then we write down the names of all the people we owe, and the amount we owe them. Then we put all the names into a hat. Next, we draw out the names one by one and pay the bill we owe. When we have exhausted our paycheck, we stop. If you don't stop sending us these nasty letters, we are not going to put your name in the hat."

Life is full of surprises, and not all of them are good or bad. Drawing up a usable plan is a good idea. My motto is to "plan your work and work your plan." At least if you have a plan, you'll have something to change and something to work on. Look life's problems squarely in the face. If possible, deal with the largest problem first, that will make the other problems seem easy.

My grandmother was a schoolteacher and the matriarch of the family. When my dad was a boy, she made him eat everything on his plate. One day, they were eating at a friend's house, and the hostess served them a big meal. At last, she served pie for dessert. My dad did not like pie-crust, but he knew he had to eat the pie-crust and all. So he broke off the crust and ate it first. Then he settled down to enjoy the pie.

The lady noticed him doing this and she said, "What a remarkable little boy. You like pie crust." Then she went around the room and broke the crust off all the pies and dumped them on his plate. He looked at his mother and her glance said, "Eat it all." We all have our uncomfortable moments.

Scripture:

Isaiah described the woes to Ephraim, people who ignored God's guidance and devotion, "The bed is too short to stretch out on, the blanket too narrow to wrap around you." ~ Isa. 28:20

Prayer:

O Lord, help us pay attention to what You are saying to us. Amen.

95

Talking Dog For Sale

An ad for a talking dog for sale appeared in the newspaper, and a person went to the address listed and inquired about the dog.

"He's in the back," was the reply.

Around the back, the dog said, "Hello! Yes, I talk. For several years, I worked for the FBI as an investigator. Then later, I had a good job with the CIA. I have also traveled all over the world and been in many countries."

The person asked the owner, "How much do you want for the dog?"

"Ten dollars," was the reply.

"Why are you selling the dog so cheap?"

"Well," said the owner, "He's a terrible liar. He hasn't done any of those things."

Looking for perfection is never a good idea. A glance in the mirror can make us all humble. While the proverbial dog was a liar, he could talk and that was a miracle. However, it did not cancel out his dishonesty. A good speech is a work of art, but saying something of substance is essential, and honesty is necessary. The world is overcrowded with dishonesty. Leadership that is going nowhere is as foolish as trying to follow a parked car.

Scripture:

"Hold fast the pattern of sound words, which you have heard from me, in faith and love which are in Christ Jesus." ~2 Timothy 1:13

Prayer:

O Lord, help me to be a follower and a leader. Give me the Wisdom to know how to do both, and the humility to give You the credit. Amen!

96

Impossible Possibilities!

Many of today's possibilities were yesterday's impossibilities. The steamboat, the automobile, the airplane, the splitting of the atom were all once thought impossible, but today all these are accepted realities!

Joel Achenbach in *National Geographic,* January 2000, recorded:

Human travel beyond earth is almost an impossible journey. Transporting our human bodies through space staggers our imagination. Our solar system's nearest neighbor is believed to be 25 trillion miles from us. If we could produce a spaceship that could achieve the speed of ten million miles per hour, which would be 25 times faster than anything we know, the journey to the nearest star system, according to scientists, would take 300 years.

As far as we know, no one has measured the speed of thought. Ideas are swift and can spring up everywhere. Greater than the human mind is the human sprit. This spirit can bear witness with God's Spirit that we belong to our Father's eternal family on earth and in heaven.

Since we find space beyond our Universe almost impossible to conceive, how can we believe and accept Heaven and all its glorious possibilities?

Like thought, there are other dimensions of the Spirit. Faith and trust in God plus many unknown and yet to be explored spiritual possibilities can make life a fantastic journey!

Scripture:

"After this I looked, and lo, in heaven an open door." ~Revelation 4:1

Prayer:

O Lord, don't let me stop. Help me to continue on my eternal journey! Amen!

97

Watch Out for Appearances

While I was a student at Perkins School of Theology during the WWII, driving an ambulance in the city of Dallas was an important part of my education. Going in and out of hospitals, especially maternity wards, made life exciting and interesting. This kind of experience made me appreciate this story.

Three men were waiting for their wives to deliver babies.

Finally, a nurse came into the waiting room and announced to the first man, "Congratulations! Sir you have twin girls."

The expectant father surprisingly said, "That's interesting, I work for the Minnesota Twins."

In a few minutes, two nurses came in and said to the next waiting father, "Look, you have triplets!"

The second father was shocked but said, "I work for 3M."

The third father got up and started to leave the waiting room. The nurse said, "Sir, wait, your wife has not delivered yet."

"Yeah, I know, but I'm out of here. I work for 7 - Eleven."

Just because something happens to others does not mean it will happen to you. The only exercise some people get is pushing their luck or jumping to conclusions. Such activity can be filled with frustration. Pray, stay calm, believe, and expect the best. Trust God for something good to happen to you.

Scripture:

"Blessed is every one that fears the LORD; who walks in His ways. For you will eat the labor of your hands: you will be happy, and it will be well with you." ~ Psalms 128:1-2

Prayer:

O Lord, thank You for having the last Word in all my activities of life. Amen.

98

A Poem by a University Student

A radical college professor took real delight in using his atheist theory on his Christian students. One student penned this bit of verse:

First, he was an amoeba beginning to begin,
Next, he was a tadpole with his tail tucked in.
Then he was a monkey swinging from a tree,
Now, he is my professor with a PhD.

Education is great training; it should add to the abundance of life. However, its value and use depends on the person being educated. It should be absorbed into the total life of the individual. In Habakkuk 2:14, it is written, "The earth shall be filled with the knowledge of the Lord as the waters cover the sea."

Living for the good, the right, and the positive values enriches your personal life. You can't go wrong and do right. The results simply will not add up. A healthy mental diet is best. Every shirt I have buttons the same. If I start at the bottom and put the right button in the correct buttonhole, when I get to the top I have no problem. The shirt is correct.

Life is like this. When I start at the bottom, if I do the right thing, when I come to the top everything comes out right.

Scripture:

"Being confident of this very thing, that He which hath begun a good work in you will perform it until the day of Jesus Christ." ~Philippians 1:6

Prayer:

Oh Lord, remind me to read the book of instruction before I try to put life together. The Holy Bible is Your great book of instruction for eternal and abundant life. Help me not to ignore it. Amen!

Mark Twain is credited with saying, "It's not what I don't understand about the Bible that bothers me, but it's what I understand."

99

Renewing Old Experiences

A lady is reported to have said, "Last year, I went on a world cruise. This year I'd like to go someplace different."

There are not many out of this world experiences. We cannot renew ourselves with new scenery. Contentment comes with our state of mind. For the Christian, being able to look to Jesus, who is the source of life, can give us new experiences of renewal and strength.

The Bible says, "Let this mind be in you which was also in Christ Jesus." Thinking like Christ is not only a great challenge, but also a refreshing event. Give this a try before you reject it or dismiss it as irrelevant.

Healthy anger may get you out of the ditch, but it will endanger your journey down the road of life.

Let us find a new excuse for living, and wake up our sleeping curiosity. Putting forth extra effort to live an abundant life now will bring new blessings to us.

I cut open a small apple and counted ten seeds. I can tell you how many seeds are in this apple, but I can't tell you how many apples are in a seed. The seeds of faith are full of great potential. Only God knows what they can produce. Surrender to the Holy Spirit, and give God a chance in your life.

Scripture:

"Who has despised the day of small things?" ~ Zechariah 4:10

Prayer:

O Lord, here is my life, surprise me with what You can do with it! Amen.

100

How to Celebrate

I was at a football game in Texas. Tennessee was playing. I don't remember much about the game since it was many years ago, but I'll never forget accidentally running into a fellow from Tennessee. To see someone in such a vast crowd that I knew was an unusual experience. The man recognized me. He had obviously had too much to drink. He asked me what the score was and I told him. Then I asked him a question.

"What are you doing here?"

"I am celebrating. I'm having a good time drinking."

"If you were going to over indulge, why didn't you stay at home? You could have gotten drunk there cheaper."

He ignored my comment and went on with what he called "celebrating."

Over indulgence is not a healthy way to celebrate.

A friend of mine was walking down a crowded sidewalk in New York City. A man confronted him face to face and said, "This is a stick up! Hand over your money!"

"You got to be kidding," my friend told him.

Then he side stepped him and went on his way!

When to take seriously what confronts us in life is an important decision. Courage and common sense can help us respond to events like this.

Scripture:

"Do not store up for yourselves treasures on earth, where moth and rust destroy and where thieves break and steal. But store up for yourselves treasures in heaven…for where your treasure is, there your heart will be also." ~ Portions of Matthew 6:19-21

Prayer:

O Lord, help me to be rich toward You. Please give me the spiritual discernment to discover and enjoy these spiritual assets. Amen.

101

Spring is Dependable

When I lived in Memphis, Tennessee, we experienced a very bad winter. On the sign in the front yard of the church, I put up these words.

"SPRING WILL COME AGAIN"

That night it snowed all over the sign. The newspaper printed it on the front page.

In spite of this storm, spring did come again. It came with all its glory and its revelation of new life.

Some years ago, I was in Panama City Beach, Florida. I was sitting on a bench at Wal-Mart watching the parade of young students enjoying their spring break. An elderly man struggled up to the bench and sat beside me.

I turned to him and said, "Are you a spring breaker?"

"No sir," he said, "my spring broke a long time ago."

Bad health can give us a hard time. Sometimes we can reject its power over us and live beyond it. Changing our focus can alter our outlook and bring new life to us.

Health begins and remains in your mind. Think healthy thoughts, they can produce their part of a healthy lifestyle.

See a good Doctor, eat healthy food, and replace worry with faith in God.

Scripture:

"In His kindness God called you to His eternal glory by means of Jesus Christ. After you have suffered a little while He will restore, support, and strengthen you, and He will place you on a firm foundation. All power is his forever and ever." ~ 1 Peter 5:10-11 New Living Translation

Prayer:

Oh Lord, I give my pain to You. I no longer claim it for my own. Thank You for taking it away. Amen.

102

Enjoying Our Heritage

A mature man was known for his financial accomplishment. For years he told everyone, "Years ago I came to New York City with the clothes on my back and a paper sack."

Finally one day after hearing this speech several times, a reporter asked him, "What did you have in the paper sack?"

He replied, "500,000 dollars in cash and 22 million in negotiable securities."

No wonder he made it big with such financial resources! However, money is neutral. It's what we do with it that determines its effectiveness.

How do we feel about money? Can we dominate money with humility, generosity, compassion, thankfulness, and responsibility? Money really talks - to me it seems to say "Goodbye!" Learn the art of making money, keeping money, using money, controlling it, and giving it away.

One of my close friends did a great job of handling money. He used his money to bless his church, many needy people, and great causes throughout the world.

Scripture:

"For the love of money is the root of all kinds of evil." ~ 1 Timothy 6:10 N.L.T.

It's not the possession, but the love of money that can damage the human spirit.

Prayer:

O Lord, thank You for people who can keep their money and material possessions in their proper place. Amen.

103

Keeping Our Bread Fresh

A contemporary renaissance of faith is a rebirth of all events, the old and the new, as they are related to one's personal faith in God and Christ and the Eternal Presence of the Holy Spirit.

Going over all of our experiences in life with the rebirth factor can produce a new vitality in our life. It brings freshness to our personality. We must avoid making only a partial review of the past. We tend to have a habit of leaving out things we need to look at and turn from.

A complete surrender of self and a direct talk with God can do wonders to your personal life. I challenge you to walk out of yourself and take a look at your life as others see you, and even as God may view you. This takes Christian imagination with objective behavior on your part. Such experiences enable you to grow and bring personal satisfaction to daily living.

Jesus teaches us to pray for our daily bread. Keeping our bread fresh makes us spiritually healthy. Stale bread is left over daily bread and produces a boring menu. In the Lord's Prayer, Jesus teaches us to ask for our bread daily. Are you feasting on stale bread or fresh bread?

Consuming daily bread from the Holy Spirit gives you moral and spiritual energy.

Scripture:

"My God shall supply all your needs according His riches in glory by Christ Jesus." ~Phil. 4:19

Prayer:

O Lord, give me this day my daily bread. Amen.

104

Comment on My Call to Preach

The Voice of God is not an echo from the scriptures, but a silent certainty at the depth of your being. Echoes come and go, but God's Spirit remains with us always!

Let us commit ourselves to prayer and dedication until we make God's Presence a permanent reality in our lives.

The call of God for me was a strong Presence in my life that clearly said, "I want you to preach the good news of God's eternal love."

I believe that God's love has transforming power over human nature. The Holy Spirit makes a permanent change in our identity. So we become God's children, members of God's eternal family both on earth and in heaven. We call God "our Father." This means we belong to an exciting and rewarding group of people. We can identify with all His children. We can love and be loved even as He loves us. We become God's people of faith. We are at home with them. We are not alone.

As Jesus said, "The Father is with me," so He is also with us. We now live and move in the company of the committed. We have exchanged presents with God. We give ourselves to God, and He gives Himself to us. What a great way to swap gifts!

Scripture:

"God's gift and His call can never be withdrawn." ~ Romans 11:29 N.L.T.

Prayer:

O Lord, thank You for Your call. I hear it not as an echo from the past, but a new Voice. Amen.

105

A Call from Beyond

Bishop Franklin opened the newspaper one morning and read the account of his death. This was obviously a mistake. After he read this story, the Bishop called his son.

His son said, "Hello!"

"Did you read the story about my death?" the Bishop asked.

"Yes, I did, Dad. Where are you calling from?"

For some, this is a chilling question. After I die, if I ever make a call, where would I be calling from?

The Bible makes it clear that eternity is divided into Heaven and Hell. Faith in God through Christ determines where you spend eternity. This is why Jesus Christ is our Savior. He saves us from our uncertain self because we can be overpowered by evil, and all the unhealthy diseases of the human spirit can attack and win.

Ideas, thoughts, plans, and purposes can take root in our lives. Without the saving and guiding Presence of God's Holy Spirit, the weeds and thorns can choke out the new life of the Spirit, who wants us to bear fruit in our lives.

Scripture:

Jesus said, "By their fruits, you shall know them" ~ Matthew 7:19 ~ This helps us identify what is growing in our lives.

Prayer:

O Lord, I dedicate my life to You. I am thankful for the blessed assurance that we belong to You forever. Amen.

106

How to Deal with Change

Crusty old fading George Bernard Shaw once said, "The only person that views me with any degree of accuracy is my tailor. Every time he sees me, he measures me." We all change. We do not remain the same. The Bible says, "The outward man perishes, but the inner man is renewed day by day."

A little boy came to the beach, and he stayed in the sun too long. His skin was blistered and after a few days it began to peel. As he pulled off a big piece of his skin, he said, "Look! Seven years old, and I'm beginning to come apart already!"

We become aware of outer changes. We grow taller, get fatter, our hair changes, and our fingernails grow longer.

But other changes are more subtle. We need to take an objective look at our ideas, our faith, our disposition, and all our behavior.

A man attended a revival. He gave the same request for prayer: "Fill me, Lord!" The person behind him heard this prayer every year, "Fill me, Lord!" He stood up and said, "Don't do it, Lord. He leaks."

Scripture:

"Let us not be weary in well doing: for in due season we shall reap, if we faint not." ~ Gal. 6:9

Prayer:

O Lord, heal the hole in my spirit that causes me to loose what You have poured into my life. Amen.

107

Controlling Rebellion

A dear mother had a son who at a very early age became rebellious. She tried many methods to help him control his temper. Finally, one day he became extremely angry. She put him in her closet and gently closed the door. After a while, he grew quiet. She went by and asked, "What are you doing?"

"I've spit on your coats - I've spit on your dresses - I've spit in your shoes - I'm just waiting here for more spit."

Anger can cause us to do many things. Once in a while, anger can get us out of difficulty. But anger can be only a temporary help. Keeping anger for very long can be self-destructive. Anger can be controlled through prayer, forgiveness and love. Here is a thought to remember: "Father, forgive me of my sins, just like I forgive others of their sins."

Scripture:

"Don't sin by letting anger gain control over you. Don't let the sun go down while you are still angry." ~ Eph. 4:26-27

Anger gives a mighty foothold to the Devil.

Prayer:

O Lord, help me to forgive everybody of everything. Those who have done me wrong do not deserve forgiveness. But Lord, I need to forgive them for my sake. Amen.

108

Surviving TV

In the early days of TV, there were two personalities who dominated the airwaves and the TV sets. One was Milton Berle who was a comic, and the other was Bishop Fulton Sheen.

After a while Milton burned out, but Bishop Sheen continued to appear on TV. Milton was interviewed on TV and was asked why the Bishop outlasted him. His reply was, "The Bishop had better writers."

The Holy Bible has outlasted all the World's literature. Scripture is presented as the Word of God. God is the Original Designer; He spoke the world into existence. God through His Word created all things; beauty shows God's handiwork. God created time and set it in motion.

Our earth and its inhabitants, especially people, are very complicated. Nature and human nature are complex factors to live with. Frequently, both of these get out of control. Jesus said to the multitudes, "Do you not yet understand that whatever enters the mouth goes into the stomach and is eliminated? But those things which proceed out of the mouth come from the heart, and those defile a man. For out of the heart - the center of our being - proceed evil thoughts, murders, adulteries, fornications, thefts, false witness, and blasphemies. These are the things which defile a man." Matthew 15:10-20

Scripture:

"Create in me a clean heart, O God. Renew a right spirit within me. Restore to me again the joy of your salvation." ~ Psalms 51:10-17

Prayer:

Again I say: "Create in me a clean heart, O God, and renew a right spirit within me. Restore unto me the joy of my salvation." Amen.

109

A Subtle Teaching

When I was a small boy in 1930, there was a famous radio show. It was a very popular show, and millions tuned their radios to listen to this program on their favorite station.

The two characters were well loved. They offered good entertainment and sound advice. One night as I listened, one of them said to the other, "There is a man I dislike. Every time he sees me, he hits me in the chest with the back of his hand. This is supposed to be a friendly greeting, but I am irritated by it. Now I have fixed him. I put a bomb in my shirt pocket, and the next time he hits me in the chest the bomb will blow off his hand."

The scripture says, "Vengeance is mine, I will repay said the Lord" (Romans 12:19). It is a dangerous practice to carry vengeance in your heart toward others, much like a loaded bomb. It could go off and destroy and hurt you as well as those for whom it is intended. Through prayer, God can heal your wounded spirit. Forgiveness toward those who have wronged you can produce amazing results in your own life.

People who hold grudges are miserable folks. Living with envy and jealousy can be bad. Compassion and love can cure many of the ills of life.

Some years ago, there was a popular saying, "God loves you and I love you!" Of course some people are easier to love than others. I always thought that a more accurate saying would be "God loves you, and I am trying to love you."

In Wickliffe, Kentucky, a man had to drive 35 miles daily to the city of Paducah. He let people ride with him. One person was a "yes man." He rode to town frequently. After a while, the driver of the truck refused to let the man ride.

"I'm sorry, sir, did I offend you?"

"No," said the driver, "you are too agreeable to be good company."

Scripture:

"In your anger, do not sin." ~ Eph. 4:26

Prayer:

O Lord, help me to disagree without being disagreeable. Amen.

110

Unbelievable Insults

There is an old story about two prominent people, Lady Ester and Winston Churchill. They were at the same party, but had a dislike for each other. Churchill continued to drink alcohol and his personality changed.

When he saw Lady Ester he said, "You are ugly!"

At first, she ignored him, but his rude comment began to get the best of her. Finally, she said to him, "You are drunk."

"That's right," he said, "but tomorrow I'll be sober, but you will still be ugly."

Great leaders have their weak moments. It seems that their "greatness" shows up their weakness. A pancake has two sides, even if one of them looks better than the other. Self-control is one of the fruits of the Spirit. We need to watch our words; they can injure others and can come back like a boomerang and hit us with embarrassing results.

The police stopped a drunk while he was driving his car. The officer said, "What do you have in that bottle beside you?"

"Water," was the drunk's reply.

The officer opened the bottle and said, "It's wine!"

The driver of the auto excitedly declared, "Jesus has done it again! He has turned water into wine!!!"

It's stupid to call on Jesus to defend us when we have done wrong. AA's big book can be summed up in one sentence, "Our thinking is stinking, and it leads to our drinking."

Scripture:

"I am writing to you, dear friends, to that we should love one another. This is not a new commandment, but one we have heard from the beginning. Love means doing what God has commanded us, and he has commanded us to love one another, just as you heard from the beginning." ~ 2 John 1: 5-6 NLT

Prayer:

O Lord, forgive me for being critical. Help me build up others in Your name. Amen.

111

Can We Get the Point?

A certain man lectured to a group of elementary students. He was warning the young children of the destructive effects of alcohol on the human body. For his demonstration he poured out a bottle of alcohol into a glass beaker. He then dropped two earthworms into the liquor. The worms promptly died. He made sure the class saw his demonstration then he asked, "What did you learn from this?"

All of the students sat in silence and finally one boy spoke up. "If you have worms, drink alcohol."

"Wine is a mocker, strong drink is raging; and whosoever is deceived thereby is not wise" (Prov 20:1).

A man checked into a hotel. There was a knock at the door. He opened the door, and a drunk looked bewildered and asked, "Is this my room?"

"No, this is my room!"

"Ok," said the drunk, and left.

About two hours later there was another knock at the door. The same drunk appeared and asked, "Is this my room?"

"No, this is my room!"

"Okay," said the drunk, and left.

Around midnight, the same drunk woke up the same man at the room. When he recognized the man who answered the door the drunk said, "Mister, do you have all the rooms in this hotel?"

Let us pray for those who seek to drown their troubles in alcohol. Our troubles can swim and all drugs only add to our misery.

Scripture:

"Look! Here I stand at the door and knock. If you hear Me calling and open the door, I will come in, and will share a meal as a friend." ~ Rev. 3:20

"God has not given us a spirit of fear, but of power and of love and of a sound mind." 2 Timothy 1:7

"Keep your heart with all diligence, for out of it are the issues of life." Proverbs 4:23

Prayer:

O Lord, I am open to Your Presence in my life. Thank You for coming and accepting me as I am. Help me to feast with You in Your joyful Presence. Amen.

112

The Preacher's Horse

The late Bishop Finger used to enjoy telling a story about a preacher's horse. When a horse was an important means of transportation, a preacher bought a young horse and personally trained the animal. He never gave the usual commands to the horse, like "Get up" for *go* or "halt" or "whoa" for *stop.* Instead he used the words, "Praise God" for *go,* and "Amen" for *stop.*

The beautiful horse was high-spirited and would go forward at a wild lunge when given the command, "Praise God!" A minister's friend borrowed the highly trained animal, and he was told the unusual commands that controlled the horse.

The new minister mounted the borrowed horse and was traveling at a rapid speed through the hill country. All at once, they were approaching the edge of a huge cliff. The horse did not respond when commanded "halt" or "stop." The clergyman began to panic, and then he remembered the ecclesiastical training that controlled the horse.

He yelled, "Amen!" The horse stopped at the very edge of the cliff. The rider looked at the deep valley below and was thankful that they did not go over the edge. Then, to show his gratitude he said, "Praise God!"

Learning the language and being able to communicate can be two different things.

Scripture:

"Even though I speak with the tongues of men, and angels and have not love I am nothing." ~ 1 Cor. 13:1

Prayer:

O Lord, help me learn the language of love. May I speak with good will, joy, forgiveness, and great concern for others. May I show that I care about them. Amen.

113

Playground Emergency

A school boy ran into the school house yelling, "Teacher, Teacher, Teacher! There are two boys fighting, and the one on the bottom wants to speak to you! "

When we are in desperate need of help and can't get out from under the pressing problems of life, we are willing and glad to ask God for help. But when we are on top of things, and we seem to be winning, we think we are doing quite well on our own. The truth of the matter is, we need guidance before events get out of hand. There is such a thing as preventative behavior. Faith and trust go together.

A man accidentally fell off a cliff. On the way down, he caught a scrubby bush and found himself dangling over the high precipice. He began to call out, but no one heard him. Then he began to call for the Lord to help him. "O Lord, help me, help me! Lord, are you up there? Please answer me, Lord. Lord?"

Suddenly, a voice from above said, "Yes, can I help you?"

"Lord, I'm about to fall. This little bush won't hold me much longer."

The voice from above said, "Do you trust me?"

"Yes, Lord I do trust you!"

"Then turn loose of the bush!"

There was a long pause from the dangling man. The voice from above repeated, "If you trust me, turn loose of the bush."

The man holding on for dear life said, "Could I get another opinion?"

Scripture:

Trust in God means "Being confident of this very thing, that He which hath begun a good work in you will perform it until the day of Jesus Christ." ~ Philippians 1:6

Prayer:

Thank You, Lord. I'm glad You are still on the job on my behalf. Amen.

114

Can Con-Men Win?

In Hollywood years ago, an actor was trying to secure a leading role in a movie. He tried to influence the producer so he could get the job. He went into a fashionable store to purchase a gift for the man making the film. Everything was extremely expensive. All the items were above his financial resources. He went into the storage room and found a very expensive vase. It was broken in many pieces. He knew the manager of the store and asked him to sell this broken, beautiful, and famous vase.

"What do you want with a broken vase?"

"Well, I want to send it to the producer of a film. I want to impress him. He will think the vase got broken in the mail."

So the storeowner agreed to almost give the man the vase. He also agreed to wrap the vase and send it with the label of his exclusive store on the box.

A long time passed, and the actor did not hear from the producer. Finally, since he did not receive a thank you note, he called the producer.

"Did you receive that expensive vase I sent you?"

"Yes, but it was broken."

"Oh, how terrible the mails are! I'm sorry they broke the vase. I had it wrapped at the store."

The producer said, "The vase was broken in many pieces, but let me ask you a question? Why was each piece wrapped separately?"

We can be too clever for our own good. Let us be honest and live with sincerity. Honesty will always be the best policy.

Scripture:

"The bread of deceit is sweet to a man, but afterwards his mouth shall be filled with gravel. The spirit of man is the candle of the Lord, searching out all his inner parts." ~ Proverbs 20:17, 27

Prayer:

Dear Lord, help me to be sincere in my behavior. Keep me from trying to force others to do for me what I want. Help me keep my relationship with others simple and true. Amen.

115

Nice to Be Unknown

In the middle of the 1960s, Grace and I were at Lake Junaluska, North Carolina. This is a great campground of the United Methodist Church. It is the seat of the Southeastern Jurisdictional Conference and our new bishops are elected at this place. I was driving all our five children through this beautiful mountain retreat. Rain in these mountains can produce a quick flood at only a moment's notice.

I noticed a man jogging in the sprinkling rain so I stopped to pick him up, but he refused to ride. I felt the cloud just above me on the mountain was going to dump all its water at any moment, so I jokingly said, "Get in the car! My mother taught me to get in out of the rain!"

He was a very stiff individual who did not appreciate my kidding. So he said, "DO YOU KNOW WHO I AM?"

"No," I replied.

"I'm a newly elected bishop of the United Methodist Church!"

I said, "Do you know who I am?"

"No!" he said.

I said, "Thank God," and drove away. However, I looked back in my rear view mirror, and the thing I saw was a downpour of water hiding and baptizing the newly elected bishop of the United Methodist Church.

I don't know whether the new bishop learned anything from this experience or not. I learned something - to keep my mouth shut and that sometimes it's not too bad to be unknown.

Let us pray for everybody, especially our bishops who have a challenging job. May they be remembered for their love and leadership, and not their faults.

Scripture:

"For I say, through the grace given to me, to everyone who is among you, not to think of himself more highly than he ought to think, but to think soberly, as God has dealt to each one a measure of faith. For as we have many members in one body, but all the members do not have the same function, so we, being many, are one body in Christ, and individually members of one another." ~ Rom. 12:3-5

Prayer:

I thank You for the wonderful bishops I have known and for their influence on my life. Help me Lord to be humble and think of others more highly than I think of myself. Let us be grateful for one another. Amen.

116

Identifying With Others

A 747 jet landed in Denver, and a Colorado rancher boarded the plane. As luck would have it, his seat was next to a big Texan. By his dress, he assumed that the man from Texas was a rancher. The ranch of the man from Colorado was small, and he hoped to avoid any conversation about land. He had no sooner become comfortable in his seat when the Texan asked, "Do you have a ranch in this state?"

"Yes" was the faint reply.

"How big is it?"

"Twenty acres."

The Texan said, "Let me tell you about my ranch. I get up early in the morning in my old pickup truck. I drive all day in my truck, and at night I'm not half way across my ranch."

The man from Colorado replied, "I can identify with that. I've got a pickup truck just like that."

Changing the subject when things become embarrassing is a great art. Doing it without the other knowing it is an even greater art. Conversation about people can turn into gossip. Talking about ideas instead can focus the conversation on more constructive things. Talking about faith in God and sharing our personal experiences in our relationship with Christ can be a great witness provided it is done humbly and in the spirit of love.

We are all sinners saved by God's grace.

Scripture:

"For I say, through the grace given to me, to everyone who is among you, not to think of himself more highly than he ought to think, but to think soberly, as God has dealt to each a measure of faith."`~ Romans 12:3

Prayer:

O Lord, help me remember that it is not what I posses, but who possesses me, that makes me acceptable in Your sight. Please take hold of my life. Amen!

117

An Unexpected Outing

An elderly couple was seated on the front porch of their home. A strong wind came up suddenly and blew the couple off their chairs and into a nearby open field. When neighboring friends found them they were a bit shaken up, but not hurt. This was declared a miracle in many ways. One miracle was that this was the first time the couple had been out together in over ten years.

What would it take to get us to change our habits? When I was a very small boy, many of the minor roads were dirt. The Model T Ford my father drove was brand new, and he disliked getting it dirty because on every trip he would have a flat tire. Changing the muddy tire was not a clean experience. Traveling on dirt and muddy roads caused huge ruts. In order to keep from getting stuck in the middle, the driver had to steer the car into the ruts. Over in the state of Missouri, there was a sign at the beginning of the dirt road. It read, "Choose your rut carefully. You will be in it for the next ten miles."

This is good advice. Habits are like invisible ruts. We need to choose them carefully. We could be caught in them for a long time. The cows on our farm walked in the same spots, killing the grass and making firm little paths over the field. Their paths were beneficial to them and made walking easier. Habits, like ruts, can be good or bad depending on what type of ruts they are.

Scripture:

"The path of the righteous is like the first gleam of dawn, shining even brighter till the full light of day." Jesus said, "I am the Way." ~ Proverbs 4:18:NIV, John 14:6

Prayer:

O Lord, help me find the way, and give me strength to walk in it. Amen.

118

His Master's Voice

In 1925, the first phonograph that impressed me belonged to a friend of my grandmother. We used to go to their house on North Six Street in Paducah to visit. Mr. Atchison and his sister were former neighbors of my grandmother, Annie Ewell Russell, until she moved out into the country with my parents.

Mr. Atchison would always let us listen to his records. The record player was called his Master's Voice. It had a dog on the front, who was listening to the big megaphone - a symbol of his Master's Voice. When Mr. Atchison would wind up the record player, I would be fascinated as I listened to the music and looked at the big horn and the listening dog.

Mr. Atchison was a very systematic bachelor. He was completely organized. He organized his records to be played on certain days. He would only play Tuesday's records on Tuesday, Wednesday's records on Wednesday, and so on. He would never change his method.

One day while we were visiting him, he asked me which record I would like to hear played. I was just a little kid and I didn't know, so I just repeated a record title that I had heard other people say was a popular song of the day. To everyone's amazement, he played it. I thought everyone was excited about the song. They weren't. The amazing thing was that he played Friday's record on Tuesday because I had requested it.

Sometimes, the needle would get stuck in the groove of the record and play the same thing over and over again until someone came and lifted it out of the stuck position. Sometimes we are like that. We get stuck in the groove of our thinking. We go round and round in a circle. Through prayer, the Holy Spirit can lift us out of this predicament.

Before medical science developed better procedures to help people who lost a leg, the cripple was fitted with a wooden leg known as a peg leg. The artificial leg had a round knob on the end of it instead of a foot. One of the old sayings of my childhood concerning people who repeated the same thoughts was, "he behaves like a man who caught his wooden leg in a knot hole in the floor." He just moves around and around in a circle talking about the same subject.

A centipede is supposed to be an animal with a hundred legs (I have never counted them), but that's not the point. One day he fell into a muddy ditch. He lay there helpless, because he couldn't decide which leg went in front of the other.

We sometimes get caught in the small details of life, trying to decide which project we should do first. Without realizing it, we are majoring in the minors of life.

Scripture:

" This one thing I do, forgetting those things which are behind and reaching forth to those things that are before, I press toward the mark for the prize of the high calling of God in Christ Jesus." ~ Phil 3:13-14

Prayer:

O Lord, I can do all things through the Holy Spirit who gives me strength. Amen.

119

A Disturbing Question

There's an old parable about mice. The mice got together in a meeting and expressed concern over the loss of their friends and family members. After some investigation, they determined that the cause of the loss was an old gray cat. He would silently slip up on them and devour them.

One young mouse came up with a solution. "Let's put a bell on the cat, then he can no longer slip up on us. We can hear him!" This was a great solution and the mice had a great party to celebrate the solving of the problem.

However, one little mouse asked, "Who's going to put the bell on the cat?" The celebration came abruptly to a halt. Nobody answered when they asked, "Who's going to bell the cat?"

Sometimes, we face difficult and unpleasant decisions. The tendency is to shift these choices to someone else. We all prefer a holiday to a horror day, but at some point in life we have to take responsibility, lie down beside the inevitable and say, "Move over bud!"

Trying events call for the use of our character reserves. Healthy habits and positive decisions that lead us to the valuable and true can later be recalled for immediate use.

Two men in prison were discussing their futures. One said to the other, "When I am in prison, I'm going to take classes in math, accounting, and bookkeeping. You are not studying anything. When we get out of jail you will still be a common thief, but I'll be an embezzler."

Real change is not found in our overt behavior alone, but in our personal motives, goals, and difficult decisions. Let us do for others what we do for ourselves. We can take our turn and put the bell on the cat. The experiences that devour us are not completely evil, they are frequently mixed with a little good; and this makes such issues hard to identify.

Scripture:

"And I heard the Voice of the Lord saying, 'Whom shall I send and who will go for us?' Then I said, 'Here I am, send me!'" ~ Isaiah 6:8

Prayer:

O Lord, help me accept the responsibility for my own acts. Please keep me from blaming others for my own problems. Instead use me to effect change and help others. Amen.

120

What's Happening?

A woman who had trouble paying her water bill turned on the faucet one cold morning and discovered she had no water. She called up the water company and asked, "Am I cut off or am I froze up?"

If nothing is happening in our lives that is interesting, exciting or inspiring, we might like to ask, "Am I cut off, or am I froze up?" Have I accidentally severed my connection with God and His people? Have I turned a cold shoulder toward those with a warm heart?

As we grow older, pain and lack of energy can bring on spiritual laziness. It's too much trouble to go to church! I can't hear, have trouble seeing, so on and on our excuses go. I'll watch TV - they have good music and better preaching than I will find at my church. I can get frozen food and canned food, but it's good to have fresh food. Watching church on TV makes you a spectator. What you are seeing is a taped version of what happened last week or some time ago.

Attending worship at your church is a live experience. The people are real, the music is live and the sermon is current. The daily bread is not stale, but fresh. The flowers are beautiful, you can smell them if you so desire. All this is happening before your very eyes and in your presence.

I love flowers, but I know that cut flowers do not have roots; their presence and beauty are temporary, they have a short life. The love of God has strong roots that keep us spiritually alive.

Scripture:

"May Christ live in your hearts by faith, may you also be rooted and grounded in love!" From St. Paul's prayer for the church. ~ Ephesians 4:17

Prayer:

O Lord, help me live all my life. Amen.

121

Thinking Backward Moving Forward

Years ago in a small rural Methodist church, the people were gathered to discuss the yearly business and decide on a new pastor. The pastor who served this church was not well liked and had many problems. The District Superintendent who was in charge of deciding the appointment of pastors for the next year was hearing from many of the members of the church, privately and in small groups. As the people left the church, the D.S. was getting into his car to leave when the pastor came across the church lawn and stopped him.

"I know what all these people are saying to you. They want a new minister, and the reason for a change is that they are saying I can't preach. Don't pay any attention to that. I've heard them say the same thing about you."

There is an old saying that "misery loves company." Looking back on our past behavior can enable us to make profitable changes, but not if we are only seeking to protect our ego by finding someone in our predicament. Every parent has had his child seek to protect his mistakes by saying, "Everybody is doing it." Thinking backward and reliving past experiences can be revealing and helpful. If we spend as much time and energy improving our shortcomings as we do in protecting our ego, we can move forward to greater and better things.

Exodus gives an account of Moses and the children of Israel fleeing from Egypt. The Egyptians came after them to take them back into slavery. More than a moment of panic swept over the children of Israel as they stood between the mighty army of Egypt and the Red Sea. They said to Moses, "It was better for us to serve the Egyptians than to die here." Moses called on the Lord while he tried to comfort and calm the children of Israel.

Scripture:

"Then the Lord spoke to Moses, 'Why are you crying out to me? Speak to the children of Israel. Tell them to go forward.' " ~ Exodus 14:15

Prayer:

O God, help us to go forward so that we may catch up with You. Amen.

122

On Finding the Right Answer

A concerned wife said to her husband, "You are drinking too much alcohol."

"No, I'm not," he replied.

"I believe you are a compulsive drinker. I don't think you can stop. I want you to see a doctor after you get off from work."

He promised that he would do this, but later he forgot all about his promise. While he was riding the commuter train home that night, it stopped at a station and suddenly he remembered his promise to see a doctor about his drinking. He looked out the window and saw a music store. He saw the word "syncopation". He decided to copy the word down and lie to his wife and tell her that the doctor said he was not an alcoholic, but that he suffered from syncopation and he would be okay.

She accepted his story. Everything calmed down, and the husband heaved a great sigh of relief. Later she came to him and said, "I was right, you are an alcoholic."

"No, no," he said, "I only have syncopation."

"Yes, you are an alcoholic. I looked up the definition of that word in the dictionary. It defined syncopation as an irregular movement from bar to bar."

Alcohol is a deceptive drug. When we become dependent on it, we are blinded to the fact that it has become a problem. One of the first letters in the New Testament was written to the Thessalonians. Paul writes, "Let us watch and be sober…let us abstain from all appearances of evil" (1 Thes. 5:6, 26). Evil is *live* spelled backwards.

As a small boy, I remember a kid saying about another boy we knew, "If you would put his brains in a woodpecker, the bird would fly upside down and backwards."

Job, the oldest book in the Bible, reminds us, "Man is born to trouble as surely as sparks fly upward" (Job 5:7). Jesus our Savior came to deliver us from this condition by inviting us to turn all our troubles over to Him and put our trust in Him to solve all our difficulties.

Scripture:

Jesus said, "Let not your heart be troubled. You trust in God. Now trust in Me." ~ John 14:1 NLT

Prayer:

O Lord, please cure my heart trouble. Amen.

123

Personal Anxiety

A traveling salesman was retiring and turned over his route to the new man who was taking over his place. The retiree went on a long extended vacation. Sometime later, he ran into the young man who had taken over his territory.

He asked, "How do you like your job?"

"I hate it," was the reply. "Everywhere I go people insult me."

"That's strange!" the retired salesman exclaimed. "I served that route for thirty years. I had people throw my sample case out in the street. They even 'sicked' their dogs on me, calling me all kinds of names; but I never had anyone insult me!"

It's not what happens to you as much as it is how you feel about it. Children may or may not remember what you said about something. They may or may not remember what you did about something. But, there is a very good chance that after they have forgotten what you said or what you did, they will always remember how you felt about it.

We all need to learn how to succeed, but we also need to learn how to fail. The chances are that if we try enough things, we are going to fail. Failure is not the end, but it is a chance to begin again.

Former Major League All Star Mike Piazza, who is married and has two daughters, was quoted in an Associate Press article printed in *The News Herald*, Panama City, Florida. He said, "At the beginning of my career, I had an 'I want to be a rock star' type of mentality. I realized once I got there that it was very empty at times. I have never been as happy as I am being a good husband and father."

"Godliness with contentment is great gain." ~ 1 Timothy 6:6.

Scripture:

Being Southern, I recognize this as biblical support for the use of the term *you all*: "Now may the Lord of peace Himself give you peace always in every way. The Lord be with you all. The salutation of Paul with my own hand, which is a sign in every epistle, so I write, 'The grace of our Lord Jesus Christ be with you all.' " ~ Thess. 3:16-18

Good fun, good humor, and good night.

Prayer:

O Lord, help me to laugh when there is no joke or anything funny. Help me to laugh frequently so that I may keep alive a sense of humor. Amen.

124

Do You Want to Get Well?

In a state hospital, there was a man who had stomach problems. He had a fixation that one day while he was asleep he had swallowed a cat. Every time he had gas pains, he said that this cat was moving around in his belly. All effort to convince the man that this was not so failed.

One night, the man had a gall bladder attack and had to have major surgery. A young doctor knew about the fellow's belief that he had swallowed a cat. The doctor went into the alley behind the hospital and ran down a cat. This old gray cat had been around a long time. He had been in many fights. One ear was almost chewed off.

As the patient was recovering, the surgeon held this old gray tomcat over him. As the patient was coming to, the doctor pointed to the old gray cat and said, "Look, you are cured. I got the cat out of your stomach!"

The man blinked his eyes and stared at the old cat. Then he said, "Oh no! The one I swallowed was black!"

John 5:1-6 records the story of Jesus' trip to Jerusalem. He stopped at the pool of Bethesada where a lot of disabled people were gathered, waiting for an angel to come and stir the water. They believed that the first one in the water after the angel had stirred it would be healed. There was an invalid who had been in this condition for 38 years. The man complained that he had no one to help him get into the pool soon enough to be healed.

Jesus looked at the man and asked an interesting question. "Do you want to get well?" This seemed like an unusual question. The man had been going there for this purpose for a long time. However, if the man got well, he could no longer lie around and do nothing. He could no longer blame other people for not helping him. He would have to get a job and provide for himself. He could no longer draw disability. He would have to compete with others. He would have to give up his complaining. He would have to do something.

Then Jesus said to the invalid, "Pick up your mat and walk." The Jews criticized the man for carrying his mat on the Sabbath. The former invalid blamed Jesus for telling him to do that. There are no signs of gratitude, thanksgiving, and joy. Later, Paul would write the following admonition to the churches:

Scripture:

"Rejoice evermore. Pray without ceasing. In every thing give thanks: for this is the will of God in Christ Jesus concerning you." ~ 1 Thessalonians 5:16-18 NIV

Prayer:

O Lord, when I am sick, I want to be made well. When I am in pain, I want relief. You can keep my mind and spirit healthy even if my leg still hurts and I walk with a limp. O Lord, I surrender all my health problems to You! Help me to see myself well, normal, and full of Your joy and Your peace. May I give thanks in all things. I turn loose of all the unpleasant memories of my life. I hold on only to You. In Jesus name, amen.

125

Ignorance is No Excuse

The LA Police Department sent out applications for new employees. One person who was turned down for the job was asked these questions:

"What would you do in a race riot?"

Answer: "I'd get the license plate number of both cars."

"What is rabies, and what would you do for them?"

Answer: "Rabies is Jewish preachers, and I wouldn't do anything for them!"

I am glad this man didn't qualify for the police force.

A man attended a revival meeting and he stood up to testify. He said, "Don't know nothing. Glory to God!"

There is no virtue in ignorance. We are never too old to learn. Two men who had nothing to do were spending the evening in a pub. They got into a philosophical discussion about the use and meaning of the words *irritation, anger,* and *frustration.* To illustrate his point, one of the men picked a number out of the phone book and dialed it. When the man at the other end answered, the caller asked, "Is Joe there?"

"No."

"OK," was the reply.

"See, the man is irritated."

Two hours later the fellow called the same number and asked the same question, "Is Joe there?"

"No."

"Are you sure? Look around and see."

"No. I told you before, there is no one here by that name!"

"See the man is now very mad and angry."

Way past midnight, the fellow called the same number again. "This is Joe. Has anybody called for me?"

There was silence at the end of the line. The man hung up.

"See, now he is frustrated."

Scripture:

"Let us not become conceited, provoking and envying each other." ~ Galatians 5:26

Prayer:

O Lord, help me not to make others miserable just to make my point. Amen.

126

A Short Sentence

In the early days of telegraphs, the sender was limited to ten words or less. There was an extra charge for any words beyond ten.

A young man away at college sent his father a short message, "No mon, no fun, your son!" His father sent back a telegram that read, "Too bad, how sad, your Dad!"

For some reason, the same stories remain in the same grade level. Not all the funny stories of childhood make it through youth, adulthood, and old age. One early childhood story was about two drops of ink that were crying. One drop of ink said to the other,

"Why are you crying?"

"My father is in the pen," the other drop replied.

"Don't cry, he will only have a short sentence!"

Such stories bring back childhood memories. Growing up has never been easy. The depression of the 1930 had its own problems. I remember my father telling me, "Son, if you can get a job making a 100 dollars a month, you will be on easy street the rest of your life." Today, such an income would be below the poverty level, tomorrow who knows?

Some years ago, I sent a telegram to a great Christian whose mother died. Under the ten-word limit, I wrote, "Let not your heart be troubled. You believe in God." These ten words can make a great difference in a person's life. Such words offer comfort, hope, assurance, and security for real believers. God has the last word. Hear Him, and trust Him.

Scripture:

Jesus said, "I have overcome the world." ~ John 16:33

"Be not overcome by evil, but overcome evil with good." ~ Romans 12:21

"Everyone born of God overcomes the world. This is the victory that has overcome the world." NIV 1 John 5:4-5

Prayer:

O Lord, my faith makes me a winner. Please increase it. Amen.

127

Frustration

A cartoon character said, "All my life I struggled to discover who I was. When I finally found out, someone stole my identity."

An epitaph on a tombstone read, "Born a man, died a grocer." Our job can be so absorbing that we forget who we are. They said of Jesus, "Is not this the carpenter's son?" That skeptical crowd did not see Him as the Messiah. He did not fit their image of a Messiah. They looked for a kingly person, perhaps riding a white horse, who would bring the restoration of Israel. They rejected a man on a donkey, a servant animal, as their leader. This was not where the people wanted to go.

Jesus said to his disciples, "The princes of the Gentiles exercise authority over them, but this is not the way I want you to act." Matthew wrote the words of Jesus, "Whoever will be chief among you let him be your servant" (20:27). Jesus advanced the role of the servant from being one who is simply does the wishes of another, to being one who serves others as a way of being a friend.

Jesus taught, "Love each other as I have loved you. Greater love has no one then this that he lay down his life for his friends. You are my friends…I no longer call you servants, because the servant does not know his Master's business. Instead, I have called you friends" (John 15:12-16 NIV). Jesus continued talking to his friends, "You did not choose me, I chose you and appointed you to go and bear fruit – fruit that will last."

On our farm there was a big old apple tree. The tree's branches were very tall and the apples grew in the very top. I would throw sticks in the tree. My friends threw sticks in the tree. All of us were trying to knock down the apples. We never threw a stick at the tree when there were no apples.

People are like that beautiful tree. When they bear attractive fruit, there are those who throw sticks of criticism at them. The fruit of their labors intimidates them. These people want either what they have, or they don't want them to have it.

Scripture:

"By their fruits you will recognize them." – Matt. 7:16-20

Prayer:

O Lord, save me from bitter and rotten fruit. I am thankful that a good tree cannot bear bad fruit. Amen.

128

Be Careful What You Repeat

A new young police officer stopped a motorist and said, "You were going ten miles over the speed limit. Let me see your driver's license!"

The motorist said, "I can't show it to you, it has expired."

The nervous officer said, "Open your glove compartment!"

Motorist, "I can't do that. I don't have a key, and you'll see the unregistered gun that I have in there."

Officer, "Open the trunk."

Motorist, "I can't do that. You'll see the dead body in there. I can explain everything, but you won't believe me."

The new officer got excited and called for back up. "I have a motorist that I stopped for speeding. He has an expired driver's license, an unregistered gun in the glove box, and a dead body in the trunk."

Two police cars arrived in a thunder of sirens. The commanding officer said to the motorist, "Let me see your driver's license."

The motorist handed over the license. The commanding officer looked at it and said to the deputy, "I thought you said his license was expired!"

The commanding officer said to the motorist, "Open the glove compartment." He searched the glove compartment and found only a road map and a pair of gloves.

He said to the deputy, "You said he had an unregistered gun in here!"

The chief said to the motorist, "Open the trunk." The trunk was empty except for the spare tire and the jack.

Again, the chief said to the new officer, "You said there was a dead body in here!"

The motorist then spoke up and said, "Chief, the next thing he'll tell you is that I was speeding."

We need to be careful when we repeat what somebody else told us; it may not be so.

Scripture:

"Only simpletons believe everything they are told. The prudent carefully consider their steps." ~ Prov. 14:15

Prayer:

O Lord, help me to be slow to speak and quick to think. May I follow what is written in Proverbs 18:19: "Any story sounds true until someone sets the record straight." Help me, Lord, to find out all the truth before I express my opinion. Amen.

129

Skillful Living

A very old story tells about a man who walked by a bakery shop early in the morning and stopped for a short time to enjoy the aroma of the fresh baked bread. The baker watched the fellow and noticed that he only smelled the bread but never bought any.

The baker was irritated by the loss of business. So one morning he stopped the man and said, "You come by here every morning and smell my newly fresh bread. You never buy any, so I'm going to charge you for smelling my bread."

An argument followed, and finally after a few attempts to collect money from the bread smeller, the man threw a coin on the sidewalk and replied, "I'll pay for the smell of your bread with the ring of my coin."

I suppose you could call that entangled business. I wonder if the taxman could figure out how to tax that transaction.

Two congressmen were discussing how to raise taxes when they overheard another member of the House comment about the political behavior of her contemporaries, "Well, I declare; that really taxes my imagination!"

The House member overheard that comment and asked, "That's a new idea. How can we tax imagination?"

At a financial meeting of the church, a report was being made of the different financial responsibilities. The treasurer read out one item called the "Bishop's Fund." One of the members stood up and said, "I'm against paying into the Bishop's Fun. I think he ought to pay for his own fun."

May our financial transactions be transparent and clear. Understanding is a big room, but misunderstanding can fill up the space very quickly.

At the inn there was no room for Jesus, but a lot of room for misunderstanding. Money is neutral. Some misunderstand the scriptures and think that money is evil.

Scripture:

"The *love* of money is the root of all evil." ~ 1 Timothy 6:18

Prayer:

O Lord, help me to posses money, and please do not let it posses me. Amen.

130

Can We Get It Right?

An elementary teacher had her pupils stand before the class and tell what their father did for a living, then spell the vocation, and tell what their father would do if he were here. A little boy stood up and said, "My father is an electrician." Then he tried to spell electrician.

"E-L-E-C-T-R-I-C-E."

No, it's "E-L-E-K-A-T-R-I-O-N."

Embarrassed, he continued to spell the word, but it got worse.

Finally, the teacher said, "You are excited. Sit down a moment and you will get calm and be able to spell electrician."

A little girl got up and said, "My father is a banker, B-A-N-K-E-R. If he was here, he would give everybody a nickel."

The next one stood up and said, "My father is a baker, B-A-K-E-R. If he were here, he would give you a cookie."

The next little boy got up and said, "My father is a bookie, B-O-O-K-I-E. If he were here, he would give you 2 to 1 that kid will never be able to spell electrician."

My mother was an orphan and lived with her Uncle Kale and Aunt Tina Langston. They were great people. Their daughter Rose was the source of great joy to me. The man she planned on marrying was killed in WWI, so she never married but showered a lot of her love on me. My Uncle Kale worked for the NC & St L Railroad. He was a foreman and told the story of a worker who used a very heavy sledgehammer to drive steel spikes in the railroad bed to hold down the tracks that the train was to run on.

At 5 p.m., a whistle would blow to signal that it was the end of the day. One day, a worker had this giant hammer over his shoulder ready to drive the spike when the whistle blew signaling the end of the day. The laborer let the big hammer fall behind him, determined not to do anything after quitting time. He missed the joy of going the second mile.

Scripture:

Jesus taught, "If someone forces you to go one mile, go with him two miles." ~ Matt 5:41

There are great possibilities in second mile living to experience real joy with the opportunity to turn a foe into a friend.

Prayer:

O Lord, Help me to give my best to others in my daily job. I count it my privilege to give more than I receive. When I am done and approach You in prayer, You will treat me the same way I have treated those who I employ. Amen.

131

The Wrong Side of the Boat

St. John tells about the frustration of the disciples. Jesus Christ had been crucified, and His disciples were defeated. They had left all to follow Jesus. They had seen many miracles and were excited and thrilled by the presence of their Leader. Now He was dead - killed by His enemies. What could they do next?

Peter said, "I'm going fishing." This was the thing he had been doing before Jesus came into his life. The disciples said, "We are going with you. Maybe this will get our minds off this horrible experience." So they fished all night, but their hearts were not in it. As they were returning with empty boats and dirty nets, to add to their despair, a stranger called out from the bank, "Friends, have you caught any fish?"

"No. We have fished all night and caught nothing."

Then the man on the bank said, "Cast your net on the right side of the boat." They reluctantly responded thinking, what does that fellow know about fishing? When they dropped the nets on the right side of the boat, the nets became full of fish.

At this point, the disciple whom Jesus loved recognized that it was Jesus and called out, "It is the Lord!" When Peter heard this, he acted in his usually impulsive manner, wrapped his garments about him, and jumped into the water and swam to the shore.

Why did the disciples not catch any fish before they received directions from the Lord? In the 21st chapter of John, we find out the reasons. First, they were fishing from the wrong side of the boat. They did not know where the fish were. They were probably so upset that they didn't care. The disciples were fishing in empty waters. It's so easy to put forth a halfhearted effort and go through the motions of fishing. Have you ever fished in empty waters?

This reminds me of a man who passed by and saw a person fishing in a water hole that the highway department had dug to get dirt to fill in for the highway.

The passerby stopped and said, "There are no fish in that old hole of water."

The fisherman replied, "I know it!"

"You do? Then why are you fishing there?"

"It's so convenient. I live next door!"

Second, the disciples caught nothing because they left Jesus on the bank. Living without Jesus is nonproductive. Because of Calvary, they left Jesus out of their lives. However, they soon discovered that because of Calvary they were forgiven. And when they learned this, because of Calvary, they were transformed. Calvary led to the resurrection, and the resurrection led to eternal life for all who followed Jesus. After His resurrection, Jesus commissioned His disciples for all ages to come to fish for people.

Scripture:

Jesus asked, "Friends, have you caught any fish?"

" No," the disciples replied.

Jesus answered, "Cast out your net on the right side of the boat." ~ John 21:25-26

Prayer:

O Lord, we do Your work today with telephone, computer, automobile, and email. We are glad to publish the glad tidings of Your love for us. We know Eternal Life is available when we turn to the Living Christ who comes to us through the mystery of the Holy Spirit. Amen.

132

An Empty Billfold

As a small boy, I had many painful ear operations. This was in the heart of the great depression from 1930 to 1940. For a long time, I had to go five days a week for post operation treatment. This procedure hurt very much, and my wonderful mother made it much easier. She took me afterwards to Woolworth's Five and Ten-Cent Store. She gave me money to spend, and I ate at their lunch counter. One day, I purchased a beautiful billfold only to discover later that I didn't have any money to go in it. I never got enough money during the depression to ever use it.

Grace and I were laughing about this, and I was wondering if this condition might now apply to some of the new banks with their impressive and expensive buildings.

When we lived in Dyersburg, Tennessee, our youngest daughter Betty Grace was a small baby. Mr. and Mrs. Arthur Hamilton were retired. They had always loved the minister and his wife and their children. Since Grace and I realized that our parents were not well and lived far away, we were glad to have the Hamiltons fill the role of grandparents to our youngest daughter Betty. Since the Hamiltons had no children of their own, it was a wonderful arrangement. Betty Grace enjoyed her daily visits with them.

One Sunday, we took her to The Hut, the town's one good restaurant. Someone there asked, "What are Grace and Hank doing with the Hamilton's grandchild." When Mrs. Hamilton died, she left Betty Grace a considerable amount of money. Mr. Hamilton took the money to a banker he knew in Union City and invested it there.

A few years late, we drove around the by-pass in Union City and saw that the bank had a new building. We commented about it and thought the building was beautiful, but from the back seat of the car, Betty Grace who was five years old said in despair, "Oh no! They spent my money!"

Whatever the investment we make, our concern follows it. Have I made a generous enough investment in the Kingdom of God that my interests follow it?

Scripture:

"But my God shall supply all your need according to His riches in glory by Christ Jesus." ~ Philippians 4:19

Prayer:

O Lord, help me to learn how to make a proper investment in the Kingdom of God. I first give myself, then my time, money, and my love for You follow my gift. This is my joy of service. Amen.

133

Everyone Has a Chance

Two natives in Louisiana were sitting on a fence at the edge of a swamp. One of the men was huge and strong. His muscles were easy to see over his large frame. The other man was healthy but small and little of stature. The little person felt intimidated as he sat beside the huge hulk. Finally, the little fellow broke the silence as he said, "If I was as big and strong as you are, I would go out in the swamp and find the biggest alligator out there and I would wrestle him out of the water, turn him over, and show him that I was stronger than he was."

This big guy was silent for a few moments, then he looked at the little guy and said, "If you want something like this to happen, there are a lot of little alligators your size out there for you to wrestle." When I lived in Dyersburg, Tennessee, years ago, I had a good friend who was good looking, healthy, and much stronger than I was. He played football for a college when you did it for fun rather than money. He laughed and said, "After the game when we won, the coach would feed us all steak. When we lost, we got hamburgers."

When he was in the shore patrol of the Navy in WWII, he told me that he got to pick a sailor to be with him. He said, "I always picked a sailor who was much smaller than I was. When we arrested a drunken sailor - I don't care how drunk he was - he wanted to fight, and he always picked a fight with the little guy. However, the drunk was surprised at how well the small person could fight!"

You can't always judge a person by his size - small can be bigger than we think.

Scripture:

Jesus said of the repentant woman, "Her many sins are forgiven, for she loved much. But he who has been forgiven little, loves little." ~Luke 7:41-50

Prayer:

O Lord, help me to go and learn what this means. Amen.

134

Laughter Lifted Me

A 90-year-old woman went to see her doctor. She had hiccups that had lasted for a week, and she was suffering with nervous exhaustion. She asked to see her regular doctor, but he was tied up with a patient and would not be available for some time.

There was a new young doctor who had just that day joined the group. This was his first day, but even though she did not know him, her hiccups had gotten the best of her so she went into the young doctor's office for an examination and treatment. In just a few minutes, she let out a horrible scream that blasted the whole office. Her regular physician came in, talked to her, and finally calmed her down. Afterwards, he called the new young doctor aside and asked, "What do you mean telling a 90-year-old woman that she was pregnant?"

"Well," said the new doctor, "it cured her hiccups didn't it?"

A shock can change our minds, as well as our focus. It can send us in a new direction. Laughter can do this too. A song leader encouraged the people to pick out a hymn of their choice, and he would lead them in a verse or two. He got no response. In desperation he declared, "Pick out a hymn or two!"

An elderly woman in the back of the church stood up and said, as she pointed her finger, "All right. I'll take him and him!"

This thawed out the cold silence and filled the house with laughter. Going to church should not be a boring experience. As church members, we have something to celebrate and laugh about.

I preached in Florida recently to Northern visitors. I told some stories and everyone laughed. Later, one person said to me, "I've been going to church all my life, but I never laughed there." How sad - what a loss of joy!

Scripture:

"The Lord reigns, let the earth rejoice." ~ Psalms 97:1

"In that hour, Jesus rejoiced in spirit." ~ Luke 10:21

"If you loved Me you would rejoice." ~ John 14:28

"I will see you again, your heart shall rejoice." ~ John 16:22

"Rejoice in the Lord, always, and again I say rejoice." ~ Phil 4:4

Prayer:

O Lord, give me a song of rejoicing for I have found victory in Jesus. Amen.

135

Still Looking!

A church member attended every service of a preaching mission that went on for four or five days. At the last service, the pastor privately said to the man, "I noticed you came to every service and heard every sermon."

"Yes," replied the parishioner, "I once heard that every preacher had at least one good sermon, and I was determined to keep coming until I heard it!"

Preaching is a challenging act of worship. Today, TV services, the circulation of many books, the Internet - all are competitors for the Sunday morning message. Ideas flow freely and subject matter is everywhere. Sometimes this makes it difficult for the local minister to preach an interesting sermon with new ideas and unheard illustrations.

Years ago, I was a minister in Fulton, Kentucky. A wonderful Christian man attended every funeral I held. One day, I said to him, "Roper, it's great that you go to every funeral."

"That's right," he said, "If you don't go to theirs, they won't come to yours!"

I had to think about this for a while. He was right – to have a friend you have to first be a friend.

Scripture:

I usually looked upon the biblical chapters of Ecclesiastes to be negative or cynical, but in it I read, "I know that there is nothing better for men than to be happy and do good while they live." - Ecclesiastes12:3

Prayer:

O Lord, help me to keep my life in focus. Amen.

136

The Right Word at the Right Time

Three men were facing the firing squad of their enemy. As he stood before the guns of the firing squad, the first man yelled, "Earthquake!"

The riflemen looked and said, "Where?"

The man to be shot ran away.

The second man faced the firing squad and he diverted their attention by screaming as they raised their guns, "Flood!"

The squad looked and said, "Where?"

The second man to be shot ran away.

The third man saw the other two divert the attention of the firing squad by proclaiming a disaster of earthquake and flood, so he decided to announce a disaster when it came time for him to be shot. He knew the squad would not be fooled by the same disaster the other two proclaimed. So when he stood before their guns he declared with a mighty voice, "Fire!"

This was an appropriate word, but it produced wrong results for him.

We can never take God's place, and we can never be smarter than He is. We must not wait until we understand all about God to enjoy his company and friendship. Ecclesiastes reminds us, "As you do not know the path of the wind, or how the body is formed in a mother's womb (or how the spirit enters into the developing embryo) so you cannot know the work of God the Maker of all things" (Ecc. 11:5).

Some people seem to never learn. Over the entrance of the old jail in my hometown the words from Proverbs 13:15 were written in large letters, "The way of the transgressor is hard."

Scripture and Prayer:

The MYF benediction of my youth was this: "O Lord, 'So teach us to number our days, that we may apply our hearts unto wisdom.' " Amen. ~ Psalm 90:12

137

Watch Out for Surprises!

A certain man told me that he knew he had married "Miss Right," but what he didn't know was that her first name was "Always!"

Marriage is a good example of people who enter into a contract without knowing all that is involved. When I was in the active ministry, it was my privilege to perform the wedding ceremony for young couples. I always insisted on a few sessions together. One of the standard questions in marriage counseling that I asked the woman was, "What do you want in a husband?" and to the man, "What do you want in a wife?" I got some interesting answers.

Most of the couples gave me a ready answer, showing that they had talked about this, but one lady when asked this question, finally said, "What do you want me to say?"

Another time I asked a man, "What do you want in a wife?" He spoke a long time describing his expectations at great length. When he paused for a breath, the wife-to-be interrupted by exclaiming, "I could *never* be that kind of a person!"

Where did we get our ideas of what a husband or a wife should be? From those we know? From movies, from TV? Are these concepts realistic?

The thing called the "Golden Rule" is a behavior pattern for all of us at all times. Another Christian virtue is forgiveness. This virtue is for everyone, and especially for active Christians.

Scripture:

" In everything, do to others what you would have them do to you." ~ Matt 7:12

"Seek good and not evil, that you may live." ~ Eternal words of Amos 5

"Hate evil, love good…let justice roll on like a river righteousness like a never failing stream." ~ Amos 5:24

Prayer:

O Lord, help me to know that marriage is never a 50-50 proposition. Frequently, it's 60-40 or 70-30, or 99 to 1, and so on. Forgive me for always remembering when I give 60% and my spouse gives 40%. Forgive me forgetting when I put forth 40% and my spouse puts forth 60%. Please help me to say, "I love you," at all times. Amen.

138

The Way to Remain Young

Up through the centuries of time, people have looked for the fountain of youth. There is great demand for food and products that can keep us young. For what its worth, my answer is that "the way to remain young" is to act your age.

Two men who were well into their mature years met one another. They were excited about their reunion. One of them said, "Let's do something exciting."

"I think that's a great idea," replied the other.

"I'll tell you what we can do, we can go horseback riding."

"But I'm too old for that," was the reply.

The next day they met, and the man furnished two horses equipped with saddle and bridle. They mounted the beautiful animals and the man who was reluctant to ride gave his account of the following events.

"I was trying to stay on my horse, but he was traveling faster than I thought. I bounced all over the saddle, and I eventually fell off, but my friend kept riding on. I panicked. My foot got caught in the stirrups and fear of pain and injury completely froze my entire body. I don't know what I would have done if the manager of the supermarket hadn't come out and unplugged the machine."

There is an old saying, "There is no fool like an old fool." The old days are not as good as we remember them to be. Everybody needs what I call a "selective memory," but we must take an honest inventory of our memory and deal realistically with past events. On the cross, Jesus repeated the 22nd Psalm. The first words He said out loud were, "My God, My God, why have You forsaken Me?" The rest of the 22nd Psalm, He may have repeated to Himself.

Note these interesting lines from Psalm 22 :

"All who see me mock me. They hurl insults, shaking their heads. He trusts in the Lord, let the Lord rescue Him. Let Him deliver Him, since he delights in Him."

"A band of evil men has encircled me. They have pierced my hands and my feet. They divided my garments among them, and cast lots for my clothing." (Verse 16)

"Posterity will serve Him. Future generations will be told about the Lord, they will proclaim His righteousness to a people yet unborn – for He has done it." (Verse 30 -31) (To compare the fulfillment of this scripture in the New Testament read Matthew 27:35 and Luke 23:34.)

"And it came to pass" - grief, difficulty, misery, did not come to stay - they came to pass.

Scripture:

The Roman officer and the other soldiers at the crucifixion were terrified by the earthquake and all that had happened. The

officer proclaimed, "Truly, this was the Son of God!"~ Matt. 27:
54

Prayer:

O Lord, I believe that Jesus died on the cross for me. He took
my sins upon Himself that I might be forgiven and changed
forever. I thank You for this Divine Mystery that has transformed
my life. Amen.

139

Road Rage

Behind the wheel, some people have a personality change. The
automobile, the airplane, or a great ship can give us access to great
power. On the high seas, the captain of a great destroyer was
traveling on a dark stormy night. Suddenly, a bright light signaled
the presence of an approaching ship directly in front of the great
warship.

The captain spoke over the loudspeaker system, "Change your
course!" The reply came back, "Change your course now!"

The captain of the destroyer was not use to taking orders. It
was his role to give orders, so again he spoke empathetically over
the PA, "Change your course, you are in our way. I'm the captain
of this US Destroyer, and I order you to change your course!"

"No" came the reply from the darkness, "I order you to change
your course now. I am the captain of the lighthouse."

It's smart to know whom you are arguing with. Frequently,
those who oppose us are doing so for our own good. We can be
blind to what is up ahead. Someone who has been there can save
us from a shipwreck. Slow down, listen, think, and change your
lifestyle - this can save you from disaster.

The inscription on the tombstone of the motorist read, "I had the right-of-way!" You can be dead right and still be dead wrong.

Jesus said, "He who has ears, let him hear."

Scripture:

"Jehosophat lived in Jerusalem. He appointed judges throughout the nation in all the fortified cites, and he gave them this instruction, 'Always think carefully before pronouncing judgment.' "~ 2 Chron. 19:1-5

Prayer:

O Lord, long ago You encouraged people to think before they speak. Help me to follow this advice. It's as good today as it was then. Amen.

140

The Mysterious Robber

There is an ancient fable that goes something like this: Once there was a dangerous and notorious robber. Not only did he rob people of their possessions, he carried on the back of his horse a little iron bed. After his robbery, he placed his victims in the little iron bed. If a person was too short for the bed, he would stretch out the individual to the length of the bed. If the person he robbed was too big for the bed, he would cut off that part that hung over. He didn't care what happened to the person, his only concern was that they fit into the mold he had for them, designated by the little iron bed.

The fable goes on to say that a great knight finally tracked down the horrible robber and killed him. The brave knight was given a hero's welcome on his return home, but the job was incomplete. The knight forgot to destroy the little iron bed. So now, all over the world there are little iron beds that people carry with them. They are constantly trying to fit the people they meet into them.

The answer to reform, redemption, and change is not made by the use of "a little iron bed." The proper use of life will ultimately bring constructive changes to others and even to ourselves, as we learn to love them without reservation.

Scripture:

"And why do you look at the speck that is in your brother's eye, but do not consider the plank that is in your own eye?" ~ Matt 7:3

Prayer:

O Lord, I was blind. I could not see myself, but thank You for opening my eyes and now I see. Amen.

141

What Do You Prefer?

A certain minister went for his annual medical checkup and after a great battery of tests, his doctor sat down with him. "Reverend, you are filled with stress. The pressure of preaching is too much for you. Your blood pressure is out of control. It's time for you to stop and retire. If you continue on, you may have a stroke. For your health, I recommend you stop preaching."

"OK, Doc," was the reply.

Time passed as it always does and the doctor and the minister parted company. The doctor was attending a medical convention in another city and decided to attend a church there. To his surprise, he found his patient was the guest preacher. The doctor could not believe what he saw. He waited until the service was over and the people had left, then he approached the minister.

"Parson, don't you remember your medical checkup. Don't you recall my recommendation - stop preaching or you will die?"

The minister said. "That's right, doctor, I tried doing that and I decided that I would rather preach and die than live and listen."

There is always stress in participation, but it makes life interesting. I used to tell my minister friend, "Remember, sit loose in the saddle, even if you don't have a horse." Long ago, I resigned as "General Manager of the Universe." It is not my place to try to put God out of work. I try to turn my problems over to God. He can do a much better job of dealing with them than I can.

Scripture:

Jesus said, "Do not worry about your life...Seek first His Kingdom...Do not worry about tomorrow, for tomorrow will worry about itself." ~Matthew 6:25

Prayer:

O Lord, I trust You with yesterday, today and tomorrow. Thank You. Amen.

142

It's Not Against the Law

A certain man had three sons. He told his friend about them, "I have one son who is serving time in a federal penitentiary. I have another son who is in a State Mental Hospital; I have another son who is at Harvard University."

"Wow, that's shocking! What is your son studying at Harvard?"

"He ain't studying nothing, they are studying him!"

We need to study people and try to find the solution to their unacceptable behaviors. The law is important for human conduct. We never get too old to obey. Nobody is above the law. The law has regulated human activity for centuries. The law is in constant need of being refined, explained, and enforced. It is something to uphold and live by.

There is a great law that Jesus came to fulfill. It is called the law of love.

Scripture:

"But the fruit of the Spirit is love, joy, peace, patience, kindness, goodness, faithfulness, gentleness, and self control. *Against such things there is no law.*" ~ Galatians 5:22-23

Prayer:

O Lord, there is no law against the fruit of the spirit. I am free to pick these from the tree of life and feed my spirit. Thank You. Amen.

Note: When I read the fruit of the spirit, these nine dynamic items blew me away, so much so that I glossed over the comment as one translation puts it - "There is no law against gathering such valuable fruit."

143

The Impossible! Live With It

It was a beautiful day at the beach. It was not too hot or cold, the weather was just right.

Two little boys had spent the day digging a large, deep hole in the sand. One of them hoped to dig to China. The other one didn't care, but he was very proud of the hole. The sun was beginning to set and the little one was told it was time to go in the house.

He began to cry. A friendly man came by and asked, "Why is your little brother crying?"

"Well, we dug this big hole - it took us all day."

The helpful man said to the crying little boy, "Son you've done a great job, this is a big hole." The boy could not be comforted. "Why is he still crying?" the man asked.

His big brother replied, "Now he wants to take his hole into the house."

It is natural for all of us to want to keep the results of our labor. We spent many days earning our money. We worked hard but now we are unhappy. At the end of the day, we suddenly find out that we cannot keep what we worked so hard for. Our problem was that at the beginning of the day, we did not have a plan to guide our efforts. We just started out, having fun. In the early part of the day, we knew we had plenty of time left to change our labor or make new plans; but we were having a lot of fun. We took time for granted - we thought we would always have morning and youth. But the days passed quickly, and before we realized it, the days were about to end.

When we come to the end of our life, will we be left like the little boy with only a hole in the sand? Is what we have spent our days working for keep-able or even worth keeping? The night comes, the tide rises, the wind blows, and the little boy's hole disappears.

Scripture:

My mother taught me, "Remember your Creator in the days of your youth…" ~ Ecc. 12:1

"Do not work for food that spoils, but for food that endures to eternal life." ~ John 6:27

"We are God's fellow workers." ~ 1 Cor 3:9

Prayer:

O Lord, You have called us to be coworkers with Jesus Christ. Help us to do a good job. Amen.

144

$40 – No more – No Less

In Moscow, after the fall of the USSR, a Christian minister was stopped by a robber who demanded that he give him $40.

The minister was with his interpreter who explained to the robber, "These are men of God. They have spent their life helping people. They have limited resources, they are not rich Americans."

The man listened attentively, but still demanded $40.

The minister pulled out his wallet and said, "I don't have $40, all I have is a 100 dollar bill."

The man took the 100 dollar bill and said, "That's okay, I can make change," and the robber handed him back $60. Obviously the man was focused on a $40 robbery, not a $100 one.

There are a lot of unanswered questions here. Was something lost in translation? Did the man need $40 for a special reason? Things in Russia were in a state of flux. The government had fallen. The Communists had all the property and money except for what the Mafia controlled. The minister was preaching Christ. Would this have been a time to go the second mile? Instead of protesting the robbery, what would have happened if the minister had inquired about his need for money that caused him to be desperate enough to rob others?

It is easy for one who is not involved to speculate. I dislike robbers for behavior reasons and criminals I care for even less. Most of these people are cruel and even have mental problems. How can we apply the words of Jesus who taught, "Love your enemies, turn the other cheek, go the second mile?" These are eternal truths that are relevant on any day.

They can only be answered by each person at the time of his living. Letting love dominate our lives can be a source of strength for us and for others.

Jesus had a reason for saying all these things. Such behavior identifies you with your Heavenly Father.

Scripture:

"For God so loved the world that He gave His only begotten Son that whosoever believes in Him will not perish but have everlasting life." ~ John 3:16 (I can't say this too much.)

Prayer:

O Lord, help me be more like Jesus. Amen.

145

The Village Blacksmith

In the days of my childhood, I lived out in the suburbs from a little town in West Kentucky called Grahamville. At that time, it boasted a population of about 500 if you counted several dogs and threw in a few chickens. The village was named for an outstanding family of Graham. The place had two grocery stores, a corn mill, and a blacksmith's shop. The owner of the shop was Shandy King. He was a hard working man and the friend of everybody. He could do many things, shoe horses, and fix almost all metal things that were broken.

It was a joy to watch him heat a piece of medal in the forge, get it hot until it turned red, then white. He took it to the anvil and beat the metal into a specific shape. The anvil was a huge piece of heavy metal. As a blacksmith, Sandy wore out a few hammers, but he never wore out the anvil.

On the way home from the country two room school, I would stop and watch all the activity. As a teenager, I took broken farm implements to him, and he would weld them together. After he finished, he would comment, "It will never break at the broken place again. It is stronger here than at any other place."

God is the Great Blacksmith, and He is the One who can put our broken life together. Henry Wordsworth Longfellow (1807-1882) was my favorite poet. I loved his poem, *The Village Blacksmith*, especially this stanza:

> His brow is wet with honest sweat,
> He earns whate'er he can,
> And looks the whole world in the face,
> For he owes not any man.

Scripture:

Jesus went to His hometown where He was rejected. The natives asked, "Is this not the carpenter's son?" ~ Matthew 13:55

This question was meant to be a criticism of Jesus. But this is what Jesus does in our lives. He is a Builder of character. His Presence in us is constructive, positive, and helpful.

Prayer:

O Lord, build a new person in me. I want to work with You for this constructive change to take place in me. Amen.

146

Tough Love Is the Best Answer

A couple in Florida found themselves in the path of a predicted hurricane. They decided to ride out the hurricane, but were concerned about their 6-year-old son who was their personal crowned prince. They contacted their relations in Arkansas, and they agreed to keep the boy until the storm blew over. His parents put him on the bus, pinned a note on him listing his special needs. Two weeks later, after the storm finally arrived and the clean up period was over, the parents contacted their relatives to return their son.

On the time and day agreed, the boy arrived at the bus station. They were excited to get their son back. After they hugged him and loved on him, they noticed a note from their relatives pinned on the boy's shirt. It read, "Next time keep this kid and send us the hurricane."

Proverbs 23:13-14 in the *Good News Bible* says, "Don't hesitate to discipline a child. A good spanking won't kill him. As a matter of fact, it may save his life." Again in Proverbs 24:26, "An honest answer is a sign of true friendship."

Self-discipline is a good practice - it makes for social responsibility. Parental discipline is transferable to the mature child. Adults, a few of them, can be defined as obsolete children. Not everybody grows up.

Scripture:

"Teach a child how he should live, and he will remember it all his life." ~ Prov 22:6

Prayer:

O Lord, help me to be patient with everybody, especially children and youth. Help me not to give up on those whose lives are still under construction. Amen.

147

The Little Country Church

As a young boy, I can remember the little church where I grew up. My first recollection was when I was in a program on children's day. I was so small that they placed me out in front of the pulpit so they could see me. One of the songs I remember, *Help Somebody Today*, was written by Homer A. Rodeheaver. We sang it nearly every Sunday. Here are some of my favorite verses:

Look all around you, find someone in need,
Help somebody today.
Though it be a little neighborly deed,
Help somebody today.
Help somebody today, somebody along life's way.
Let sorrow be ended, the friendless be friended,
O help somebody today.

This is not a bad message. In fact, the message may be better than the tune. But being a follower of Christ is more than just getting to heaven, as great as that may be. Life's purpose is helping someone into heaven today.

John Ruskin who lived in 1819-1900 wrote: "There's no music in a REST, Katie, that I know of, but there's the making of music in it, and people are always missing that part of life – the melody."

This is a word from God. He says, "Remember Me, give Me a chance in your life. You can share in My divine nature through Jesus Christ. You can be empowered by My Holy Spirit."

Scripture:

We have these words of assurance: "The grass withers and flowers fade, but the word of our God endures forever." - Isaiah 40:8

Prayer:

O Lord, You stabilize my life with the Presence of Your Holy Spirit, and I thank You for this. Amen.

148

A Shocking Discovery!

A married man came home from his work. His wife met him at the door and hit him several times with a broom!

"What are you doing?" he said.

"I found this name on a piece of paper in your shirt pocket and it said,

'Mary Jane.' "

"Oh," he said, "that's the name of a horse a friend of mine is trying to get me to bet on."

She apologized and said, "I'm sorry."

He came home the next evening and she met him at the door and again hit him many times with a broom.

"What's the matter with you?'" he asked.

"Your horse called today!"

We finally get caught. The Bible says, "Be sure your sins will find you out" (Numbers 33:22).

Have you ever been caught doing good? That is the best surprised of all. A lot of secret givers never get caught. And they have blessed many.

Scripture:

"For my people have committed two evils; they have forsaken Me, the Fountain of Living Water, and they have hewed them out broken cisterns that can not hold water." ~ Jer. 2:13

Prayer:

O Lord, we repent; we confess that we have made wrong choices. Please forgive us and show us the way everlasting. Amen.

149

A Remarkable Decision

A football team was losing the game by just a few points. The coach was desperate. All his quarterbacks were hurt and out of the game. The coach decided the game was lost so he substituted the only quarterback he had left, a guy who had been around for several years but who had never been good enough to play. The fellow got everyone in a huddle and called the play. It was put in motion and they won the game. Everybody was amazed, shocked, and overcome. Later, the coach called the quarterback and asked what happened.

"I called play No. 15," he said.

"We haven't used that play in years," said the coach. "How did you think of it?"

"Well, I didn't know what to do. I looked at the opposition and there was a number 9 in front of me and a number 5 standing beside him, so I added them together and called number 15."

The coach said, "You are dumb, 9 and 5 do not equal 15."

"That's right, coach, but if I had been as smart as you, we would have lost the game."

Sometimes people stumble into being a winner; they just happen to be at the right place at the right time. They may win the lottery - but remember, a great number of people had to loose for one person to win.

My newspaper expired, and for a few days, I bought one at the corner store. Everyday, I saw the same lady come and buy a lottery ticket. After a few times, I asked her what she was doing. She said, "I'm working on my retirement."

I stood silent in amazement at her logic. How many things do we leave to chance?

Scripture:

"The Kingdom of God is not meat and drink, but righteousness, peace, and joy in the Holy Ghost." ~ Romans 14: 17

Prayer:

O Lord, help me pay close attention to my spirit, for it is my spirit I will take to heaven, and my body I will leave behind. Amen.

150

Your Last Six Months

In a Sunday School class, a teacher posed a hypothetical question: If you were told by your doctor you had only six months to live, what would you do?

The first one said, "I would travel all over the world. There are so many things I would like to see."

The second one said, "I would go to my preacher and ask him to line out some jobs I could do help other people."

The third one said, "I would invite all my relatives to come and spend six months with me."

"Why would you do that," asked the teacher?

"My relatives are the only people I know who could make six months seem like six years."

Many of the conflicts that end in disaster are family related. There are many people who have wonderful families that support and enjoy one another. These families never make the news. Unfortunately, good events are not defined as news by the media. The reader decides and makes a demand for the shocking and bazaar.

Scripture:

"The Kingdom of God is within you." ~ Luke 17:21

Prayer:

O Lord, You are my King. You rule in my life. Amen.
Good news, God loves you always!

151

Are We There Yet?

Children always ask this question when they travel with their parents. Growing up is a process of untying the apron strings without cutting the family ties.

A friend who lived in the East had a close family friend who lived in Texas. The Westerner was proud of Texas. When the Eastern friend visited him, he took him across the ranch. They drove for miles in a Jeep through the hot, dry desert sun and wind. The person from Texas never let up about how great Texas was and the fact that everything in Texas was bigger and better than anything else.

Finally, a beautiful multicolored bird flew up in front of the men. The person from the East asked, "What kind of beautiful bird is that?"

"That is a bird of Paradise," said the Texan.

The friend from the East commented, "He sure is far from home."

Scripture:

"A scribe (a teacher of the Law) overheard Jesus talking to the Sadducees and was impressed with Jesus' teaching. He asked which was the most important commandment?"

Jesus replied: "There is only One God. Love Him with all your heart, soul, mind and strength. The second one, love your neighbor as yourself."

The scribe repeated what Jesus had just said, and Jesus replied, "You are not far from the Kingdom of God." ~ Mark 12:28:34

Prayer:

O Lord, I'm standing in Your holy Presence, and I crown You King of my life. Amen.

152

Jones

The wife of a man named Jones gave birth to a beautiful baby boy. Jones was a proud father, but he thought, "Jones is a popular name, so I'm going to give my boy a distinctive name to go with Jones." He then gave his baby the name "Fantastic"- Fantastic Jones. Such a title would make his son stand out from among the Jounces of the world.

But the boy, like a lot of people, did not like his name. The children he grew up with teased him unmercifully. He grew to hate the name Fantastic. He left specific instructions in his will to put only the good name JONES on his tombstone. His children set up the tombstone with only the word JONES on it. But the word did not give him personal identity.

So his children listed all the favorable characteristics of their father on the tombstone.

> Here lies a man by the name of Jones.
> He always said something good about people.
> He was never angry.
> He always agreed with his wife.
> He was forever on time.
> He paid his taxes gladly.
> He appreciated all politicians.

People driving by the cemetery read all these great things about the man named Jones. Their comments were, "He was fantastic!"

It's hard for us to escape who we really are. Our name and our reputation follow us throughout life to the grave and beyond. It is wise that we pay close attention to what we do and what we want to become. It takes real insight to get out of ourselves and see ourselves as we really are.

In his gospel, Matthew records the hard and challenging words of Jesus. I list a few of them:

> Love your enemies.
> Bless those who curse you,
> Pray for those who spitefully use you and persecute you.
> If you love only those who love you, what do you more than others? You shall be perfect, just as your Father in heaven is perfect.~Matt. 5:43-48

Jesus' words, "You shall be perfect," is a goal for your life. The ancient sailors set their course pointed to the North Star. They never expected to arrive at the North Star, but it was their guide that brought them safely home. John Wesley taught everybody who would listen, "To go on to perfection." So did the Apostle Paul.

Scripture:

"You shall be perfect, just as your Father in heaven is perfect." Matthew 5:43-48

Prayer:

O Lord, help me to be perfect. This will help me be humble and teachable all my life. Amen! (I will never be perfect except in love.)

153

The Wheel of Faith

My concept and appreciation of many of the divisions of the Christian Faith can be illustrated by the design of a wagon wheel: The hub is Jesus Christ. The spokes are the different Christian churches. They go out in different directions.

The Wheel - The Kingdom of God

Where Those Who Go Out from Christ Come Together

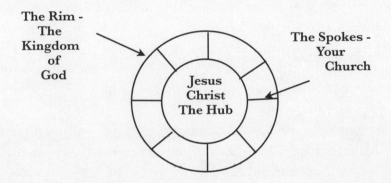

**The Rim -
The
Kingdom
of
God**

**Jesus
Christ
The Hub**

**The Spokes -
Your
Church**

All those who go forth from Christ finally meet in the Kingdom of God. The Kingdom of God is in motion - it is moved by the Holy Spirit. The Holy Spirit is God's Great Guarantee that He is with us. This is God's great news for all believers. We are the community of faith.

Scripture:

"Remain united to me and I will remain united to you." ~ John 15:4

Prayer:

O Lord, help me to respect the churches of all Christians and the Christians of all churches. Amen.

154

Confused Logic!

A farmer was unloading watermelons while a little boy was watching with great interest. The eyes of the lad fell on one beautiful watermelon.

The farmer said, "Do you like that watermelon?"

"Oh, yes, yes!" replied the lad.

"Well, I tell you what I'll do. If you can eat that melon, I will give it to you. But, if you can't eat it all, you will have to pay for it."

The boy replied, "Will you give me thirty minutes?"

"Yes," said the farmer.

The young boy disappeared and was gone for half an hour. He came back and declared that beyond a shadow of a doubt, he could eat the large melon. After finishing all the big red melon the farmer was astonished and commented, "You ate it all! But, why were you gone for thirty minutes?"

"Well," replied the boy, rubbing his stomach, "I had a melon at home that very size. I went home and ate it, and after that I was sure I could eat yours."

Sometimes our logic can be as confused as this young boy, and often we need greater wisdom. For ages, the Bible has exhorted us to get wisdom for the issues of life. But where can this wisdom be found? The Bible tells us, "The fear of the Lord is the beginning of wisdom and the knowledge of the Holy One results in understanding" (Prov. 9:10).

Scripture:

"If you need wisdom--if you want to know what God wants you to do--ask Him, and He will gladly tell you. He will not resent your asking" (James   1:5).

Prayer:

O Lord, I ask You for wisdom for all the decisions that I face. Show me Your will. Show me what to do. Help me make the right decision. I thank You for the answer in advance, because You have promised to give me the wisdom I have asked for. Amen.

155

Why? How?

"Why" is one of the great words of the English language. "Why" is a word of inquiry. This is the word of understanding, depending on the answer we receive. Frequently our answers are unclear, confusing, and lead to more questions.

One of my favorite stories comes out of England during WWII. Hitler was destroying London and much of England. My friends from England related this very distinct incident from the war:

During the war, a bomb would come out of the blue and destroy whatever it landed on. One day, one of these bombs fell on a half empty apartment house. The rescuers came quickly to drag out those caught in the ruins. One building was shattered, leaving the plumbing standing in mid-air. The second story plumbing was intact and a bathtub was dangling there. In it was a man.

The rescue crew put a ladder up to the old fellow in the bathtub. When they reached him he was holding the stopper in his hand, and he said, "I don't understand what happened. All I did was pull out the plug."

Life can suddenly fall apart all around you. The first question is usually "Why?" However, the real question should not be "Why?" but "How?" "How can I put my life together again?"

Scripture:

"Everyone who is born of God overcomes the world." ~1 John 5:4

Prayer:

O, Lord, help me put my life together again. Amen.

156

Learning to Think Before You Speak

Sam Rayburn served as Speaker of the House for seventeen years in the mid-twentieth century. This was the longest tenure in American history. Rayburn was from Texas. In a position like this, a person can receive a lot of criticism, as well as a great amount of cooperation.

Legend has it that after a stressful political agenda he commented, "Several good carpenters and some strong and able laborers could work hard and in a few weeks they could build a nice barn. Even so, any jackass could kick it down in thirty minutes."

D.D. Crisp, my high school principal in 1939, commented, "Any fool can criticize, complain and condemn," and added "and most fools do."

Criticism does not require previous experience or prior knowledge. All that is required is to open your mouth and put it in gear. You can leave your mind in neutral while you are doing this. You can even think about something else. A thoughtless mind is a dangerous situation that can produce unhappy results.

Scripture:

"Keep on loving each other as brothers!" ~ Hebrews 13:1

Prayer:

O Lord, I am thankful that I belong to Your eternal loving family on Earth and in heaven. Amen. ——

157

Rural Responsibility

When I was a boy in the early thirties, I went to a two-room school. It was in a little town called Grahamville, Kentucky. Once a year, a fine gentleman and a successful farmer, Mr. Emerson Jett, a member of the School Board and Trustee Chairman, would make his annual visit. All of us would gather in one room and sing out of a yellow songbook.

There are several songs I remember - *America, the Beautiful, My Old Kentucky Home,* and *My Country 'Tis of Thee.* This was before Kate Smith made *God Bless America* a well-known anthem. We didn't sing *The Star Spangled Banner.* The kid on the French Harp didn't know it. We memorized the words until the school got a piano and a county music teacher came in to teach us how to put the words together with the tune. Mr. Jett would always make a speech. I can still remember one line he said, I quote:

"Every tub sits on its own bottom."

I was familiar with washing tubs, but it took me a long time to fully appreciate the meaning of this proverb.

Scripture:

"Let us hold fast the profession of our faith." ~ Hebrews 10:23

Prayer:

O Lord, thank You for forgiveness that keeps me going. Amen.

158

Escape

Escape is a great word. It's the dream of all prisoners - whether they sit behind bars or desks and work places of all sorts. Escape can take us away from boredom. However, escape can be destructive when it takes us away from personal responsibilities.

Many children have thoughts of threatening to run away from home. When I was a young boy, I suggested this desire to my mother. She helped me pack my bag, and by the time we finished I decided that such an effort was a lost cause, a dead end street that led to nowhere.

In Christmas of 1946, I graduated from the School of Theology at Southern Methodist University. I was appointed to a church in Wickliffe, Kentucky, so I left Dallas, Texas, with my lovely wife and a little baby girl who was in a basket in the back of our car. The bridges across the Mississippi and Ohio Rivers were toll bridges, and the last bridge took the last dollar I had.

I left behind a host of wonderful people. I had paid for seven years of university life. I had worked for the Colonial Bakery and Lambuth College in Jackson, Tennessee, where I received my Bachelor's degree. I had helped pay for my seminary degree at SMU by working at a funeral home in Dallas, Texas. What a terrific change and happy challenge to go to a town on the banks of the Mississippi River.

While there, I met all kinds of people. They were amazing, exciting, and unforgettable. Some people were such characters that I stopped telling stories about them and quoting what they said after I left Wickliffe because nobody would believe that my stories were true.

One of the interesting characters of the town was Bob Moore. Bob was a hard working barber that everybody liked. His shop was a great place to go for a haircut and to wait and listen to gossip and receive political advice. The comments made there on people, life, and religion were amazing. One day, the people in the barbershop were discussing a person with a bad reputation.

Finally, Bob Moore spoke up, and since he was the town's only barber and the shop belonged to him, he ended the character assassination by saying, "He is not a bad man. He wouldn't go to Hell for a dollar, but he would chase it around the edge 'till he fell in."

Underestimating the power of temptation, the very nature of evil, and the weakness of our own character can cause us to fall. Too much unhealthy TV and too little time in prayer can weaken our faith. Surrendering to the Holy Spirit can make us strong again and enable us to be "more than conquerors through Him who loves us."

Scripture:

"How shall we escape if we neglect so great salvation?" ~
Hebrews 2:3

Prayer:

O Lord, I know it takes a few days to grow a squash, but it
takes a lifetime and beyond to grow a mighty oak tree. Help me to
remain loyal and open to Your guidance. Amen.

159

A Boat in the Middle of the Lake

For over ten years, I lived near Reelfoot, Tennessee. Reelfoot
Lake was formed by an earthquake in 1812, on the New Madrid
fault. Rumor has it that during the earthquake the Mississippi
River flowed backward for 24 hours and formed this lake. The
lake is a great place to rent a boat and enjoy the sport of fishing.

The Memphis paper reported the story of two men who rented
a boat, rowed out into the middle of Reelfoot Lake, and started
catching fish.

After a while, the man in the back of the boat said to his
partner in the front who was catching a lot of fish, "This boat is
leaking."

"Don't worry about it; the fish are biting like crazy."

"But the boat is leaking"

"Don't worry about it; bail out the water."

"But the boat is leaking faster than I can bail it out."

"Don't worry about it; it ain't our boat."

There is a temptation to disregard other people's property. Events that happen to others are of no concern to us. It is worth remembering that we all are together in the same boat. Ultimately, we all experience the same results. We hurt, we suffer, we get sick, and we die. Let us remember that God comes to our rescue. Peter in the storm, as he began to sink, cried out, "Lord save me!" God is available in the storms and in our moment of fear.

Scripture:

"Lord, save me!" Matthew 14:30

Prayer:

O Lord, help me realize that if I want to walk on water, I have to get out of the boat. Amen.

160

Somebody with a Mission

Many stories came out of WWII. The following is one that it is worth pondering.

The draft brought everybody who was physically able into service. One young man was taken from a satisfying career and drafted into service. He was given the rank of private and posted at the entrance of the military camp. His instructions were to guard the gate and let no automobile in that did not have the proper insignia. He stood at the gate all day long. After an hour of this boring job, it began to rain and he became rain-soaked.

Finally, a big car appeared. A sergeant was the driver, and in the back was a high-ranking officer. The auto did not have the proper marking. The private commanded the vehicle to halt. The high-ranking officer was irritated and commanded the sergeant to drive on through and disregard the lowly private at the gate. When this happened, the private stepped in front of the big car, threw a shell into his rifle and said, "Sir, I'm new at this job! Who do I shoot, you or your driver?"

This private was saying, "I am *somebody* acting under orders. I have a mission, a purpose - you can't push me around." If God has called you, let no one stop you.

Scripture:

"But Jesus said, 'Somebody touched Me, for I perceived power going out from Me.' " ~ Luke 8:46. The sick and bleeding woman touched Jesus and was healed. To the disciples, she was just one of the multitude, but to Jesus she was *somebody, a real person.*

Prayer:

O Lord, help me find Jesus in the midst of life's crowded experiences. Help me to touch Jesus by faith, so He can heal me with His Presence. Amen.

161

Being Clever is Not Enough

When I was a boy growing up in rural West Kentucky, there was a practice of raiding watermelon patches. I had worked very hard growing watermelons on our farm. Several times someone came in the middle of the night and stole some of my watermelons. I finally stop raising the melons because of this. In fact, one time they took a melon and stomped on the rest. The people who did this were full of mischief. Such rural behavior seemed to be par for the course.

A farmer thought he would prevent such behavior, so he put up a sign that read: "Warning! One of these melons has been poisoned." A few mornings later he came to his melon patch to find that in the night someone came and changed the sign to read: "Warning! Two of these melons have been poisoned."

Before the farmer knew which melon had been poisoned, now the thief and the farmer were on equal terms - neither of them could eat any of the melons. To be clever is not enough. There is no substitute for honesty and responsibility.

Scripture:

"Jesus replied, 'If you only knew the gift God has for you and who I am, you would ask Me, and I would give you living water.'"
~John 4:10

Prayer:

O Lord, if I had known the gift of God I would have acted differently. Now that I have found out, help me. Amen.

162

What Do We Have in Common?

A bus stopped and picked up a man who promptly pulled out a gun and took a man's hat and passed it down the aisle.

"Put your wallets, your jewelry, watches, and all your money in the hat. I'm coming down to collect everything!"

About half way down the aisle of the bus, he came upon a man sitting in the seat crying. He leaned over with his gun and demanded, "What's the matter with you?"

The little man sobbed: "I'm a poor Methodist Preacher. I've never had much in life, and you are about to take all I have."

The robber looked at the fellow for a moment, reached in his pocket, and pulled out $5 and gave it to the man. He leaned over and whispered to him,"Here, take this! I understand! I'm a Methodist myself!"

Who we are, and what we believe, should make a difference in the way we behave.

Scripture:

"The thief comes only to steal, kill and destroy. I have come that they may have life." ~ John 10:10

Prayer:

O Lord, save me from people and things that steal from me. Amen.

163

Alphabetically Correct, But Wrong

Some years ago, my wife Grace and I took a hundred young university students and adults to England and Europe. On the last leg of the trip, we had reservations on a night train from Glasgow, Scotland, to London. The Scots had taken all the names and assigned sleeping compartments to each person. They alphabetized the names of all on the tour and placed their room assignments on the coach. The lists were printed and pasted on the glass window of each coach. They had students sleeping with faculty members of a different sex.

We explained that we could not do this. "For example," we told them, "you have a prominent retired dean of women bunked up with a male student. While the names are alphabetically correct, men and women who are not married cannot sleep together in the same compartment on your train."

They listened attentively to what I said, and when I finished explaining the mix up, they again repeated their operational procedures. When I tried to explain why this would not work, they repeated their procedures and added that they had been doing things on this train this way for 100 years. I don't know whether they exaggerated the time factor or not, but this I knew, they were not going to change the way they ran the train from Glasgow to London.

Since they did not know any of us, I told everybody to get their traveling companion, go in a train berth, and shut the door. When they come by to check the room, don't open the door. We finally arrived in London the next morning, but not without a night of confusion. "I have made up my mind; don't confuse me with the facts," is not a good slogan.

Scripture:

"Seek first the Kingdom of God and His righteousness." ~ Matt. 6:33

Prayer:

O Lord, help me to remain spiritually correct, so that I might not sin against You. Amen.

164

Don't Touch the Buttons

A grandmother enjoyed talking to her daughter and little granddaughter by way of video camera over the Internet. This new method of communicating is a great way for children and grandmothers to enjoy each other's company. Among her granddaughter's favorite things at the tender age of one was punching buttons.

One day her grandmother was visiting with her over the Internet when the little girl's mother said, "I have to go in the other room for just a minute and check something on the stove. You may keep talking to your grandmother, but while I'm gone do not touch the buttons on the computer."

When her mother left, the little girl moved closer to the video camera. You could see the gleam in her eyes as she reached out to touch the buttons. She waved her hands over the buttons. Her mother called out from the other room, "Remember, don't touch those buttons."

You could see the excitement all over her face as she reached for the buttons, and said over and over again, "I touch the butties, I touch the butties." Then she heard her mother coming and ran across the room.

Temptation has been around a long time. The story of Adam and Eve is a tale of temptation. God showed them everything in the garden. The tree of the knowledge of good and evil was off limits to them. God's last word to them before leaving was, "Don't touch the buttons."

As soon as God left, Adam and Eve remembered God's last words, "Don't touch the buttons - Leave the tree of knowledge of good and evil alone." When they heard God coming back into the garden, they hid because they had eaten the forbidden fruit.

The garden story is a beautiful story of God placing his last creation, "human beings," in His lovely garden. You can see that God adjusted the events of the garden to play just like they were designed to happen, but man and woman couldn't wait for God to leave so they could touch the buttons. Consequently, life got out of focus. They were cut off from intimate fellowship with God.

Scripture:

"There is no temptation taken you but such as is common to man: but God is faithful, who will not allow you to be tempted above what you are able to bear." ~ 1 Corinthian 10:13

Prayer:

O Lord, don't let me mess up what You have so bountifully furnished and beautifully made. Amen.

165

Motivation

From 1958 to 1965, we lived in Dyersburg, Tennessee. Our family consisted of Grace and our five children and me. Peggy was the oldest and graduated from Dyersburg High School. About twenty years later, they had a high school reunion. They invited Mrs. Poore, their retired teacher, to the reunion. Later in the evening, one of the men made a speech.

"Mrs. Poore, you were my teacher years ago. I want to thank you. Because of you I went to college. I am grateful to you! You motivated me to go to medical school and finally become a doctor."

Surprised Mrs. Poore asked, "What did I say to you?"

"You called my name before the class and said, 'The day you graduate from college, butterflies will be pulling box cars down the railroad tracks.' "

It is amazing what will motivate a person. Good teachers know how to motivate students.

Scripture:

"With God all things are possible." ~ Matt.19:26

Prayer:

O Lord, increase my faith. Amen.

166

Rice and Grits

Church ushers are very valuable members of the church. They are the people with whom visitors and members interact. They represent the church more than any other person.

At one church, a man by the name of Rice was the head usher. On Sunday morning, he greeted each person with a firm handshake saying, "Rice is my name."

He never listened to what the person he was greeting was saying. He never bothered to learn their name. Over and over again, he repeated each week the words, "Rice is my name."

Finally, after a month of Sundays, a certain man got tired of being treated this way. So the next Sunday this man stood at his usual place at the front door. When he came in, the usher chanted his usual greeting, "Rice is my name."

The weary person, tired of being greeted like this Sunday after Sunday, replied, "Grits is my name."

But usher Rice never heard Mr. Grits.

Scripture:

"God's secret plan is Christ in me." ~ Col. 1:27

Prayer:

O Lord, save me from being timid. Help me speak up for You. Thank You for doing a great work in me. Amen.

167

Watch Your Step

In a certain southern town, a circus arrived, and during the night, the show people staked out a big burley elephant in a vacant field outside the city limits. Her huge foot was tethered beside an anthill. Early the next morning, an ant crawled out to get some morning sun. Shocked, the ant looked up at the elephant and said, "Look lady, let's not start stepping on each other."

Regardless of our size, we need to watch where we step. It is also good for us to observe where we walk and in what direction we are going, for all our movement takes us somewhere. If we go to the air terminal and get on a plane that is headed for San Francisco, but we wake up and find that we are in Chicago, it is evident, beyond a shadow of a doubt, that we caught the wrong plane.

Wrong habits, wrong ideas, and wrong decisions can take us to wrong places. Our steps take us in one direction at a time. Let us be careful where we walk.

Scripture:

"Watch and pray so that you will not fall into temptation. The spirit is willing but the body is weak." ~ Mark 14:38

Prayer:

O Lord - Jesus was tempted - I am tempted; please help me deal with it and use it to strengthen my faith. Amen.

168

Replacement

One Sunday morning, a new preacher stood in the pulpit. His appearance was an unexpected shock to the congregation. The visitor explained his presence.

"Your regular pastor is sick, and I am a substitute. For example, if you were to break out one of the panes in your window, and you temporarily replaced the pane with a piece of cardboard that would be a substitute."

The visiting clergyman continued talking and delivered a long boring message. In fact, he passed two overtime periods. After the service, the substitute preacher stood at the door and greeted the weary people. A man shook his hand on the way out and said, "Preacher, you weren't a substitute today, you were a real pain."

Listening can be hard work. TV has shortened the attention span of most listeners. Hard pews make it difficult. One end can only absorb what the other end can endure.

Scripture:

"Now certain Greeks came saying, 'Sir, we would see Jesus.' " - John 12:31

Prayer:

O Lord, I want to see Jesus. Amen.

169

Did You Get My Message?

One Sunday morning, a minister was in the midst of developing his sermon when he noticed that a piece of paper was being passed up through the congregation. It distracted his attention and aroused his curiosity. The slip of paper was coming from his wife. It finally got to him. He glanced at the short message and continued on with his sermon. After the morning message was over and the minister and his wife were on the way home, his wife asked, "Did you read my note this morning?"

"Yes, I did."

"Why didn't you respond to it?" asked his wife.

"Well, the note said KISS! I appreciate your affection, but I didn't think that it was appropriate to respond to KISS before all those people."

"You misunderstood the message. KISS meant Keep It Short STUPID."

This is funny, however, humor can be destructive when used in a harmful way.

Scripture:

"When you ask, you do not receive because you ask with wrong motives." ~ James 4:3

Prayer:

O Lord, help me be kind to those I love. Amen.

170

Dog Gone!

A certain man was walking down the road, and a sad, frail, mangy looking dog was following him.

"What's wrong with your dog? How long has he been ill?"

The man replied, "My dog's not ill, he's just lost his sic-em."

On the way home, a little girl asked her father, "Dad what is sic-em?"

When we find we don't have the energy that we need for life, we have a profound promise from the word of God, "Even youths will become exhausted, and young men will give up. But those who wait on the LORD will find new strength. They will fly high on wings like eagles. They will run and not grow weary. They will walk and not faint" (Isa. 40: 30-31).

Scripture:

"His truth endures to all generations." ~ Psalm 100:5

Prayer:

O Lord, help me keep up my zeal and enthusiasm for You. I agree with the prayer of Saint Paul: "I pray that I will begin to understand the incredible greatness of Your power for us who believe You. This is the same mighty power that raised Christ from the dead." Amen. (Ephes. 1:19-20)

171

Big Ben

One year for Christmas, I got an alarm clock. It was a thrilling experience for a little boy. Years later, I spoke in London and enjoyed the thrill of being in the presence of the real and original Big Ben. This beautiful and historic clock is the centerpiece of historic London.

One of the stories about Big Ben comes out of World War II. This majestic clock survived the reign of terror that Hitler let loose on England and London with his horrible bombs. During this chaos that fell from the skies in the night, Big Ben, the great clock over the British Parliament, kept accurate time. Although the explosions had shaken the great clock tower, it was off only a few seconds during this terrible ordeal.

When Grace and I visited London where I was scheduled to preach, the papers were reporting a problem with Big Ben. It was mysteriously losing time. Its faithfulness as a significant timepiece had never been questioned before. What was ailing the great old clock? The government brought in experts to find out the problem and bring about a cure for the loss of time. After an examination of Ben, they could find nothing internally wrong with the old fellow. After further observation, they discovered the problem.

It seemed that sixteen starlings would light on the hand of the clock and ride it for a few seconds and then fly away. The birds repeated their ride frequently. What a story! Sixteen starlings! What Hitler and all his fury could not do, what time and its power of aging could not do, sixteen starlings did by merely sitting on the hands.

We can survive many trial and tribulations. We can overcome injury, sickness, and financial disaster; but we can slow down progress and development in our life by sitting upon our hands. Inertia can defeat us. Sitting on our hands and doing nothing about our personal needs can be disastrous for us. God has called us to greatness. We are to be a people with a mission. We cannot work for others or ourselves while we are sitting on our hands.

Scripture:

"It is time to seek the Lord until He comes to rain righteousness upon us." ~ Hosea 10:12

Prayer:

O Lord, You are the source of time. Help me find time for You. Amen!

172

Class Reunions Can be Revealing

A certain high school sponsored a class reunion. After twenty-five years, they asked everybody to come back to the old alma mater. During a recess in the festivities, three men gathered in a group. They began to reveal their success, telling their favorable experiences. One man bragged that he was a stockbroker, had a seat on the Exchange, and dealt in millions of dollars every day.

The second of the three men was not going to be outdone, so he colored his life as a physician. He bragged about his skill as a surgeon and the many complicated and successful operations that he had performed.

There was a lull and the men turned to the third person and asked, "What do you do?"

The reply was, "I'm just a poor Methodist preacher."

An awkward pause followed and one of the men said, "Yeah, I know, I heard you preach last Sunday."

How do we see ourselves? Our view of ourselves can reflect on who we are and what we are able to accomplish. God gives worth and dignity to our lives. Being a co-laborer with God can be the greatest job on earth. We do not have to be ordained to fulfill this task.

Scripture:

"We are colaborers together with God." ~ 1 Cor. 3:19

Prayer:

O Lord, You have called me to colabor together with Christ and Your Holy Spirit. I answer yes, so my life may be interesting and exciting for me and helpful to others. Amen.

173

Leadership Failure

A certain man moved into a rural community. He had spent most of his life in the city, where he made a considerable amount of money. He decided that he would retire to a farm. He bought beautiful and finely bred cows. When he moved in, a resident farmer was attracted to one of the new farmer's cows. He approached this man and offered to purchase this beautiful cow.

The farmer offered an extraordinary price for the new man's cow. When they loaded the cow in the truck, the farmer said he would like to buy the cow on credit. He offered as his collateral a reference that he was a deacon in the Baptist Church. Since the cow was on the truck and the farmer wanted the cow very badly, the man agreed.

When Saturday rolled around, the new farmer went to the little town and visited its only store. He had a few doubts about the fellow who had purchased his cow. He explained the situation to the local merchant, "He said he was a deacon in the Baptist Church. I'm not familiar with the offices, what is it?"

The merchant replied, "A deacon in the Baptist Church is the same as a steward in the Methodist Church."

"Oh, good grief! I done lost my cow."

When leadership in the church fails, we all suffer.

Scripture:

"Trust in the Lord with all your heart, and lean not unto your own understanding." ~ Proverbs 3:3

Prayer:

O Lord, help me to be a good follower of Your Holy Spirit, so I can be a better leader in the faith. Amen.

174

Walk-In Clinic

In an effort to help people with their medical needs, doctors built walk-in clinics. Like anything new, it took time for people to accept such a thing as a "walk-in clinic." For the most part, these clinics have proven to be very useful. However, some have failed because of circumstances not in any way related to the competence of the doctor and the people who staffed these units. In those days of new beginnings, I ran across the following story that I found amusing, but it was not related to any historical facts.

A doctor opened a new walk-in clinic as part of what he hoped would be a successful enterprise that would serve a lot of people. One day, a man rushed in to the newly opened clinic and excitedly said, "Doc, your last patient walked out on the front porch of your clinic and had a heart attack and died."

One of the medical staff turned promptly to another staff member and said, "Quick, go out there and turn him around so it looks like he's just coming into the clinic."

Medical science and hard working doctors have done much to extend our life and make us more comfortable. But life can be uncertain even with the best of medical attention. Make your peace with God and your fellow man. This will help you live longer and enjoy life more.

Scripture:

St. Paul had what he called a "thorn in the flesh." He asked God to remove it three times. Three has always been a powerful number. But Paul's request was denied. God's message to Paul was "My grace is sufficient for you." ~ 2 Corinthians 12:7-10

Prayer:

O Lord, I keep searching for something that will make my life complete. Help me redirect my search, and seek Jesus in my life. His Spirit and Power can bring new life to me. Amen.

175

How Much Information is Enough?

In a certain town in Tennessee at a local bank, the president asked his vice president to step into his office.

"There are some rumors going around about one of our ex-employees. Would you find out more about this?"

In about an hour, she returned to report to the bank president.

"I couldn't find out much about this situation, but I understand that your wife knows all about it. When you go home for lunch, why don't you ask her?"

The bank president promptly replied, "Oh, no. I don't want to know that much about it."

Frequently an "ear full" can be too much.

The old saying, "a little knowledge is a dangerous thing," has some truth to it. But on the other hand, too much knowledge can leave us over informed and at a loss as to what to do with all the extra information. Such an experience can tempt us to gossip or to pose as an expert. Common sense should be the regulator of what we say.

A redneck sign at a yard sale in Middle Tennessee read, "Chester drawers for Sale." Of course, it should have read "chest" of drawers. The seller needed more information about what he was selling. In all probability, the buyer called the stack of drawers "Chester" drawers, too, because it was sold so quickly.

Scripture:

"If any of you lacks wisdom, let him ask of God, who gives to all liberally and without reproach, and it will be given to him." ~ James 1:5

Prayer:

O Lord, forgive me for laughing at the man who put the wrong label on the object he wanted to sell. Like him I am ignorant, perhaps in a different way, and there are those who find me amusing. To the best of my knowledge help me know what I am doing. Forgive me for making mountains out of molehills. Amen.

176

Sunsets

Albert Schweitzer, famous and renowned musician, theologian, and medical missionary, had compassion for the needy and isolated people of the world. His fame drew people to him.

In 1913, he set up a medical clinic in Africa and treated thousands of patients in the crudest of circumstances. He was visited by an admirer who loved his music, but his visitor was irritated and unhappy over the crude surroundings that he was working in and felt miserable during her visit with him. However, she felt she should say some positive remarks about the place where he was serving.

"Dr. Schweitzer," she remarked, "you have such beautiful sunsets for such a remote place."

When God created sunshine, He was generous with it. An artist by the name of J. M. W. Turner (1775-1851) was known as "a painter of light" and was famous for his ability to paint sunsets. One day, a female art critic complained, "Mr. Turner, I have never seen a sunset like you have painted."

Unmoved by the woman's criticism, Turner said, "Madam, don't you wish you could?"

Those who have eyes to see, dear God, let them see!

Scripture:

"Jesus touched their eyes. Instantly they could see! Then they followed Him." ~ Matthew 20:4

Prayer:

O Lord, open my eyes to let me see and appreciate Your beauty. Amen.

177

Anonymous Letters

Anonymous letter writers are cowards. The people are mean spirited and want to cause trouble. I once lived in a community where there was a group of anonymous letter writers. I got one of these letters, the contents of which I don't remember. I stated publicly that I thought one anonymous letter showed ignorance. I defined gross ignorance as one hundred forty-four anonymous letter writers. Laughter filled the room.

A certain man was making a public speech in the open. A sheet of paper was being passed up through the crowd. It was intended for the speaker. When he received the sheet of paper, he stopped speaking and looked at it. There was only one word on it, the word was "FOOL."

The speaker said, "In all my years, I have received many anonymous letters, but this is the first time a person has signed his name and forgotten to write the letter."

Being anonymous encourages behavior that the person would not indulge in if his or her name were known. I was speaking in a West Tennessee town, and I enjoyed the company of the postmaster. He told me that one day he received a post card from a man. It read:

> Dear Postmaster,
>
> Please forward my mail to "The Birmingham Jail." I am not signing my name since this is a post card, and I am afraid some people might read it. I don't want them to know I'm in jail.

The postmaster said, "How was I to know who he was?"

People do things in foreign countries they would never attempt at home. When I was preaching in Cuba in 1957, a Cuban told me he disliked the people who came from the USA to Cuba - "They come over here to drink our wine, gamble in our clubs, and be immoral with our women."

Scripture:

"A good name is more desirable than great riches." ~ Proverbs 22:1

Prayer:

O Lord, let us be faithful to You even in a foreign land. Amen

178

Diplomacy

A cartoon showed a minister standing in front of a high building in a metropolitan city. The man was small and not very impressive physically. He was being interviewed by a TV reporter.

Holding the mike, the reporter said, "It's my understanding that you have been pastor of this church for almost a lifetime. You have seen many changes. You have pastored during civil strife when there were marches and protests. You have survived civil-rights problems. You have been here when this city became completely urban. Can you explain to the TV audience how you have managed to survive all these disruptive changes?"

The minister replied, "I have always avoided two controversial subjects - politics and religion."

These are certainly two controversial subjects. They mean a lot to people. A county seat town in the South, when weather would permit, had groups of men who sat on park benches on the courthouse lawn, told stories, whittled on wood, chewed tobacco, and argued about the Bible they had never read. Most of these men were retired, but one of them said he was employed. He seemed to be doing nothing, and I asked, "What do you do?"

He replied, "I'm a go-getter. My wife has a job over at the plant. She gets off from work at 3 p.m., and I 'go get her.' "

Life is a shared experience, especially in a healthy marriage. When two married people love God and are committed to Him, they can't help but love each other.

Scripture:

"The Eternal God is Your Refuge, and underneath are His Everlasting Arms." ~Deut. 33:27 ~This is God's great safety net.

"Jesus said, 'I am the resurrection and the life. He that believes in Me, though he were dead, yet shall he live. And whoever lives and believes in Me shall never die.' "~ John 11:25

Prayer:

O Lord, I believe, please make my belief stronger. Amen.

179

Unbelievable Experience

In 1944, I worked in Dallas, Texas, at Brewer Funeral Home. I was a student at Southern Methodist University. The Second World War made housing difficult. I worked every other night driving an ambulance, so I lived in the dorm at the Home. I enjoyed the friendship of a lot of people because of this job.

After midnight, the people on the streets of Dallas changed. I think a few of them lived in the sewer and came out after the midnight hour. One of the men I worked with was named Wallace. After 9 p.m., we closed the downstairs of the funeral home for the night. Wallace and I were closing a casket when I heard him give out a wild scream. The funeral home was a big place, so it took me a while to find Wallace. When I got to him, he was shaking.

"What's the matter, Wallace?"

"I was closing this casket, and when I looked over my tie dropped on the dead man's hand. I felt my tie being jerked hard. For a moment, I thought he grabbed it. It turned out there was a catch that held the lid to the casket closed. It was next to the man's hand. My tie got caught on this catch."

A lot of people are afraid of the dead, especially the ones they do not know. The dead will never bother you. The people who lived in that body are not there.

As a Christian, I believe that they have gone on to have a wonderful family reunion with their loved ones and friends.

Faith in the resurrection of Jesus takes the sting out of death and gives me meaningful hope and peace while I am alive.

Scripture:

"The thief believed in the dying Christ, 'Jesus, remember me when you come in to your kingdom.' Jesus said, 'I tell you the truth, today you will be with me in paradise.' " ~ Luke 23:42,43

Jesus stopped dying long enough to lift a bloody nail scared hand to open the door of paradise that a poor, penitent thief might enter in and have eternal life.

Prayer:

O Lord, what You did for the thief on the cross, please do for me now! Amen.

180

Frustration

A man spent time in a penitentiary. A cockroach shared his cell. He trained the roach. Then he carved a miniature piano out of wood. He built a stool, put the roach on the stool and taught the bug to play the miniature piano. After hours of tedious labor, he got the cockroach to play very well. He put the bug and the little piano in a matchbox. He was excited. This would be a way for him to make a living when he got out of the pen.

That day arrived at last, and he was free. He decided to try out his great achievement. So he entered a bar, took out the piano, placed the stool beside it, and put the cockroach on it. He called the bartender over and showed him the cockroach playing the piano. The bartender looked at the roach and said, "Yeah, I've got a hundred of them in the kitchen." With that, he took his thumb and squashed the bug.

Most people do not understand or appreciate the achievements of others. Our careless living can destroy the hopes and aspirations of others. It is a great experience to get out of ourselves, so we can be free to enjoy others.

I heard about a man who had been single for many years. When he got married, he had been alone so long that for his honeymoon he bought only one ticket. Loneliness can dictate our present and future. Being free with responsible behavior is the very best way to live.

We used to like to go to a restaurant called the Home of the "Throwed" Rolls. Its décor was unusual. A waiter would walk through the restaurant with bowls full of hot rolls. The waiter would throw the rolls to the customers. For the sake of humor, I guess you could stretch the following scripture and apply it to this restaurant:

Scripture:

"Then I turned and lifted up my eyes and I looked, and behold a flying roll." ~ Zachariah 5:1

Prayer:

O Lord, help me to throw blessings to those around me. Amen.

181

The Most Expensive Item

A lady said to a man she knew but had not seen for a long time, "I've missed you at church."

"I'm not coming back to church, the Devil has got the church."

"Well," replied the lady, "he may have your pew, but he doesn't have mine."

The most expensive item in the church budget is not:

The money sent overseas to help others
The money invested in higher education
The cost for insurance, electricity, and building maintenance
The salaries of ministers and staff

The most expensive item in the church budget is the empty pew. As a preacher, I have never liked empty pews, especially at the front of the church. They remind me of talking to a lady who has her two front teeth missing. You can't help but notice their absence, even if you are trying not to concentrate on them. Without people the church becomes an empty building. If we don't show up, the church has lost her pew power, her most valuable asset.

Pew Power is the secret power of the church. It is in the pew that we experience the real meaning of spiritual power. It is in the pew where we have an opportunity to have an exciting and personal ministry. Serving God in the pew is a dynamic opportunity for Christian activity. Touch the person beside you by silent prayer. Prayer can jump across the aisle of pews and your life can be blessed.

Pew Power:
1. Define It
2. Enjoy It
3. Show It
4. Use It

Morning worship is the place where the people of God show up. Our presence at our church services makes a significant statement about who we are and what we believe in. The pew is not only a place we can receive inspiration for our daily service to God, our very presence there is an inspiration to others. We do not realize our influence on others. Our faith in God and our joy over the meaning of the resurrection makes us a person of joy and power. This we share mysteriously with others.

Scripture:

"May you be filled with all the fullness of God." ~Ephesians 3:19

Prayer:

O Lord, I open up to You; fill my empty life with all Your fullness. Amen.

182

When is a New Experience Not New?

Years ago, a man who lived in the mountains of East Tennessee decided to send his son to UT at Knoxville. He was very proud of him. He wrote him a penny post card telling him that he was coming to visit him at UT and asked him to meet him at the Greyhound Bus Station. The father arrived and his son met him with great joy and enthusiasm.

"Dad, we are going to have a great time together. I've planned a great weekend. Saturday night, I'm taking you to see the fight. It will be a great time, you will see more action for $2.00 than you have ever seen in your life."

The old mountaineer was skeptical and replied, "I doubt it son. I didn't pay but $2.00 for my marriage license."

New experiences are not always as new as they seem. They are not to be avoided, but they are to be viewed and entered into with care and wisdom. Not many things are new. Most of them are events and circumstances that we are unfamiliar with. The longer we live, the more we observe people making the same mistakes over and over again.

Most any event can be an opportunity for learning, however some of them are more expensive learning experiences than others. It is hard to believe, but true, that a person can master the challenge and skills of technology, yet fail completely on the basic questions of right and wrong.

It's smart, and it makes good sense to tell the difference between right and wrong, good and evil.

Good is easy to identify because it has the same characteristics, while evil's job is to be deceptive. Evil is never 100% evil. If this were the case, everyone would identify it right away. Evil never gives up. When defeated it retreats, but it comes back to us disguised as good.

The problem is that the good people get tired of being good before the bad people get tired of being bad. How we start in life, and how we end or finish, is an indication of what went on between these two events. Stay on the job. Be loyal to what you believe and faithful to who you are.

Scripture:

"Behold, I make all things new." ~ Rev. 21:5

Prayer:

O Lord, change me and make me new. Amen.

183

Learning to Preach

Learning to preach is more than reading, writing, and speaking. Learning to preach not only requires content and communication skills, it requires that you connect with your audience.

A young man was trying to learn how to deliver his message in the church service of a small country church.

His sermon began, "I come…"

After these first two words, his mind went blank. He had tried to deliver his sermon by learning each word. He started his sermon again.

"I come..." The other words were lost in his memory bank. He tried again, "I come..." Still stage fright kept back the words. He felt that surely the third time all the words would come spilling out. So he stepped forward with new enthusiasm and hit the pulpit.

"I come..." he blurted out. The pulpit was not fastened down. It went over the communion rail, and the preacher fell over it into the lap of an elderly lady who had always inhabited the front pew. He got off her lap and apologized to her.

She was unperturbed and said, "That's all right son. It was my fault. You told me you were coming three times, so I should have gotten out of the way!!!"

Getting a grasp on life and a strong handle on what we are about to do is a good and safe beginning. Life has many skills, and mastering the art of living is very basic in whatever job we are doing.

Failure can come to all people. Learning how to fail is very important. People who have always been successful are overwhelmed when failure comes upon them.

I'm not much into boxing. I have watched a few rounds of boxing, and I did observe one thing. If a boxer falls on his back, he is usually counted out. But if he falls on his knees, he will rise to fight another round. When you feel sorry for yourself, it is like falling on your back, while falling on your knees for a Christian means going to God in prayer. From this position Christians can rise to fight again and possibly win!

Scripture:

"For this cause I bow my knee unto the Father of our Lord Jesus Christ." ~ Eph. 3:44

Prayer:

O Lord, by Your Spirit give me strength within. Amen.

184

What's in a Name?

On my return to my home in Kentucky from Panama City Beach, Florida, I took a beautiful back road trip through Red Bay a little village. A store beside the road attracted my attention. In the gable in large letters was painted: NO NAME STORE!

I went in the place, and it was a very nice country store. A small restaurant was beside it. I asked the lady cashier the origin of the label "NO NAME STORE." She told me that the owners discussed several names, and they finally decided to call it NO NAME STORE.

The lady explained that when they went to the bank to borrow the money to open the store, the banker asked, "What is the name of the store?"

"No Name Store," the owners replied.

"You have to have a name for the store."

"That's it. No Name Store."

Finally, they convinced the banker that the name of the store was "No Name Store!" Every place has to have a name and even a place without a name has that for its name.

The lady said the name has actually attracted a lot of attention. Spring breakers have stopped by to talk and take pictures.

I have heard people say, "I don't have a philosophy of life." In reality that is their philosophy of life. I have heard some say, "I don't have any religion." That is their religion, a negative belief in

NOTHING. Zero is a good number. But zero by itself means nothing. You have to put another number with zero for it to have any meaning or significance.

I have heard of people who said, "I don't know nothing! Glory to God!" There is no virtue in ignorance.

My college roommate once said about a person like this, "If ignorance was bliss, he would be a blizzard."

Scripture:

"I know your works, you have a name that you are alive, but you are dead." ~ Rev. 3:1

Prayer:

O Lord, help my image to be really me. Amen.

185

Art ???

My wife Grace is a beautiful artist. It is amazing how she can take a worthless piece of paper and in a little while turn it into an attractive, interesting and exciting piece of art.

All professions I guess have their equal number of absurd people. I guess art has its equal number of them.

In Washington, D.C., an art gallery was having an exhibition of abstract art. A farmer from Virginia wandered into the gallery and look at amazement and interest at this odd display. One of the attendants went over to offer help and guidance to the rural man. Finally, the attendant said, "You have to view this art with the same imagination the artist had when he painted this."

The old fellow from out of town said, "If I had an imagination like that, I wouldn't expose it."

Art sometimes is a reflection of what is going on in the world. Art can be a mirror that reflects what is happening in our society. Art, like everything else, needs to be practiced with responsibility.

A lot of public toilets do not have the graffiti on the walls they use to have. Most of these dirty minds are now employed writing script for TV and movies.

It would be tragic to live a life, die, and stand on the day of accountability before Eternity, and at that time be asked, "What did you do with your talent and time on Earth?"

And your reply would be, "All I did was write on restroom walls until I finally got a job writing that stuff for cheap novels, useless TV, and movies."

We all have a ministry of influence. Other people are watching, listening, and using us as their guides.

Scripture:

"He has showed you, O man, what is good; and what does the Lord require of you? To act justly, and to love mercy, and to walk humbly with your God." ~ Micah 6:8

Prayer:

O Lord, guide me in my appreciation of art, music, and literature. Help me to take a stand for the beautiful, the good, and wholesome expressions of life. Amen.

186

Give Careful Thought to Your Ways

Two men named Walter and Johnny operated an auto repair shop in Paducah. Before they retired, I was in the office talking to Walter. He began working the combination to a very large safe. I started to leave because I didn't want to pry into his business affairs, but he motioned for me to stay.

Finally, he finished the combination, and with some effort, he opened the heavy safe door. With the safe wide open in front of me, I could not help but see its contents. To my amazement, the thing was completely empty except for one box of small chocolate Oreo Cookies. He opened the box and offered me one. He said, "I have to eat to keep my strength up, so I keep this box of cookies in here. If I left them out, the fellows working here would eat them all."

I could imagine some future thief spotting the safe, coming back in the night, breaking into the shop, drilling the safe, opening it, turning on his flash light, and expecting to find it full of money - only to discover a small box of cookies.

Is everything we do worth the risk we take?

My generation grew up in the great depression. We never threw anything away because we might need it someday. A certain lady who lived during the depression died, and in going through her things, they found a big ball of string. There was a label on it that read, "Pieces of string too short for any good use."

Scripture:

"Give careful thought to your ways. You have planted much, but have harvested little. You eat, but never have enough. You drink, but never have your fill. You put on clothes, but are not warm. You earn wages, only to put them in a purse with holes in it. Give careful thought to your ways." ~ Haggai 1:5-7

Prayer:

O Lord, save me from dropping my bucket into an empty well, growing old, and drawing up nothing. Amen.

187

Passing on Good Habits

Many, many years ago my dad went to a place where a lot of men were working on a farm. While waiting to discuss business with one of them, my father said to a little boy, "Everybody has a job here, what do you do?"

The little lad promptly replied, "I do the running and the cussing!"

Our children pick up our bad habits. In fact, they also pick up the bad habits of other people. Children seeking to be adults try to be grown up. Cussing by little people seems cute to some people at the time, but later it limits one's vocabulary and can be very offensive. Some people who are trying to stop smoking said they started smoking when they were little and now the habit is very difficult to break.

I spent the night with one of my boyhood friends years ago. His father was our pastor, a good man, and well loved. He had several wonderful children. While we were sitting on the front porch enjoying the beautiful sunset, one of the children came out on the porch very excited and said that the baby who was just learning to talk was mad, "He's under the kitchen table and he won't come out, and besides that he is cussing."

This was shocking news in a preacher's family, so we all ran in the house to see and hear this act of rebellion.

When we got there. sure enough he was under the kitchen table. He was also angry and was definitely cussing. We listened as he muttered beneath table, "Cuss; cuss; cuss."

That was all he knew at least at the time. Perhaps people who use profanity are only expressing all they know. Cussing and praying do not mix together any more than water and oil. For an effective prayer life, clean up your language. No one drinks water from a dirty pitcher. It is also true that no one can praise God effectively with a dirty mouth.

Scripture:

"Cleanse me with hyssop, and I will be clean." ~ Psalm 51:7 Alexander Fleming, discoverer of penicillin, declared this verse to be the first known reference to this wonder-working drug.

Prayer:

O Lord, create in me a clean heart, O God, and renew a right spirit within me. Amen.

188

Rainbow Ties

Men's ties come and go. First, there are bow ties, then long ties knotted by hand - wide ties, narrow ties, expensive ties, hand painted ties and all silk ties. There are bright and beautiful ties – these I called rainbow ties. I tell all my friends that you can always tell a man's rainbow tie, because it has a pot at the end of it. As men get older, what they eat no longer goes to muscle, but everything seems to go to pot. A friend of mine called this "his nutrient reserve."

After my son Steve finished medical school, I mistakenly talked him into wearing a tie. For years now he has been an emergency room specialist. But the first day he wore the tie, they brought a drunk into the E.R. room. The drunk was stretched out on the table. He looked up, saw my son with the tie on, and pulled it really hard. He was sorry that he wore the tie.

Emergency medicine is a difficult task. Long hours and a variety of medical problems are very challenging. Lives are lost or saved in a matter of seconds. Hurt and needy people are brought in, and doctors are asked to put together the broken segments of the victims. We owe a word of thanks to people who are prepared and stand ready to help us in a time of great need.

Scripture:

> "Finally beloved,
> Whatsoever things are true,
> Whatsoever things are honest,
> Whatsoever things are just,
> Whatsoever things are pure,
> Whatsoever things are lovely,
> Whatsoever things are of good report,
> If there be any virtue,
> And if there be any praise,
> Think on these things. ~ Phil 4:8

Prayer:

O Lord, please take control of my thoughts so I can remain spiritually healthy. Amen.

189

A Sick Horse

Years ago, around the first world war, horses were important means of transportation. My mother learned that an old gentleman's horse had died. She sympathized with him and asked, "What was wrong with your horse?"

"I don't know, I think he was just internally defective."

Not a bad analysis for a person who knew nothing of veterinary medicine.

Morally, all of us are internally defective. John Wesley described this "internal defect" as a flaw known as "sin." The Bible says that all of us have sinned and fallen short. Jesus taught that what comes out of the mouth of a person gets its start in the heart. This concept is explained in the Bible, "As a man thinks in his heart so is he."

Animals are not morally responsible, but it is amazing how their behavior can follow the guidelines of good and evil. Training for a horse can turn him into a winner, but it is also true that what he inherited from his ancestors can make him a winner.

As a young boy, I was impressed with the behavior of the cows. One red cow was the head boss. She stood at the barn door and was the first in line. We always put food out in every place. Each cow had her own place. We did not know where each cow was supposed to eat, but they knew, and if a cow ate at another cow's place, a fight would occur. The red cow's name was Blossom. When she went in first, she would stop and eat food from other cow's troughs. We could not break her of this.

Some people are like this – they dominate others. Amos of Tekoa was a great prophet who spoke out against the wickedness of his day. The wealthy were irresponsible and made their wealth greater by making the poor, poorer. The religious were not sincere, and they bragged about their sacrifices. Amos spoke out against all corrupt behavior. He called the wealthy women of Samaria well-fed cows of Bashan (Amos 4:1).

This seems insulting, but these women mistreated the weak, oppressed the poor, and demanded that their husbands keep them well supplied with liquor. Amos went on to say, "You people will fill your mansions with things taken by crime and violence. You don't know how to be honest. You try to cover up your sins by loud religious celebration. Stop your noisy songs. Amos called the wicked to repentance.

Scripture:

"Let justice be like a stream and righteousness like a river that never goes dry." ~Amos 5:24

Prayer:

O Lord, help me come against a corrupt world with the strength and power of Your justice. Amen.

190

Vacation Experiences

A certain man went to visit his barber. He got in the chair and said, "Give me a good hair cut; I'll be gone for three or four week. I'm on vacation."

"Where are you going on your vacation?" asked the barber.

"Europe."

"Where in Europe?"

"Italy. I want to go to the Vatican."

"Why?"

"I want to see the Pope."

"You won't get to see him. He'll be on vacation," said the barber.

The customer left and was gone for a month. He returned, seated himself in the barber's chair and said, "Well, I went to Italy on my vacation."

"Is that right?" replied the barber.

"I saw the Pope."

"You Did!"

"Yeah, I knelt down and the Pope came by and put his hand on my head, then he bent over and spoke to me."

"That's amazing! What did he say to you?"

He said, "That's the worst looking haircut I have ever seen."

Haircuts and beauty parlors for women can be big business. In men's haircuts, it is a known fact that the difference between a good haircut and a bad one is about two weeks. Hairstyles for men change, and some men let their hair grow long. It is not the length of a man's hair that is important, but the length and strength of his character.

We frequently make up our mind about people by their physical appearances. We must overlook the styles of people who are not like us. The Bible tells us to shun all appearances of evil. Long hair on a man is not an appearance of evil. But porn and child molesting are. Such behavior indicates mental illness, but the mentally unbalanced can also be evil, especially if they indulge in evil acts.

Scripture:

"Do not put out the Spirit's fire. Hold on to the goal - avoid every kind of evil." ~1 Thes 5:22,19

Prayer:

O Lord, I hold on to You. Thank You for holding on to me. Amen.

191

First Aid

One of the stories I like telling reminds of the days in WWII when I was an ambulance driver for the Brewer Funeral Home. At that time, the City of Dallas did not have a citywide ambulance services. Each funeral home was responsible for this service. As a student at SMU this job provided my housing and a salary. This job has nothing to do with the story I'm about to tell, however it does help my appreciation of the story.

A man was driving a motorcycle with a sidecar when a hitchhiker asked for a ride. The sidecar was empty so the cyclist stopped and picked up the man. They rode along a little way and the man in the sidecar yelled to stop. The driver pulled over.

"I'm freezing to death. The air is too much," the hitchhiker explained.

"Take your coat off and put it on backwards. This will keep the air from coming down your open shirt collar."

With this instruction from the driver, the two got on the motorcycle and the man in the sidecar was warm with his coat covering his open shirt. After traveling for along time, the man driving the motorcycle fell asleep. As a result of this, they had a horrible wreck. An ambulance was called to the scene. The ambulance drivers got out to help.

One of them radioed back to the hospital, "Two men were in a motorcycle, and they hit the end of a concrete bridge. The man driving the motorcycle was dead when we arrived on the scene. The fellow in the sidecar died after we got his head turned around."

As we travel down the road, we are at the mercy of another person's knowledge and experience. Highway courtesy and golden rule behavior is essential to public safety. Everybody is in a hurry. Getting there is the real goal in traveling, and it is our job to make our journey and the traveling of others a pleasant experience.

A cartoon showed two people in a car on the freeway. Traffic was bumper to bumper. "When are we going to get there?" asked the passengers.

"I don't know," replied the driver, "I've been out of gas for ten miles."

Exaggeration? But not much. Any way you look at it, a traffic jam is a traffic jam. As we sit on the road backed up in traffic, we can fret and fume and worry and cuss the situation, or we can make this a time of value by turning our heart to God in prayer.

Scripture:

"Then said I, 'Wisdom is better than strength.' " ~ Ecclesiastes 9:16 KJV

Prayer:

O Lord, when I get stuck in the traffic jams of life, help me redeem these situations by turning my heart and my thoughts toward You. Help me to remember that it is during these times that I have the opportunity to have a greater awareness of Your Presence, receive new creative ideas, victory over trouble, and answers to prayer. Thank You. Amen.

192

Race Horse

I'm from Kentucky. Horses are beautiful animals to us. Here in Kentucky *horse sense* is defined as the intelligence that God gave a horse to keep him from betting on the human race.

A certain man had a famous racehorse. The horse's name was a household word. Everybody knew this horse because he had won a lot of races and great amounts of money. An eager promoter sought to buy the horse from the owner. The owner refused to sell the horse, but the man kept trying to buy the horse.

The fellow made a pest of himself, and just kept nagging the owner, "Sell him to me, you don't need him."

Then a veterinarian examined the famous horse and said to the owner, "I hate to tell you, but your horse is gravely ill. He probably won't live more than six months."

That afternoon, the same man called the owner and wanted to buy the famous horse. He offered a very large sum of money. So the owner sold the insistent man the racehorse. The owner took the money and went on a trip around the world. He was gone for a year. At times, he thought about the sick horse he sold to the man who kept pestering him. A year and a half later, he accidentally met the man and asked, "How is the horse I sold you?"

"I owned him for six months and then he died."

"I am sorry you lost money on the horse."

"I didn't loose money on the horse. I had a raffle sale and sold chances on the horse. I kept his death a secret and sold a million chances."

"What did you do when the person who bought the ticket found out that he was the winner of a dead horse?"

"No problem. I just have him his money back."

Be alert. There are people who are out to cheat you. These people can make money out of a dead horse.

Scripture:

Jesus said, "Be on your guard against the deceit of the Pharisees and the Sadducees." ~ Matt. 16:16

Prayer:

O Lord, help me be alert to ideas and teaching that reduce me to ineffective living. Amen.

193

A Good Way to Earn Money

A man went to the racetrack. He watched the races and studied the winning horses. He noticed that a priest went up and blessed one horse, and the horse won. He observed that the priest blessed another horse, and that horse also won the race. This went on several times.

Finally, he watched the priest bless another horse. So the man went up to the window and put all of his money on this horse. The race started, and the blessed horse ran halfway round the track and fell over dead. The man sought out the priest later and said, "I saw you bless several horses, and they all won. After you blessed the last horse, I bet all my money on him, and he ran halfway round the track and died."

"You're not a Catholic?" said the priest.

"No, but what does that have to do with it?"

"Well," said the priest, "if you were a Catholic, you would know the difference between a blessing and the last rites of the church."

Those who look for some great event to suddenly change the circumstances of their life, without any effort on their part, are living with great, unrealized disappointment.

I asked a lady to speak to her husband about becoming a Christian. I had talked with him, and I realized he depended on her. She said to me, "You know he rides a motorcycle, and I have to kick-start him to get him to go to work."

Everybody should learn to be a self-starter. Try out the message of Jesus for your own life.

Scripture:

Jesus said, "Present your requests over my signature." ~ John 16:26

Prayer:

O Lord, when I pray I ask You to grant my desire, and I ask in your name. Great things happen in prayer that are serious and unselfish because we ask in Your name. Amen.

194

What is the Right Message?

Years ago, when telegrams were the popular way to send messages, a man had two women friends who were celebrating special events. One was in the hospital with another baby, and the other woman was celebrating her birthday. He sent the two women telegrams with appropriate messages. The only problem was that the congratulatory notes got mixed up.

The lady with the new baby received the message, "Congratulations, I hope you have 100 more."

The lady celebrating her birthday received the message, "Congratulations, I hope you had a great time of it, and it was not as painful as you thought it might be."

Communication can be a real problem. The English language has many words that are alike but different. When my two boys were in high school, we bought each one a horse. Steve's horse could do a few tricks. You could pat her on her front leg and say, "Count to ten, Trixie," and she would tap her front foot on the ground ten times. This was one of the few tricks that she would do.

One day, we were having her do this, but she stopped at six. I stroked her leg again and said, "Count to ten, Trixie." She lifted her foot up in the air and stomped out the other four. She wasn't about to start over again. Everybody looks for the easy way out. Even animals have figured this out.

What do we need to help us live wisely and victoriously? We need the power of God's Spirit.

Scripture:

Elijah, the great prophet, was about to ascend into heaven and he asked Elisha, who was to be his successor, "What can I do for you?" Elisha's reply, "Let a double portion of your spirit be upon me." ~ 2 Kings 2:9

Prayer:

O Lord, I know I can count on You to help. May I be certain that what I want You to do is right for me, and it will not harm others. So, Lord, I ask that not my will but Yours be done. Amen.

195

E or I?

A certain man took a great deal of pride in knowing the names of a lot of people. One day, he met a man he did not know. Not wanting to admit that he did not know his name, he decided to fudge it.

"Do you spell your name with an E or an I?"

The stranger looked at him and with a little bit of anger in his voice he said, "My name is Hill!"

Trying to impress people can get a person into trouble. It is important for us to develop every part of our lives, so we can live a well-balanced life. Inner strife can produce outer conflict. A person riding on a public bus made almost everybody uncomfortable from the time he boarded the vehicle until he got off.

As he started to leave, much to the pleasure of everyone, a passenger called out to him, "Hey fellow, you left something!"

With an abrasive sneer he said, "What did I leave?"

"A bad impression!"

Personal irresponsibility can cause us to leave a bad impression. Selfishness is always unpleasant. In a crowded theatre, a man sitting in the middle section got up after the show had started, staggered down the row, and stepped on the toe of the man sitting on the end of the aisle. The injured person squelched a cry of pain, but said nothing. Later the man came back down the aisle, stopped, and said, "Did I step on your foot as I came out?"

"Yes, you did," said the injured man, waiting for an apology.

"Hey, Mable, this is the row where we were seated."

The world is short on courtesy, responsibility, and sincere concern. It is great for us to spread a little of this around.

Scripture:

"Hate the evil, love the good." ~ Amos 5:15

Prayer:

O Lord, I take the time to pray a prayer of silent love to those who are rude and filled with road rage. Please heal their hurting spirits. Amen.

196

Signs

Across from the church building was a roadhouse. The noise of singing and dancing filled the air on Saturday night. The roadhouse had a sign out in front that read, "In this place never a dull lull."

One Saturday night, the place caught on fire and burned to the ground. The only thing left was the sign. Sunday morning when the preacher came to lead worship, he saw everything burned to the ground and only the sign left. He took it and placed in front of the church a sign saying, "In this place, never a dull lull."

It's one thing to put a sign up in front of your church declaring it to be an exciting place, but it is another thing to make the sign come true. Has the Holy Spirit made you an interesting and exciting person?

Years ago, I walked into our house to find the TV was playing. Someone had left it on. I went over to turn it off, and the program was a guitar-playing hillbilly. He said, "Someone has requested that we sing a hymn. I don't know no hymn, but I'll sing you a sad song instead."

I turned the TV off and thought, I can't believe this guy's idea of a hymn was a sad song. The gospel is set to music with notes of joy, forgiveness, everlasting love, and Christian Assurance.

Scripture:

"Restore the joy of my salvation." ~ Psalm 51:12
"Rejoice in the Lord always, and again I say rejoice." ~ Phil. 4:4

Prayer:

O Lord, please brighten my spirit. Help me get out of myself so I can love and appreciate others. Teach me how to serve You by loving others. Amen.

197

When Is it Time to Wake Up?

A mother came into her son's bedroom, shook him and said "Wake up, son, it's time to go to church."

"I'm not going to church today. The people there criticize me, they are not friendly, and I'm bored with the whole thing."

"But son, you have to go to church."

"Why mama, give me two reasons."

"Well, one, you are forty years old, and two, you are the pastor of the church."

There comes a time when we grow up and put away petty things. St. Paul tells us this, "When I was a child, I thought as a child, I spoke as a child, but when I become a man I put away childish things" (1 Cor. 13:11). We hurt other people, and other people hurt us. In church, we think things should be different and that people should not hurt each other. The church is a redemptive fellowship; we should be above such experiences. Things should be different. This only works if all of us are different. We all should build up one another. We all should forgive one another.

The church fails when only a third or only a half of its members are practicing Christians. What we say will be heard, what we do will be observed, but the way we feel about everything will long be remembered after all else has been forgotten. Let us give, receive, and enjoy genuine Christlike love. A Christian is not an observer. We are there to share our love and our presence with others in Christ's name. Let me radiate love, joy, and peace as a member of the family of God.

Scripture:

"A friend loves at all times." ~ Proverbs 17:17

Jesus said, "You are my friends, I have called you friends." ~ John 15:14-15

Prayer:

O Lord, it is a joy to give thanks to You. I am so glad You have forgiven me, and I am delighted to forgive others in Your name. Amen.

198

For Those Who Have Ears to Hear

A man with a hearing problem was having coffee with his friend at the country club. "I finally solved my hearing problem. I have purchased the best and most expensive hearing aid available. I paid $16,000 for it."

"My goodness. What kind is it?"

"Fifteen minutes to eleven o'clock," was the reply.

Hearing is not just a problem for the deaf. Long ago, Jesus commented about those in His audience, "Those who have ears let them hear." Ears can also be turned off from the inside by those who do not want to listen. Being a good listener is an important part of being a good conversationalist. We all need to improve and develop our ability to listen.

There are many wonderful sounds in the world, including the songs of the birds. There are many things in the world that have no voice but need to be heard. The voice of the unborn person needs to be heard. Obviously, the human embryo does not have to speak to say "I'm a child with two parents. I am a person with mind, body, and spirit getting ready to enter into your world."

We can learn a lot when we listen to our own voices. Talking to ourselves is a human pastime; however, the greatest achievement can be accomplished by those who have the ability to answer themselves. The ability to hear God's voice in a noisy and blasphemous world requires great spiritual attention.

A friend expressed appreciation for the book of Proverbs in the Bible and said these proverbs speak to our present age. Although they were written thousands of years ago, they still give guidance to the world simply because human nature has not changed.

Jealousy, criticism, hatred, unforgiveness, and self-centeredness are still what they were in Solomon's day. Try something new, and try today to listen to the Voice of the Holy Spirit as He witnesses to your spirit.

Scripture:

Thoughts from the Epistle of James: "Draw near to God and He will draw near to you. You do not have, because you do not ask. You ask and you do not receive because you ask wrongly." ~ James 4:2-3,8

Prayer:

O Lord, when I talk to myself about something important, may I listen as I talk back to myself, because the Holy Spirit may be entering the conversation, and I want to hear from Him. Amen.

199

What Do You Belong To?

It is not easy to become and remain a new and healthy spiritual person. There is always a human struggle to make good our good intentions.

When I was a small kid, I had a job carrying drinking water to the men working on the backfield of our farm. I didn't keep the job long. I started the journey with a jar of cold ice water. But along the way, I accidentally dropped the jar and a lot of the contents spilled.

Jesus said, "We have the treasure of life in an earthen vessel." Along the way, we fall and lose some of the contents of life. The heavenly prayer of the Holy Spirit can mend the broken places in our lives.

A little girl in biology class was asked to classify herself.

"Do you belong to the vegetable, mineral, or animal kingdom?"

She stood up and proudly proclaimed, "I belong to the Kingdom of God."

How do you classify yourself? Plants are identified by their fruits.

Scripture:

Jesus said, "By their fruits you shall know them." ~ Matt. 7:20

Prayer:

"O Lord, help me to be fruitful and bring people into Your kingdom one person at a time." Amen.

200

Dog Trouble

A little boy went to visit a neighbor. The owner's big dog overpowered the little boy, and the boy began to cry.

"Did my dog bite you?" the neighbor asked.

"No," the boy replied.

"Then why are you crying?"

"He tasted me."

How much affection is enough and how much is too much? There is an old saying "he's as friendly as a wet dog." The late Dr. Charles Grant, who was pastor in Memphis, Tennessee, was a friend of mine. They were building a lot of new houses in Memphis, and Dr. Grant called on a lady who visited his church whose home was in a new subdivision. The streets were still being built. There was mud everywhere. Because her house was the first being built, she had a lot of mud in her yard. Dr. Grant rang the doorbell, and when the lady opened the door, a big beautiful muddy dog darted into the house. He jumped on the couch with muddy feet and went wild.

Dr. Grant said, "Nice Dog."

The lady agreed and asked "Dr. Grant, is that your dog?"

"No ma'am. I've never seen him before."

The lady opened the door and with an old newspaper she drove out the dog.

I have known people who were as thoughtless as the wet muddy dog. These people run into the lives of others and make a mess of them. Cheap living is funded by thoughtless people. When we encounter strange intruders, we must identify them and cast them out of our lives. But beware, they may be angels in disguise. Both "No" and "Go" are two good words. We must deal firmly with all forms of evil. Moral hostility is a good defense against unhealthy and destructive people and ideas.

Scripture:

"Give not that which is holy unto the dogs, neither cast your pearls before swine, lest they trample them under their feet and turn again and rend you." ~ Matt. 7:6

Prayer:

O Lord, help me to use wisely the resources You have given me. I want to be thoughtful and kind. Help me to be able to protect myself without being obnoxious. Amen.

201

Tough Days

In the days of the great depression, people came to my father and begged for a job. The hours were from sunrise in the summer to sunset. It was hard physical work they begged for. The going rate was 75 cents a day. My father needed help, but his resources were limited. He hired people who he couldn't afford financially, because they were hungry and needed a job. We had lots of food, and my mother was a great cook, so the food was delicious. One young man pleaded for a job. When the mealtime came, there was plenty of wonderful food. My mother saw this young man not eating.

"Why aren't you eating?" she asked.

"When I left home, my wife and baby had less than a quart of milk between them. I can't sit here and eat all this food when they are so hungry."

My mother said, "Son you eat all you want. There will be plenty left over at the end of the day. I have a big box, and I'll give you all the food you can carry home."

At the end of the day, my mother gave him all the food he could carry, and while he had agreed to work for 75 cents a day, my father paid him a dollar. He was one happy man.

While a dollar would buy a lot more in those days, it was still difficult to manage financially. Farmers who raised their own food had plenty to eat but no money. Once a year they sold their crops and got a little money.

My dad bought two little boys each a candy bar. You could get a big bar of candy for a nickel. One boy ate his right away; the other put his chocolate bar in his pocket. It was a hot August day. My dad said "Son your candy will melt in your pocket."

"No it won't," he said. "Look in my pocket - see all the shade down there."

Decisions are made frequently without considering all the consequences. All of life's signals must be on "go" for the best results. Going off half-cocked has often explained many a failure.

Scripture:

"Whosoever shall give you a cup of water to drink in my name, because you belong to Christ ... shall not lose his reward" ~ Mark 9:41

Prayer:

Oh Lord, thank You for generous parents, who taught me to give and forgive in Your name. Amen.

202

Just When I Think I've Heard it All!

One day, I read of 30 cats and 6 dogs in a house along with a few more animals. In the same newspaper two weeks later, I read that on March 13, 2008, in Tucson, Arizona, the sheriff's department reported they found 800 dogs in the triple-wide mobile home of an elderly couple. The dogs were small, but when the welfare office removed the dogs, they also found 82 caged parrots in the house. All the animals were healthy, only the owners were starved.

I remember when I was a small boy in the rural area of Western Kentucky that it was said of some people there that "they go to bed with the chickens." It was obvious that these people did not sleep with the chickens. They went "to bed" at the same time their chickens did, but they did not sleep in the hen house.

Rural Kentucky was a miserable place to live in the dead of winter. Darkness brought life to a close. The church sang songs like, "Work for the night is coming, when man can work no more." Darkness ended the work of the day. I recall an eclipse of the sun in the middle of the day; it was so dark that the chickens went in the hen house and climbed up on the roost and went to sleep.

Scripture:

"If the light in you is darkness, how great is that darkness." Matt. 6:23

Prayer:

O Lord, let my light shine. Let me be transparent so that I can share with others. Help me keep the light within me burning. Amen.

203

Do You Know Me?

Lawyers should never ask a Mississippi grandma a question if they aren't prepared for the answer. A friend of mine sent me the following story.

"In a trial, a southern small-town prosecuting attorney called his first witness, an elderly grandmother to the stand. He approached her and asked "Mrs. S., do you know me?"

"Why yes," she responded, "I do know you, Mr. J. I've known you since you were a boy, and frankly you've been a big disappointment to me. You lie, you cheat on your wife, and you manipulate people and talk about them behind their backs. You think you're a big shot when you haven't the brains to realize you'll never amount to anything more than a two-bit paper pusher. Yes, I know you."

The lawyer was stunned. Not knowing what else to do, he pointed across the room and asked, "Mrs. S. do you know the defense attorney?"

She again replied, "Well, yes I do. I've known Mr. B. since he was a youngster, too. He is lazy, bigoted, and he has a drinking problem. He can't build a normal relationship with anyone, and his law practice is one of the worst in the entire state. Not to mention, he cheated on his wife with three different women. One of them is your wife. Yes, I know him." The defense attorney nearly died.

The judge intervened and called the two lawyers to his bench and quietly said to them, "If either of you men ask this woman if she knows me, I'll send you both to the electric chair."

I personally know lawyers who are moral, upright, and adhere to Christian principle. They are as different from these people, as daylight is from darkness. I know judges personally who are honorable and beyond reproach. In fact, the lawyers and judges that I know personally are the very best of citizens. It seems the reprobates are the only ones we hear about in the news.

Judges, lawyers, doctors, bankers, and clergymen are supposed to be examples of honesty, justice, and good behavior. When these people fail to live up to their position of responsibility, we are shocked and dismayed. We have a right to hold people with such important positions in the community to a higher standard. As Jesus taught, "If the blind lead the blind, they both fall into the ditch."

Tammany Hall was the Democrat Party political machine that controlled elections in New York to elect Irish immigrants from the 1790's to 1960's. The machine's definition of an honest politician was, "When you've bought him, he stays bought."

All of us are called to practice honesty. I am thankful that there are a great number of lawyers, judges, and public officials who are honest and honorable to their core.

Scripture:

"For all the law is fulfilled in one word, you shall love your neighbor as yourself." ~ Galatians 5:14

"Bear you one another's burdens and so fulfill the law of Christ." ~ Galatians 6:2

Prayer:

O Lord, help me be honest with You and forgive me for not being open to others. Amen.

204

A Mountain Top Experience

The government was trying to improve the way of life for the mountaineers. A government official arrived in a small mountain village and went into the little country store and asked, "Who among the villagers is in the greatest need of help?"

One of the mountain men spoke up, "Well, I guess it would be old Zeek over there at the end of the road."

The government official thanked him and walked down the dirt road. At the end of the road was a rundown shack that backed right up to the mountain. The official opened the gate that led to the shack and out came two hound dogs. Zeek followed the dogs out the door and greeted this strange visitor.

The official remarked, "It costs a lot to feed those hound dogs. For the same price of upkeep, you could have a nanny goat that would produce milk and a brood sow that could produce a lot of hogs. They would keep you fed."

Zeek tipped his hat and thanked the man kindly. Later, Zeek went down to the old country store. All the villagers were gathered around talking. "Ya'll will never guess what happened. A high falootin' government official came down to my house this afternoon. You will never guess what he just told me!"

Everyone looked in silence, waiting for Zeek to continue.

"He said I should sell my hound dogs and buy a nanny goat and a brood sow. Now isn't that just ridiculous. Can you imagine how silly I would look going coon huntin' with a nanny goat and a brood sow?"

My son Henry Ewell Russell III (Rusty), who is the head of Miracle Life Ministries, went on a mission trip to the Himalayan Mountains, trying to help out the mountain people there. Rusty's team flew in to the top of a nearby mountain at an elevation of 8500 feet where there was a dirt airstrip. The village they were going to was two valleys away and 1000 feet below. There were no roads. The only way to get to the village was to climb down the steep incline and walk - a journey of about 4 hours. The village is made up of 225 people who live in 31 houses.

Rusty and his friends brought new ideas to this little village that sits high up on the mountainside. The team brought solar panels and stoves for light and for warming the homes which they carted down the mountainside on burrows. Their homes are barn-like structures, and they cook and keep warm with open fires on the dirt floor of their houses. Their life expectancy is short because the smoke from these unventilated fires have caused many of the villagers to get sick from smoke inhalation.

The villagers were very appreciative for the new conveniences that Rusty and his team brought. Although these people were backward in so many ways, Rusty found that there was someone else who had found this remote village - a cell phone salesman. The whole village had cell phones. I'm not quite sure who they were trying to call, nor am I certain how they managed to charge their cellphones - maybe in the far away village at the top of the mountain where the plane landed which had already installed solar panels.

This villagers did not know who Jesus was. They had never heard of Him. They were more steeped in witchcraft than anything else. Rusty and his friends brought the message of the love of Jesus Christ to these village people for the very first time.

Ninety-nine percent of them had never heard of the Bible. Rusty's team brought Bibles in the Nepali language for the people to read.

One man from the village came to their campsite. He said, "I was given a Bible by a school teacher long ago, but I haven't been able to understand it. I have never seen a Christian before, and I do not understand how they live."

The team answered, "Just watch us while we are here - we are Christians. We are a demonstration of Christ's love to the village and of Christ's giving."

That night the team invited the villagers to come to the camp site to watch a movie about Jesus. They shared about Jesus' love. That night, four people, two who were elders in the village, repented and gave their hearts to Jesus. A little girl with a deaf ear was instantly healed - along with many others who had various ailments.

The next day, an older man came to the campsite and said, "My daughter's friend was healed of a deaf ear last night. Can you pray for me. I have one deaf ear and I have only a little hearing in my other ear. Rusty prayed for him - his ear was opened, he was totally healed, and he gave his heart to Jesus.

The team, went around the village with their Nepali translator Sabin and announced to the village to bring all the sick and anyone who needed to be healed to their campsite. 27 people came - the team preached about Jesus. As a result, 19 were saved and 23 were totally healed of fevers, rashes, blurred vision, and other aliments.

Over the next few days, the team put up solar panels, lights, and installed the stoves. The last house they worked on was the home of a man who was a deaf mute. He was married and had four children. He had never heard or spoken in his life; he communicated with others through sign language. Through sign language interpretation Rusty asked, "Would you like to be able to hear? I will pray for you and Jesus Christ, the God of Heaven and Earth, will heal you." The man eagerly agreed.

Rusty prayed for this man, and he was healed instantly of deafness. Then Rusty prayed for his vocal cords, and the man was able to repeat words in a clear tone of voice. He spoke for the very first time. With great joy, this man received Jesus in his heart as his Lord and Savior.

A demonstration of miracles - signs and wonders from God - brought the revelation to the village people that there is a God, His name is Jesus, He died for your sins, and He wants you to be a part of His eternal family. The team started a church there. Within 5 days, which was the duration of the team's visit there, 51 people were saved - that is 1/9 of the village. The team believes that soon the whole village will become Christians and give their hearts to Jesus as their Lord and Savior.

Over the years, I have been privileged to be a part of many of Rusty's ministry adventures from the comfort of my home in Paducah. Rusty hooks me up with Skype on the Internet, and I have the privilege of getting to speak to people in Asia - half way around the world - about the love of Jesus.

Scripture:

Jesus told all His followers, "Go into all the world and preach the Good News to everyone, everywhere!" ~ Matt. 16:15

Prayer:

Lord, You did not call me to convict others of sin and their need for you. You called me to preach to others and tell them the Good News. Help me to remember that if I will just share my faith in You, the Holy Spirit will do the rest. Amen.

205

The Children's Hour

The following stories are about children. In fact, they are about my great-grandchildren, who are the youngest additions to our family at this time. They are stories that their grandmothers told me, and I believe that they furnish an example of true spirituality for all of us. Jesus told us to not only study the children, He told us that it is by learning the secret of children that we are able to enter the kingdom of God.

As adults, Jesus' disciples had fallen into the trap of competing with each other for the spot of "top dog." Matthew records, "The disciples came to Jesus and asked, 'Which of us is greatest in the Kingdom of Heaven?' Jesus called a small child over to Him and put the child among them. Then He said, "I'm telling you once and for all, that unless you return to square one and start over like children, you're not even going to get a look at the kingdom of God" (Matt. 18:3- *The Message Bible*).

What are some child-like principles we are to remember?

1. We are still immature.
2. We must not close our minds. There is still much to learn.
3. We need to keep our lives new.
4. We must trust in the Right - in God our Father.
5. We are members of God's eternal family. He is our Father.
6. We must keep our imagination alive.

7. We must remember to not only believe in God's Word, but let our actions show that we trust in His Word and believe His Word is true.

8. We must open our eyes to see the beauty, joy, and the miraculous in the small things.

9. We must enjoy the absolutes that come to us from God - they do not loose their value with the passing of time.

The following accounts of my great grand children are meant to be funny, you can draw your own conclusions about their meaning.

206

Childlike Faith

My daughters, Peggy and Rose, were at the beach with Peggy's granddaughter Julia, who was then three years old. Peggy was trying to get Julia to come up the stairs to get ready to go to bed. Julia did not want to come up, so she didn't.

Peggy kept calling her to come up, but to no avail. Finally, Rose yelled down to her, "Julia there are billy goats in the closet that will bite your toes. You had better run up stairs as fast as you can!" In less that a second and faster than a speeding bullet, Julia ran up the stairs and stood beside her grandmother.

Evil can often conquer us because we cannot imagine that it is real. If we simply act on the Word of God in faith, our fears will be relieved.

Another thing that is striking about this story is the simple faith of a child. A child uses his imagination to believe the impossible. Do we trust in God's word and believe in His promises? Do we believe He can do the impossible? Jesus assured us that "With men this is impossible, but with God all things are possible." (Matt. 16:26).

Although Julia could not see the billy goats, she could see them in her imagination. They were very real to her because her aunt said so. She believed in her aunt's word, and she acted on it immediately. The Bible teaches us that faith is believing before we can see it.

There is something in us that wants to see it, before we can believe it. This is not faith. If you can see it, you don't need faith at all. Faith in God is believing before we see it, because God says it is true. James reminds us about Abraham, "You see, he was trusting God so much that he was willing to do whatever God told him to do. His faith was made complete by what he did--by his actions... because of this he was called God's Friend." (James 2:22-23)

Scripture:

"What is faith? It is the confident assurance that what we hope for is going to happen. It is the evidence of things we cannot yet see." ~ Heb. 11:1

Prayer:

Lord help me to live by faith, especially faith that is invested in the Presence of Jesus in my life today. Amen.

207

The Power of Imagination

The "billy goat" saga that my great-granddaughter Julia had encountered at the beach started a great game in the family. Billy goat stories were passed around. The children were told that the billy goats were often invisible. You couldn't always see them, but you could tell they were in the treetops by the way that the leaves rustled, or by the way sticks mysteriously fell from trees. To my great-grandson Jacob, the billy goats were real.

One day, when Jacob was 7, he had to make a report about a mammal for his first grade class. Jacob chose billy goats. He told his teacher that he knew a lot about them. The day for the report came, and Jacob got up to give the following oral report to his class. He said, "Billy goats are different from other mammals because they live in the tops of trees. Most of the time they are invisible. In fact, when billy goats see me, my sister, or any of my cousins, they always turn invisible. You can always know that they are there because they shake the leaves of trees or throw pine cones.

"When this happens, we know we have to get rid of them, or they will break the tree tops. We know what to do because our Aunt Rose showed us how to get rid of them. We get cans from the recycling bin and fill them with dirt. Then we beat sticks together real loud, and throw the dirt at the bottom of the trees. This scares the billy goats and they run away, but they are invisible, so we can't see them. We know they are gone, because the leaves stop shaking."

The teacher of the first grade class sat there with her mouth open. After Jacob finished his story, the children asked him lots of question. At lunch break, the teacher called Leigh Ellen, Jacob's mother, and told her that Jacob had the most vivid imagination of any first grader she had ever seen. The teacher related, "Jacob was supposed to give a factual report on a billy goats, and instead, he told the tallest tale I have ever heard."

Leigh Ellen told the teacher that it was a game, but that Jacob was convinced that all this was real. The teacher said, "Well, I have a whole class of first graders that believe it is true, too."

Just when Jacob and his cousin had filled their grandmother's garage with sticks and cans of dirt they had gathered to chase away the billy goats, Jacob's aunt called him and told him she had taken all the bill goats with her to Florida.

They were disappointed, but not for long. Soon, evidence began to stack up everywhere that proved to Jacob that the billy goat stories were absolutely true, regardless of all the nay-sayers. It wasn't long before Peggy took Jacob and the rest of her grandchildren to the beach in Panama City Beach, Florida. Just as they crossed the Florida state line, there at the edge of the road was a billy goat farm! Jacob was convinced that here were the billy goats in Florida, just where his aunt had left them.

When Jacob returned home from vacation, the local Decatur paper reported that a farmer had come into town with a billy goat in the back of his pick up truck. The billy goat had gotten out of the truck and run away. The farmer could not find the goat, but the billy goat had been spotted in people's yards tearing up their gardens. Whenever anyone would try to catch the billy goat, he would disappear. Jacob was convinced that the reason for this was that the goat was turning invisible, just as his aunt had told him they do. Here were more facts to back up his theory.

These billy goat sightings became a human-interest feature in the Decatur, Alabama, newspaper. Everyday there was another billy goat sighting. With each newspaper sighting, evidence kept stacking up for Jacob in favor of the invisible billy goat story.

One day, a picture of the mysterious billy goat appeared in the paper. Jacob was convinced that this was the very billy goat he had seen when he was chasing them away from the treetops with sticks and dirt. His faith in the existence of the invisible billy goats that he had seen in his imagination was invincible. He was convinced that the reason the people could not catch this billy goat was because it would turn invisible and jump into the tops of trees. Jacob believed that all this evidence proved that everything he believed about the billy goats were absolutely true - it was the adults who were trying to take him out of it who were mistaken.

Imagination is a wonderful thing. Great things for the improvement of our life on earth were once only dreams in someone's imagination. We should do everything we can to cultivate a vivid imagination because it is the major engine of creativity.

On the other hand, over the centuries, faith in wrong premises has erected elaborate scientific explanations that have only proved later to be false. Human reasoning does not discriminate between what is true and what is false. It is capable of erecting theories on false premises and can even find evidence to back those theories up. It is important that we base our life and what we believe on truth.

We must be careful that we don't base our faith on defective facts. We need to examine the facts before we accept it as reality, but where can truth me found? St. Paul reminds us that God's word is truth. Jesus said, " I am the Truth!" (John 14:6)

Scripture:

"If the light in you is darkness, how great is that darkness." ~ Jesus, Matthew 6:23

Prayer:

O, Lord, show me Your truth. Illumine my darkness. Amen.

208

Look for the Rainbow

One day, my little great-granddaughter Reagan, who lives in Alabama fell and hit her eye. It turned black. Reagan was four-years-old at the time. She was so embarrassed that she didn't want anyone to look at it because she felt it looked ugly. Reagan would walk around with her hand over her eye and refused to look in the mirror. She didn't want to go to preschool or play with anyone else. She wanted to put a patch and put on her eye so no one could see.

Her grandmother, Peggy, tried to solve the problem. "Why, Reagan," she said, "you have a rainbow eye! Everyone is gong to want to see it because it is going to change colors from day to day. It will start out in the darkest colors, violet, indigo, and blue - like the rainbow in the sky. It will be three colors of purple." This got her attention because she likes to color.

Peggy continued, "Then your eye will look green, yellow-green, organ and red, and finally it will be light pink. Suddenly, it will be gone from your eye, just like rainbow in sky. You can look for the bright side of this injury and enjoy seeing the colors of the rainbow as your eye heals."

Reagan told everyone about her rainbow eye at preschool. Everyday, the children could not wait to see what color Reagan's eye would be next. Since then, any time she sees a child with a black eye, she tells them the story.

When we see the rainbow in the sky, it is the story and promise of God that He will never again destroy the earth with a flood. The dark foreboding storms in our life can seem horrible as we anticipate what the storms might mean. But like the storms in the sky, they will clear, and many times a rainbow will be seen the rainbow eye, we can have a hope and a promise that God will bring us through the ordeal with His blessing and His promise. The promise of the rainbow stands true today, no matter what the adversity - no matter how dark the smudge. God can turn our adversity into a rainbow and heal us and strengthen our faith, changing the dark spot in our lives to the light of hope.

Scripture:

"God is our refuge and strength, a very present help in time of trouble. We will not fear, even if earthquakes come and the mountains crumble into the sea. The LORD Almighty is here among us; the God of Israel is our fortress. God will help us at the break of dawn. ~ Psalm 46:1-2,5

Prayer:

O Lord, help me to remember that You are walking with me through the storm. After the storm is over, help me to see the rainbow. Amen.

"All my I looked for a pot of gold at the end of the rainbow, and I found it at the foot of the cross."

~ Dale Evans, Wife of Cowboy Actor Roy Rogers

209

Understanding the Main Thing

Several years ago, all our family went to Nashville for the wedding of my granddaughter Christina Houser and her husband Corey. Several of my great-grandchildren were in the wedding. My great-grandson Preston, who was five years old at the time, was not in the wedding and was disappointed. The church building where the wedding was held was a Methodist Church that had a high steeple with a big bell in it.

Preston's cousin, Jacob, was the ring bearer. Preston kept telling his grandmother Peggy, "I can't believe Jacob is going to be the bell ringer in this wedding, and I'm not going to get to do anything."

Peggy didn't think anything about Preston calling the *ring bearer* the *bell ringer*. She though he was confused about the name. Right before the bride came in, Jacob walked down the aisle carrying a pillow.

Preston asked, "Why is Jacob carrying that pillow down the aisle?"

His grandmother said, "That is his job in the wedding."

"What? What?" Preston exclaimed. "I thought he was going to be the bell ringer!"

"It's called a ring bearer, and that is just what he is doing. There are two little plastic rings on the pillow," said his grandmother.

"What?" Preston continued. "I thought he was going to be the bell ringer!"

"What do you mean?" asked his grandmother.

"The bell, the bell in the steeple! I thought he was going to get to ring the bell!"

"No, Preston, this is what Jacob was going to do," she said.

At the end of the wedding, as Jacob was walking with his pillow back down the aisle and out the door, Preston leaned over to his grandmother and said, "I'm supposed to be the ring bearer in my dad's wedding next summer. Is this what I'm supposed to do?"

"Yes," she replied.

"Oh no, I thought I as going to get to ring the bell," he said in great disappointment.

" No," said his grandmother. "You are not supposed to ring the bell. The church where your daddy is getting married doesn't even have a bell."

"Well," said Preston, "I'll tell you what. If I have to carry that pillow down the aisle, at least I am going to make sure the rings are real. I want to make sure my Dad and Amy are really getting married, and it's not some kind of fake wedding!"

Preston actually thought because the rings Jacob was carrying were plastic and that because of this the whole wedding was a fake, a sham. In the same way, it is possible to get caught up with the symbols of Christianity or the positions that different people hold in the church and miss the main thing.

What is the main thing? The main thing is knowing Jesus Christ as our personal Savior and Friend. In fact, it is what the Bible calls the "marriage of the Lamb." The Bible tells us, that "the marriage of the Lamb has come and the bride has made herself ready" (Rev. 19:7).

As true Christians, we are called in the scripture the Bride of Christ. Instead of focusing on the symbols of Christianity, we should focus on making sure we are able to enjoy our relationship with Christ. How can we do this?

Jesus tells us, "I advise you to buy gold from Me--gold that has been purified by fire. Then you will be rich. And also buy white garments so you will not be shamed by your nakedness. And buy ointment for your eyes so you will be able to see. I am the one who corrects and disciplines everyone I love. Be diligent and turn from your indifference. Look! Here I stand at the door and knock. If you hear me calling and open the door, I will come in, and we will share a meal as friends" (Rev. 3:18-20).

Scripture:

Jesus told the Jewish leaders, "You search the Scriptures because you believe they give you eternal life. But the Scriptures point to me! Yet you refuse to come to me so that I can give you this eternal life." ~ John 5:39-40

Prayer:

O Lord, help me to see clearly so I can participate in the main thing in Christianity - a deep, loving, abiding relationship with You. Amen.

210

A Do It Yourself Job

My daughter Rose was visiting her daughter Stephanie and her granddaughter Liberty Grace, who live in Switzerland. Liberty Grace was two years old at that time. Liberty wanted to go outside and play and Stephanie asked Rose to make sure that Liberty had on a hat because it was windy.

Rose got out the hat from the closet and put it on Liberty's head. Liberty protested and took the hat off. Rose put the hat back on Liberty's head. Liberty continued to insist that she wasn't going to wear the hat and took it off. Finally, her grandmother said, "Liberty, if you don't wear this hat, you cannot go outside and play." After some more protesting, Liberty reluctantly let her grandmother put the hat back on her, and then she went out the door to play on the front porch. Rose went back to vacuuming the stairs.

A few minutes later, Liberty came in the door, made sure her grandmother was looking at her, and took the hat, threw it at the bottom of the stairs, then ran back outside. Not wanting to make a big scene in front of Stephanie's house, Rose was not sure what to do next, so she decided to finish vacuuming the steps to think about it.

After a few more minutes, Liberty ran back in the house, took off her coat and her boots, and went in the bathroom and slammed the door. She stood in the bathroom and cried out, "No, No, No Nein, Nein, Nein!" (Nein is German for "No"). She cried and sobbed. Suddenly, everything got quiet. She came out of the bathroom and went in the living room and sat down to look at a book. She had given herself her own punishment – a time out!

There wasn't anything wrong with the hat - Liberty just didn't want to wear it. Liberty, like most children has a very tender conscience that stung her because she had disobeyed. Obviously, her disobedience bothered her conscience. She didn't want to wait to receive her punishment; she wanted to get it over with so she could experience the peace of mind and joy of a clear conscience.

Liberty's parents have taught her that when she disobeys, she has to go in the bathroom and shut the door and pray until she is sorry for what she has done wrong. Then she must ask Jesus to forgive her. So she did just that.

Jesus said, "When you pray, go away by yourself, shut the door behind you, and pray to your Father secretly. Then your Father, who knows all secrets, will reward you" (Matt. 6:6). If we go to God secretly and work out our problems, we have this promise from Jesus, He will reward us.

The purpose of discipline is ultimately to teach me self-discipline. When I am growing up, hopefully, someone who loves me helps to control me, until I take over the task of disciplining myself.

Socrates said, "Know yourself."
Marcus Arelius said, "Control yourself."
Jesus said, "Deny Yourself."

Everyone who tries to please himself will never be pleased. Jesus taught us to deny ourselves by going into our closet to pray to deal with ourselves and bring our lives into obedience to His word and back into fellowship with His Presence in our lives.

Scripture:

"We use God's mighty weapons, not mere worldly weapons, to knock down the Devil's strongholds. With these weapons we break down every proud argument that keeps people from knowing God. We bring every thought captive to the obedience of Christ. With these weapons, we conquer rebellious ideas, and we teach them to obey Christ." ~ 2 Cor.10: 4-5, NLT, NKJ

Prayer:

O Lord, help me deal with myself because I will be with me all my life. Help me bring my life in obedience to Your commands, so I can enjoy fellowship with You everyday and receive the blessings that come from submitting my life to You. Amen.

211

Cheers!

One day, my great-grandson, Judah came to visit us. His family lives in Switzerland, so I had not had the occasion to get to know him very well. I could not believe that Judah was less than two years old, and yet he was so smart. Judah found many things around the house that I had lost. He found a good paintbrush that I had misplaced sometime ago. He found a hammer and screwdriver that I hadn't been able to find for over a year.

Needless to say I was amazed. After Judah had accomplished

all of this, he found the cap to a plastic bottle that had been dropped on the floor. He picked it up, went to the bathroom, dipped it in the toilet, and took a drink.

Judah can speak two languages - Swiss German and English. I know people much older than Judah who speak more than two languages, but they still drink from a polluted fountain. What are the signs of intelligence?

Scripture:

Jesus said, "If you only knew the gift God has for you and who I am, you would ask Me, and I would give you living water. But the water I give them takes away thirst altogether. It becomes a perpetual spring within them, giving them eternal life." ~ John 4:10, 14 NLT

Prayer:

O Lord, lead me to the fountain that never runs dry. Amen!

212

The Source of Self-Confidence

My daughter Betty Grace picked up her granddaughter, two-year-old Anabelle, at the airport. Anabelle had come with her mother to visit grandmother Betty in Austin, Texas. As Betty was fastening Anabelle in her car seat, Anabelle said, "Its okay grand-mommy, you can look at me because I'm so cute and my dress is so beautiful."

It's not bad to have a good opinion of yourself, if you keep it balanced with humility and an appreciation for others. If you do, then this concept will be a source of strength for you all your life.

It is important that we base our confidence not on ourselves, but on who God says that we are. Anabelle thought she looked pretty because everyone she knew and loved said that she was. She believed that what everyone said about her was true.

God has said some wonderful things about us as His children. If we have a childlike spirit, like Anabelle, we will believe that the things He says about us is true. And since we are His children, and the God of Heaven and Earth, who is the Redeemer of the world is our Father, we should be the most confident people on earth.

Scripture:

"So you should not be like cowering, fearful slaves. You should behave instead like God's very own children, adopted into His family, calling him "Father, dear Father." For His Holy Spirit speaks to us deep in our hearts and tells us that we are God's children. And since we are His children, we will share His treasures--for everything God gives to his Son, Christ, is ours, too. ~Romans 8:15-17 NLT

Prayer:

O Lord, I deposit my confidence in You, the source of my strength and the assurance of my identity. Amen.

213

Keeping Excitement for Life Alive!

Elijah Houser, my youngest great-grandson is a Texan who lives in Louisville, Kentucky, with his parents, Philip and Ranelle. Elijah's father is a medical doctor. Elijah is not quite two and is trying to talk. He has a hard time because his sister Anabelle talks a lot and dominates the conversation. To solve the problem for the moment, Anabelle now goes to play school once a week so her parents can enjoy a quiet time, and Elijah can have a chance to talk.

Of course, Elijah has fun being the center of attention. When he sees something for the first time, he calls out, "Whoa! Whoa!" in amazement over his excitement of seeing something new. Perhaps this is a refection of his Texas roots.

With his one word vocabulary, Elijah, in his childlike way, expresses the excitement over the commonplace things that we often miss or take for granted. In our adult way of thinking, our minds are often filled with worries or cares, so much so that we are blinded by them and miss God's wonders that surround us.

To become childlike, we need to clear our minds by giving all our worries to the Lord, and then we will have room in our minds for observation and reflection on the things around us. When those things that block our interaction with God are out of the way, we can participate in an uninterrupted conversation with our heavenly Father. It is up to us to take advantage of this opportunity.

Scripture:

"I have set before you an open door, and no one can shut it." ~ Rev. 3:8

Prayer:

O Lord, help me to enter into dialogue with You, which is the true meaning of prayer. Help me to turn all my worries and cares over to You and maintain the excitement of a little child over the common place things and the wonders of life that I have been missing. Amen.

214

Still Under Construction

My great-granddaughter two-year-old Abigail lives in Florida, and loves to go for a drive with her grandmother, Mildred Russell, who she calls Neenie. She loves to talk about all the places she recognizes as they drive by in the car. When Abigail sees Starbucks, she will always say, "There is Starbucks."

One day as they drove by Starbucks, her grandmother said, "Abigail, when you are older, we can go to Starbucks and have coffee."

Two weeks later, Abigail and her grandmother drove by Starbucks again. Abigail said, "Neenie, there is Starbucks - I am older now. Can we get coffee?"

A lot of times, we think we are ready to do a thing. Even though we are very sincere, we may not be ready. We need to be patient with ourselves. Sometimes, we are still under construction.

Another time, Abigail went with her grandmother to work. She had gone into the back room where the snacks were kept and was in the process of eating a bag of Famous Amos Cookies. Her Uncle John came into the snack room and asked, "Abigail, did Neenie say you could have those cookies?" Abigail didn't answer.

Her uncle told her, "Abigail, eat the cookie you have and put the rest away."

Abigail responded, "Go back in the other room Johnny - go away."

Some people think that if you do something that is not good for you, and no one sees you, it is okay. Nobody likes to be called up short. We all avoid people who try to make us accept responsibility, frequently to our own detriment. The passing of time does not assure our growth. Something has to be going on besides the passing of time. It is our obedient actions that count and bring transformation.

Scripture:

Jesus told us, "Pray that you enter not into temptation, the spirit is willing but the flesh is weak." Matt. 26:41

"But remember that the temptations that come into your life are no different from what others experience. And God is faithful. He will keep the temptation from becoming so strong that you can't stand up against it. When you are tempted, He will show you a way out so that you will not give in to it." ~ 1 Cor. 10:13

Prayer:

O Lord, help me to be like Jesus and "to grow in wisdom and stature and in favor with God and man." Amen!

215

A Memory of Joy!

Looking back 50 years ago, when I was pastor at the First United Methodist Church in Dyersburg, Tennessee, is a joyful experience. While I was in Dyersburg, I once invited Dr. Charles Allen to preach a revival meeting. At that time, he was pastor of Grace Church in Atlanta, Georgia. He had written over 22 books and several newspaper columns. He was much in demand as a preacher and public speaker.

I remember one night he preached on the 23rd Psalm. He did a tremendous job presenting this beautiful psalm of David. Dr. Allen told of going to New York and seeing the beautiful and talented Mary Martin on stage. He explained that she sang this song, "I'm stuck like a dope with a thing called hope. I can't get it out of my mind." Dr. Allen then said, "You know David would have liked that song." He paused a moment and then said, "Come to think of it, David would have liked Mary Martin!"

The people of the Bible were real human beings. They had their weak points. They were people of both doubt and faith.

Scripture:

I have read the book of Job many times. Here are some high points of this book:

- Job's response to his troubles: "The Lord gives and the Lord takes away, blessed be the name of the Lord." ~ 1:21

- Job's prayer: "Oh that I knew where I might find Him." ~ 23:3

- Job's wife advised Job: "Curse God and die.'" ~ 2:9

- Job's philosophy: "Though He slay me, yet will I trust Him."~ 13:15.

- God's question to Job: "Where were you when the morning stars sang together, and all the sons of God shouted for joy?" ~ 38:4

- Job's observation of the uncertainty of the wicked, "Why do the wicked prosper, growing old and powerful?" ~ 21:17

- Job trusted in God despite his problems: "I know that my Redeemer lives, and He will stand upon the earth at last. And after my body has decayed, yet in my flesh I will see God! ~19:25-26

Through suffering, doubt, and failure Job held on to God. Job taught me that if I will hold on to God, when I can no longer hold on, God will hold on to me!

Prayer:

O Lord, I take a firm grip on faith so I can hold on to You.

Biographical Information

Dr. Henry E. "Hank" Russell was born in Paducah, Kentucky, in 1921. His parents were Henry Ewell and Margaret Wurst Russell. His great-great-great grandfather was Major Charles Ewell, the only Revolutionary War veteran buried in Paducah.

Hank grew up on his father's dairy farm. He attended a one-room grammar school at Grahamville, Kentucky, and graduated from Heath High School. He worked his way through Paducah Junior College, Lambuth College in Jackson, Tennessee, and Southern Methodist University School of Theology (now called Perkins School of Theology) in Dallas, Texas.

In 1972, Lambuth awarded him an Honorary Doctor of Divinity Degree. Hank married Grace Jarrell Williams of Humboldt, Tennessee, in 1945. They have five children, seventeen grandchildren, and eleven great-grandchildren.

Among Hank and Grace's direct descendants - children and grandchildren there are:

- 4 Ministers
- 2 Medical Doctors
- 2 Teachers
- 1 Engineer
- 1 Accountant/Worship Leader (Masters in Accounting)
- 4 Entrepreneurs (2 with BS Degrees in English,1 with BS Degree in Art)

The grandchildren who are still students are pursuing degrees in the following:

- 1 Medical Degree and is finishing her Internship

- 1 PHD in Physics at the University of North Carolina 1 Masters Degree in Documentary Films at Wake Forest University
- 1 English/Writing Degree at the University of Texas,
- 1 will pursue a History Degree to become a History Professor
- 1 Bachelor's Degree at the University of Florida to pursue a Law Degree to become a Judge
- 1 high school student who will pursue an Art Degree

Among the spouses of those children and grandchildren:

- 3 Ministers
- 1 College Coach/Professor
- 1 Lawyer
- 1 Engineer
- 1 Toxicologist

Hank served the following Methodist Congregations over the years:

- 1942 - Oakgrove Methodist Church near Jackson, Tennessee

- 1943 - Gilbersville Circuit near Gilbertsville, Kentucky - when they were building Kentucky Dam - this included Gilbertsville, Calvert City, Palma, and Oakland

- 1945 - Associate at Grace Methodist Church in Dallas, Texas

- 1946 - Nevada Circuit, including Nevada, Pleasant Valley, Lavon, and Rowlett, Texas

- 1946 - 1949 - In the Memphis Conference: Wickliffe, Kentucky

- 1949 - 1950 - Reidland, Kentucky

- 1950 - 1955 - Ellendale, Tennessee and founded St. Stephen's in Memphis

- 1955 - 1958 - Fulton, Kentucky

- 1957 - Hank participated in a nation-wide revival in the Methodist Churches in Cuba shortly before Castro took power.

- 1958 - 1965 - Dyersburg, Tennessee

- 1963 - One of 12 American ministers, Delegates to the World Methodist Conference Ministerial Exchange. Exchanged with Rev. Reginald Mallett at the Albert Hall in Manchester, England. Following that trip, Hank and Grace took the whole family on a camping trip in eleven countries in Europe. Over the years after his children were grown, Hank and Grace subsequently took a number of tour groups to Europe and Israel.

- 1965-1967 - Brownsville District (Name changed to United Methodist Church)

- 1967 - 1972 - Broadway United Methodist, Paducah, Kentucky

- 1972 - 1978 - St. Luke's United Methodist, Memphis, Tennessee

- 1974 - Chairman of the Board of Education and on other boards and committees in the Memphis Annual Conference.

- 1974 - Delegate to the Reopening of City Road Church in London

- 1978 -1984 - Dyersburg District Superintendent

- 1978 - Delegate to The Christian Heritage in Government Conference

- 1980 - Delegate to the World Methodist Conference in Honolulu

Offices and Community Associations

- Junaluska Associate

- Secretary of the Board of Trustees at Lambuth College for twelve years

- Board Member of the Methodist Hospital in Memphis and Dyersburg, Tennessee

- Dyersburg Housing Authority

- Initiator of Wesley Homes of Dyersburg and Wesley Homes Tiptonville, Tennessee.

- Charter Member of Reidland Lions Club, Member of the Kiwanis Club, and the Rotary Club. Hank was active in other civic organizations in various communities where he served.

- In 1977, Hank and Grace bought a condo at Pinnacle Port in Panama City Beach, Florida. Since Hank's retirement, he and Grace spend their winters in Panama City Beach and are active members at Gulfview Methodist Church. Hank has preached the Snowbird Sunday sermon there for years.

- The year Hank retired, he traveled and preached with Maranatha Campus Ministries which was a university fellowship his children Rose and Bob Weiner and Rusty and Mildred Russell founded. He traveled with Maranatha Ministries and spoke at Parent's Weekends in Australia, New Zealand, Indonesia, the Philippines, Korea, and Japan with a week off to visit China. He also spoke at many university campuses in the United States.

- In 1992, Hank ministered in Finland and traveled and preached in Russia. Since his retirement, Hank has continued to preach revivals in many American churches over the years.

Children

- Margaret Lill (Peggy) and husband Bill Rudolph of Decatur, Alabama

- Rose Ellen and husband Bob Weiner of Gainesville, Florida

- Henry E. Russell III (Rusty) and wife Mildred Cooper of Gainesville, Florida

- Dr. Stephen A. Russell – MD Knoxville, Tennessee

- Betty Grace and husband of Philip Houser, Austin Texas

Grandchildren

- Leigh Ellen Rudolph and husband Brad Atkins of Decatur, Alabama

- Bill Stephen Rudolph and wife Amy Dillon of Decatur, Alabama

- Stephanie Weiner and husband Andreas Keller of Winterthur, Switzerland

- John David Weiner of Gainesville, Florida

- Evangeline Weiner of Seattle, Washington

- Catherine Grace Weiner of Winston Salem, North Carolina

- Jason Russell and wife Susie Correia of Gainesville, Florida

- Rebekah Russell of Gainesville, Florida

- Cameron Russell of Washington, DC

- Madeline Russell, MD of Atlanta, Georgia

- Katherine Ann Russell of Knoxville, Tennessee

- Daniel Wiseman of Knoxville, Tennessee

- Christina Houser and husband Cory Colley of Nashville, Tennessee

- Dr. Philip Houser, MD and wife Ranelle Butala of Louisville, Kentucky

- John Russell Houser, PHD University of North Carolina

- Taylor Houser of Austin, Texas

- Elizabeth Houser of Austin, Texas

Great-Grandchildren

From Decatur, Alabama

- Jacob and Reagan Atkins
- Julia and Preston Rudolph
- Brittany and Dillon Bullard

From Winterthur, Switzerland

- Liberty Grace and Judah Daniel Keller

From Gainesville, Florida

- Abigail Russell

From Louisville, Kentucky

- Anabelle and Elijah Houser

Acknowledgments

Thanks to my daughter Rose Russell Weiner, who is also a writer, artist, and Bible teacher, who along with her husband Bob has traveled to college campuses and reached out in an intense and effective way to thousands of university students in the USA and in many of the nations of the world. Rose worked to help me get this manuscript into book form. Thanks to my grandson, John David Weiner for the cover design. Thanks to Mildred Russell, my daughter-in-law for proofreading this book. My thanks to family and friends who have read and typed the words into a manuscript. Thanks to all my family and friends who have encouraged me to write down these stories.